SIDETRACKED

FRANCESCA GINO

SIDETRACKED

Why Our Decisions Get Derailed,

and How We Can Stick to the Plan

HARVARD BUSINESS REVIEW PRESS

BOSTON, MASSACHUSETTS

Library of Congress Cataloging-in-Publication Data

Gino, Francesca.

Sidetracked : why our decisions get derailed, and how we can stick
to the plan / Francesca Gino.
 p. cm.
 Includes bibliographical references and index.
 ISBN 978-1-4221-4269-1 (alk. paper)
 1. Decision making. I. Title.
 BF448.G49 2013
 153.8'3--dc23   2012034918

The paper used in this publication meets the requirements of the American
National Standard for Permanence of Paper for Publications and Documents in
Libraries and Archives Z39.48-1992.

To Greg(orio)
Choosing to explore life hand in hand with
you has been by far my best decision

CONTENTS

SIDETRACKED

What Gets Us Off Track?

On a sunny day a few years ago, my husband, Greg, and I were wandering the streets of the Gold Souk in the old part of Dubai. Both my sister, who was living in Dubai with her family, and my travel guide had described the *souk*—a marketplace where you can buy products ranging from fresh food and spices to handicrafts and even gold—as a "must-see." Our plan for the afternoon was clear: Greg and I wanted to have an enjoyable day and buy something authentic that would help us remember the experience vividly once we were back home.

As we went from one tiny, packed store to the next, we noticed that amid the traditional shops lining the souk's enchanted streets were other shops filled with fake designer handbags and knockoff designer clothing. Vendors ran after us, hawking "Nike" shoes, "Versace" T-shirts, "Louis Vuitton" bags, "Prada" wallets, and "Ray-Ban" sunglasses—all of them at bargain prices, and all of them closely resembling the authentic products we were familiar with from home.

One vendor was particularly persistent. He convinced Greg to follow him to the back of his store, where the two spent almost an hour haggling over "Rolex" and "Panerai" watches—identical copies of the real thing. Greg thought a fancy watch would make him look and feel good, and he doubted any of his friends or colleagues would be able to tell the difference.

After quite a bit of negotiating, Greg was ready to make a purchase: a copy of a Panerai Luminor Power Reserve men's watch, which typically sells for about $7,000 in the United States. Greg bought his perfect (in his mind) replica for just over $100.

He was thrilled, but his euphoria over getting such a good deal was short-lived. By the time we got back to our car, Greg said he couldn't help but feel a bit fake while wearing the watch. Ironically, this was exactly the opposite of our initial plan: having an authentic experience at the souk.

The decisions that we expect we will make based on our finely developed plans are often different from how we actually behave. We get sidetracked.

We set a new career path, we choose a diet to follow, we make plans to save for retirement, we set a new direction for the management team, or we promise to carefully research our next big purchase. And yet, like Greg, you may have found yourself following a course of action that took you completely off track—putting off your job search, sabotaging your diet, spending too much on trivial items, and so on. In the end, your outcome bore very little resemblance to your initial goal. Such results can be discouraging, demoralizing, and baffling.[1]

We have a rose-colored view of who we are and what we do, and we aim to behave in ways that are consistent with our self-image as capable, competent, helpful, and honest individuals. We care about following through on our goals and wishes. And yet, even when we have spent time developing our plans and are fully committed to our best intentions, our decisions often veer off course in unexpected ways.

Greg set off to choose a souvenir that would enhance our authentic experience abroad, but left the souk feeling just the opposite—inauthentic and false. And Greg is not alone. I have observed experienced managers plan carefully for their negotiations but end up with very different deals than those they had planned because they were caught up "in the heat of the moment." I've seen friends make plans to improve their relationships but fail to follow them due to their inability to put themselves in their partners' shoes. I have watched thoughtful managers planning new incentive schemes to motivate their employees, only to find the employees focused more on cheating the system than on working harder. And I have also noted similar inconsistencies in my own behavior. Why do our plans so often go astray, and how can we keep on track?

Over the last ten years, I embarked on a number of research projects that focused on answering just those questions. In *Sidetracked*, I'll share my findings.

Three different sets of forces influence our decisions in ways we commonly fail to anticipate: (1) forces from within ourselves, (2) forces from our relationships with others, and (3) forces from the outside world. Throughout *Sidetracked*, I will describe the results of various studies examining the power of these forces and how they operate. I will suggest that we can make more successful decisions by understanding these forces and that we can learn to account for them as we set goals or clarify plans of action. I will conclude each chapter by describing one principle for you to consider to avoid getting sidetracked in the future.

Forces from within are factors that reside in both our minds and our hearts, and exist because of the very nature of being human. We will explore the accuracy (or lack thereof) of our beliefs about our abilities and competence (chapter 1), the effects of our emotions on unrelated decisions (chapter 2), and the consequences of having an (overly) narrow focus when evaluating information and making decisions (chapter 3).

Forces from our relationships are factors that characterize our relationships and interactions with others. We are social human beings, but our bonds with others often derail our plans. In the second part of the book, we will examine how this happens. I will discuss the difficulty of putting ourselves in others' shoes (chapter 4), how sharing even superficial features with others (such as having the same first name) colors our viewpoint and decisions (chapter 5), and how we are affected by comparing ourselves to others (chapter 6).

Finally, *forces from the outside* are factors that characterize the context in which we operate and make decisions. We will explore the effects of irrelevant information on our decisions (chapter 7), examine why subtle differences in the way a question is framed lead to different solutions (chapter 8), and discuss how the structure of our environment can cause us to veer off track (chapter 9).

To a certain extent, all these forces were at play when Greg was deciding what to buy at the souk. Forces from within made him concentrate on how wearing a Panerai (albeit a fake) would make him feel, a prediction that turned out to be shortsighted and inaccurate. Forces from his relationships made him focus on the fact that he would look good relative to others, but at a much cheaper price; this focus may have clouded his understanding of the power of wearing counterfeits. And forces from the outside—the heady atmosphere of the souk—may have had an impact as well.

Whether in a souk, on the streets of New York City, or in a nondescript shop, many of us have probably been in a situation similar to my husband's. We focused on the fact that we could show off our fashion sense by wearing Armani sunglasses or a Zegna suit bought at a fraction of the retail price. Wearing these products should send a very positive message—both to ourselves and others—about who we are.

Psychologists and behavioral decision scientists refer to this type of behavior as *self-signaling*—making decisions to communicate the type of person we are to ourselves. Here's an example of how self-signaling works. A few years ago, Joe Marks, Disney's then vice president of research, visited Tokyo Disneyland and was struck by the long line that had formed outside a shop in the park's Frontierland. Marks learned that people were queuing up for hours at a time—about four hours on average—simply to buy a leather bracelet, which cost less than $10, on which they could have their name painted or embossed.[2] Most waited in line with their sweetheart or spouse. Marks learned that the lines formed because of a tradition in Tokyo that equated the exchange of leather bracelets with bonding. *Why didn't Disney open another store selling the exact same bracelets?* Marks wondered. As far as he could remember, standard economics suggests that supply should match demand—and, in this case, this principle meant making it easier for customers to buy what they wanted. If the product was so popular, why not make it more easily available? The answer turned out to be simple but counterintuitive: the long lines contributed to the product's popularity. Waiting in line signaled to park visitors that their commitment to their romantic partners was exceptionally strong.

Given how common self-signaling is, we might assume that it thrives in the realm of fashion. Wearing a pair of Hugo Boss pants, a silk Prada scarf, or a Panerai watch could make us feel differently about ourselves—that we are more worldly, suave, and sophisticated than we were before we donned these products. Wearing them may trigger emotions we would not have experienced otherwise, such as confidence or pride, which in turn could influence our decisions (for example, confidence might inspire a risky investment), even if no one else knew the products were authentic. But what if these items were knockoffs, as in the case of my husband's fake Panerai watch? What would we be signaling to ourselves if we purchased a fake product instead of an authentic, brand-name one? Is it possible we would feel like a fraud? This is what my husband seemed to have experienced.

Let's take it one step further: is it possible we would then behave like a fraud, acting less ethically than usual while wearing a counterfeit product? The choice between purchasing a knockoff versus spending more money on the real thing is another interesting case of the inconsistencies I mentioned earlier. The signal we believe we are sending to ourselves by wearing a knockoff may not match the actual signal, and it might not be consistent with our subsequent actions. I felt this was a theory worth testing empirically before thinking carefully about its implications. And so, inspired by my visit to the souk with Greg, I teamed up with some collaborators, and we designed a simple experiment.

With my colleagues Mike Norton (professor at Harvard University) and Dan Ariely (professor at Duke University), I recruited a group of female college students and had them wear pricey Chloé sunglasses during part of the experiment. The glasses were the real thing (they cost more than $300!), but we led some of the young women to believe they were wearing knockoffs. We wanted to see if thinking they were wearing counterfeit shades would make our participants feel and act differently from those wearing authentic sunglasses. We hypothesized that participants would expect that wearing an inauthentic product would have a positive impact on their self-esteem but that, in fact, the product's lack of authenticity would cause them to feel less authentic themselves. In turn, we predicted these feelings would cause them to behave dishonestly and to view other people's behavior as more dishonest as well. In short, we suspected that feeling like a fraud might make people more likely to commit fraud.[3]

For our first laboratory experiment, we recruited eighty-five female students and told them that they would be participating in a marketing study in which they would have to evaluate the quality of different pairs of sunglasses. We informed them that their first task would be to express their preferences for various products. Specifically, we showed them twelve pairs of products from different categories (including clothing, technology, and jewelry) and told them that one product in each pair was authentic and the other was a counterfeit, without identifying which supposedly was which. Participants were asked to indicate which option they preferred in each pair. Regardless of which product they chose, we randomly assigned them to receive a particular response from us.

Namely, we told them that, relative to other people in the study, they seemed to have a preference for either authentic or counterfeit products (depending on the condition).

Next, we asked them to go to an adjacent room and take a pair of sunglasses from one of two boxes that were placed side by side. The group of participants in the "authentic" condition was asked to wear sunglasses from a box labeled "Authentic Sunglasses by Chloé." The group of participants in the "fake" condition was asked to wear sunglasses from a box labeled "Counterfeit Sunglasses." The sunglasses in the two boxes appeared identical (and, in fact, unbeknownst to the participants, they were).

Once everyone was wearing their sunglasses, we had them leave the room and asked them to test the quality of the lenses by looking out the windows and at posters hung on the wall while walking down the hallway. We informed them that we would later ask them to describe the experience. After about five minutes, the group of women returned to the lab room. It was time for them to engage in a second task.

In this task, participants were told they would be presented with twenty matrices to solve. Each matrix included a set of twelve three-digit numbers (for example, 6.14), two of which added up to ten. The participants' task was to find the two numbers. To make the task especially challenging, we put them under time pressure: we gave them five minutes to correctly solve as many problems as possible. Five minutes is not enough time to solve all twenty matrices; people correctly solve only about six or seven matrices, on average, during this amount of time. Participants received a worksheet with the twenty problems and a collection slip on which to record the number of matrices they solved correctly when the five minutes was up. We also gave them an incentive to do well by telling them they would receive 50 cents for each correctly solved matrix. Figure I-1 presents a sample matrix.

Now put yourself in the position of our participants. Imagine looking through these numbers on a worksheet to quickly find a solution before moving to the next matrix while wearing

FIGURE I-1

Sample matrix for the counterfeit sunglasses experiment

8.19	6.46	1.62
8.29	2.91	2.03
2.73	7.89	9.86
6.21	3.54	3.18

your sunglasses. Although you're good at math, after a few minutes, you realize you've solved only three matrices. "Hurry up!" you tell yourself, and spend the next few minutes adding numbers in your head. All too soon, time is up.

The experimenter tells you to quickly count the number of matrices you solved, fold your worksheet, and place it in the recycling box positioned in the corner of the room. To your surprise, you discover that you solved only seven matrices. After you put the worksheet in the recycling box, you are asked to write down your score on the collection slip you received initially. You know you will be paid based on your self-reported performance—and it appears that your worksheet will be recycled. There doesn't seem to be any way for the experimenter to know what your actual performance was.

Would you be honest or would you inflate your score? Would your honesty depend on whether you were wearing real or fake sunglasses?

Without the participants' knowledge, we monitored both their actual score and their self-reported scores. (We matched one of the digits in the matrix used as an example on the back of the collection slip to one of the digits in one of the matrices in the test sheet that participants recycled. This digit was unique for every participant.) The actual score and the self-reported one were different from each other for a large number of participants. More notably, wearing counterfeits rather than authentic sunglasses made a difference: the women who thought they were wearing the fake Chloé shades cheated more than those who thought they were wearing an authentic pair—considerably more. Fully 71 percent of those in the fake condition inflated their performance when they thought nobody was checking on them—in effect, they stole cash from the experimenter. By comparison, 30 percent of those who knew they wore authentic Chloés cheated.

After the matrix task, the participants, still wearing their sunglasses, engaged in a third task: a perceptual task on the computer. This task included three hundred trials (one hundred practice trials and two hundred trials for real money). In each trial, they were presented with a square divided in two by a diagonal line. The square included twenty dots, some on the right side of the diagonal and some on the left side. After glimpsing the square for just one second, the women had to identify which side of the diagonal (right or left) contained more dots by clicking either a button labeled "more on left" or a button labeled "more on right." Figure I-2 shows a sample square.

A glance at this square suggests there are more dots on the left side than on the right side. But the experimenter also informed our participants that they would earn 0.5 cents for each click on the "more on left" button and 5 cents (ten times as much!) for each click on the "more on right" button. Thus, the task presents a conflict between giving an accurate answer and maximizing profit.

FIGURE I-2

Sample square for the counterfeit sunglasses experiment

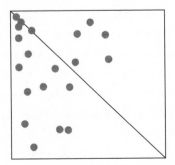

How did our participants resolve this conflict? Those wearing counterfeit sunglasses pressed the "more on right" button more frequently than did those wearing authentic sunglasses. Of course, the glasses were actually the same in both conditions, so it wasn't as if the "fake" Chloé shades affected the wearers' vision. But, as in our previous task, wearing a supposed counterfeit product increased dishonesty.

Intrigued by these results, we pushed our initial hypothesis a bit further. One possibility is that the presumed "fakeness" of the sunglasses made our participants behave more dishonestly than they would have otherwise. But it is also possible that participants who were told they were wearing an authentic version of the product behaved more honestly than they would have otherwise. In the first case, our results would be explained by a negative signal the women sent to themselves when wearing the seemingly fake sunglasses: "I am fake." In the second case, the results would be explained by a positive signal the women sent to themselves when wearing the authentic Chloé sunglasses: "I am authentic." Which explanation drove our results?

To answer this question, we recruited another group of female college students, one hundred of them. This time, we added a third condition: a control condition in which participants did not receive any information about the sunglasses; the box containing their sunglasses had no label on it. After walking around the hallway for five minutes, the women returned to the lab to engage in the matrix task, on which they had an opportunity to cheat.[4] We also asked them to answer a series of questions about how authentic they felt and whether they felt in touch with the "real you." Consistent with our previous findings, 30 percent of participants in the authentic condition cheated by overstating their performance, and more than 70 percent cheated in the fake condition. The level of cheating in the no-information condition was about 42 percent—statistically, no different from the authentic condition. This suggests that wearing authentic sunglasses did not make our participants more honest. Instead, wearing what they believed to be fake sunglasses caused them to behave more dishonestly than usual. The answers the women gave to the questions posed at the end of the study were consistent with this conclusion: wearing seemingly fake sunglasses made them feel less authentic, a feeling that apparently predisposed them to cheat during the study. We tested the robustness of our findings with other experiments, and further evidence pointed us to the same conclusion: wearing a fake product increases the odds that people will feel inauthentic and behave unethically.

Wearing fake sunglasses impairs your ethics. Who would have guessed? Just in case this finding was self-evident to everyone but us, we recruited another group of students to test whether our intuition was correct. We gave these students information on the average performance of past participants in the matrix task and asked them to predict self-reported performance in each of our three conditions: fake, authentic, and control. The students correctly predicted that, overall, participants would cheat by overreporting their performance on the task. However, they did not anticipate that cheating would vary across the three described conditions and, specifically, that those wearing counterfeits would cheat the most. These results led us to conclude that people do not realize that counterfeit products may have an unexpected influence on their ethicality.

Together, this set of experiments suggests that what we wear (counterfeits) influences how we feel (inauthentic) and behave (dishonestly), whether we realize it or not. I find these results quite worrisome. Virtually all of us have a strong desire to behave morally and to be viewed by others as honest. That's our plan: we want to choose the right path when facing complex ethical choices. And yet, as the results of these experiments indicate, subtle factors can lead us astray. If the seemingly minor decision to look fabulous on the cheap can impair our ethics, how might more significant forces take us off track in other domains?

Inconsistencies between what we had in mind (wearing a faux luxury pair of sunglasses to look good) and what we ended up doing (cheating to earn more money) are surprisingly common and systematic. Moreover, the forces that lead to these inconsistencies are so subtle that it is hard to believe they could affect us.

To understand these forces, I'll tell you about some additional experiments—my own and those of my colleagues—that will clearly show how seemingly innocuous factors, such as the amount of lighting in a room, the bitterness of a cup of morning coffee, or the way the furniture is arranged in an office, can have a significant impact on our decisions and behavior—a far greater impact than we might wish to admit.

The fact that we could unearth such seemingly counterintuitive findings reveals the power of the experimental approach (as opposed to, say, storytelling or drawing solely on our own experience). The contexts in which we make our decisions are often complex, with various forces influencing our decisions and behaviors at once. Understanding the individual effects of these simultaneous forces on our decisions is a complicated endeavor. Experiments allow scientists to study one force at a time while keeping all other features of the decision context constant, singling out the effect of each change on how subjects behave. Through this method, social scientists can identify the forces that influence us and, even more importantly, why they have the effects that they do. Experiment after experiment, we can uncover precisely what derails our decisions.

Although simple, the experiments I will discuss provide vivid illustrations of general principles that explain how we make decisions and why these decisions are often inconsistent with our initial plans. I hope each one will give you the opportunity to reflect on past experiences where the same principles may have guided your actions and to identify corrections you might want to apply to similar situations in the future.

Understanding the forces that lead us astray can also help us decode the sometimes mysterious, hurtful, or unwise decisions of our friends, spouses, neighbors, leaders, and colleagues. When we evaluate or judge the behavior of others, we often assume their actions reflect their personalities. For example, if a new colleague arrives late to an important business meeting, you might infer that he has a problem with tardiness or disorganization rather than considering that he may have been delayed by forces beyond his control (for example, being stuck in traffic or having a flat tire). And if your spouse makes a poor investment decision, you might assume she is bad with money rather than considering that your family's financial adviser unduly influenced your spouse's emotions at the time of the decision. In other words, we fail to recognize that the same forces that sway our own decisions may be at play when other people make theirs. Being human makes all of us vulnerable to subtle influences—from the anxiety triggered by an authoritative person to the type of watch we wear—that can dramatically impact our behavior. These subtle factors can completely overshadow the effects of our underlying personality on our behavior.

I also hope to prompt you to apply the principles behind these ideas to your own life. How do they affect how you think about your past decisions and those you will face in the future? As a remedy, I'll also offer some advice about how to counteract the three kinds of forces that derail our decisions so that you'll be more likely to stay on track.

PART I

Forces from Within

CHAPTER 1

Better Than Mother Teresa

Inaccurate Views of Ourselves

During a visit home to Tione di Trento, Italy, a few years ago, I started a new after-dinner routine: watching the TV show *Affari Tuoi* (translated literally, "Your Business") with my family. Before each episode, an independent notary company randomly assigns monetary prizes and nonmonetary ones (such as a cork or a one-year supply of soap) to twenty boxes. The monetary prizes range from 1 euro cent to hundreds of thousands of euros. The maximum prize is €500,000 (about $630,000), which is always contained in one of the boxes. The twenty boxes are sealed, consecutively numbered from 1 to 20, and randomly assigned to twenty contestants, who represent different regions of Italy. At the start of each episode, the contestants have the opportunity to answer a general knowledge question. The person who answers the question in the shortest amount of time is selected to be the first contestant.

The structure of the game is rather simple. The contestant has a sealed, numbered box in her possession (the one she was assigned at the beginning of the game). The nineteen other numbered boxes are arrayed before her. In each of five rounds, she is given an opportunity to choose a fixed number of boxes to open: six boxes in the first round, then groups of three boxes in the remaining rounds. The contestant is responsible for choosing each of the boxes to open. Once a chosen box has been opened, the cash value of that box is revealed and then eliminated from the list of possible prizes. A screen keeps track of the available prizes and those that were eliminated in earlier rounds.

At the end of each round, "the bank" (a disembodied male voice) makes a proposal: he offers the contestant either a "swap"—that is, the opportunity to exchange her box for one of the remaining boxes of her own choosing—or a definite amount of money to quit the game. If the contestant accepts the bank's offer to quit, the game ends; if she chooses a different box, she proceeds to the next round. If the contestant reaches the final round (after opening all nineteen boxes) and rejects the bank's offer to quit in this round, she receives the contents of the box in her possession at that time.

Imagine that you are a contestant in this game. Your lucky number is 8, so you choose box number 8 first. After quite a bit of suspense, the host opens the box, revealing a prize of €25. You feel relieved and quite excited to have eliminated this minor prize, and you keep on going. Eighteen boxes are left. You come up with another lucky number, the date of your college graduation, and soon discover that it was another lucky day: the hidden prize is another humdrum prize, a chair. You are feeling great about your ability to pick numbers, and you keep on going.

The game progresses, and the number of unopened boxes declines. You have eliminated fifteen of the boxes, and you know that the grand prize is still hidden in one of the remaining ones. When only five boxes are left (including yours), you receive a call from the bank, which offers you the opportunity to sell your box for €46,000 (and walk away with this amount of money) or exchange it for another box. The €500,000 is still out there, together with the following prizes: €50,000, €50, €1, and a picture frame. You can keep opening boxes (a risky move), or you can say yes to a sure amount (the bank's offer of €46,000). What would you do? Would you keep going through your lucky numbers?

There is a third possibility for you to consider: you are allowed to ask the audience for advice about whether to accept or reject the amount offered. If you do this, you will learn which percentage of the audience thought you should accept the monetary offer and which thought you should reject it.

You know the rules: the game will end if you accept the bank's monetary offer. Alternatively, you can continue to choose boxes to open. You might get the grand prize, a prize better than what the bank offered you, or a better offer from the bank later on—or you might get next to nothing. You are not sure what to do. You have successfully opened so many boxes already, and you want to trust in your streak of good luck. After much deliberation, you decide to consult the audience. Do you think your decision would be influenced by their advice?

If you are like most contestants, you would likely ignore the audience's advice. In fact, the audience's advice has little impact on the decisions contestants make in this game, even if following that advice would be the best objective choice. In fact, more generally, in situations where others' opinions are available to us on the right decision to make and these opinions are independent from one another, we're better off listening to them than to ourselves.[1] Evidence collected from over one hundred television episodes and four hundred decisions suggests that contestants tend to ignore the audience's advice, even though a later analysis of contestants' decisions indicates that following the advice would have increased their earnings.[2]

I know what you are thinking: this is just a game. In real life, when facing high-stakes decisions (such as how to invest retirement savings, whether to accept a job offer, or how to best propose to a significant other), we would not ignore useful advice from others. We would be open to what others who are just as knowledgeable or more knowledgeable about the decision have to say. We would surely consult others for their independent opinions, weigh their advice carefully, and make a decision after rationally weighing our opinion with theirs.

Actually, I bet we would not.

In support of my claim, I offer the fact that the business press regularly covers stories of CEOs and other leaders who failed to listen to the advice of colleagues, peers, or other constituencies and suffered the consequences. In early August 2008, for example, the *New York Times* reported an interesting tale of advice ignored: the story of Richard Syron, then the CEO of the mortgage giant Freddie Mac.[3] As recounted in the article, in 2004, David A. Andrukonis, then the company's chief risk officer, warned Syron that the firm's underwriting standards had slipped and that the company could face significant losses. According to Andrukonis, many of the loans the company had bought "would likely pose an enormous financial and reputational risk to the company and the country" and that Syron ignored the advice, insisting that "we couldn't afford to say no to anyone." Freddie Mac continued to purchase riskier loans over the next three years and at a faster pace. And though Syron was warned that Freddie Mac needed to expand its capital, he allowed the company's safety net to shrink.

At the time the *New York Times* ran its article, Freddie Mac was in trouble. Its stock price tumbled 60 percent between February and August 2008, destroying more than $80 billion in shareholder value. The company had just posted a second-quarter loss of $821 million, and it clearly needed good advice to change its fortunes. Yet Syron released a statement calling the *Times* story "superficial" and defending the company's records. He called the company's mortgage default and credit loss rates "a fraction of the industry averages."

Interestingly, this was not the first time Syron had ignored advice from trusted advisers. Beginning in 2001, Federal Reserve governor Edward Gramlich began to warn Syron about the risks of subprime mortgages (home loans to high-risk borrowers).[4] Gramlich's advice was supported by solid 2006 data from a Merrill Lynch analyst indicating that companies could suffer as a result of their subprime investments. But Syron refused to listen. In September 2008, the US Treasury placed Freddie Mac into a conservatorship overseen by the Federal Housing Finance Agency, thus allowing the government to temporarily run the company until it was on stronger footing. Syron was no longer in charge.

Or consider the story of Ken Olsen, a leader in the minicomputer sector as a cofounder of Digital Equipment Corporation (DEC) back in 1957.[5] During the following two decades, DEC dominated the scientific and engineering workstation market and, by the late 1970s, was number two in the computer industry under Olsen's leadership, thanks to the company's development of a unified hardware architecture and operating system. But in the early 1980s, Sun Microsystems appeared on the market with a superior technology, a leaner business model, and a more aggressive sales force that used its "open" Unix operating system as a compelling pitch. Throughout the 1990s, Sun's revenues exceeded $2 billion as the company came to dominate the workstation market that DEC had once ruled. As DEC lost ground in the marketplace, Olsen ignored advice from board members to retire. The decline of DEC's advantage continued until 1992, when the board finally decided to replace Olsen with an insider.

Let me add one more example to this list of valuable advice ignored: Walmart's 2006 failure to expand its success into Germany. Walmart landed in Germany with what appeared to be an unbeatable business model, but the model quickly failed, and the company started selling its German stores at a loss. So spectacular was Walmart's failure that it is cited in textbooks as an example of how leaders should *not* behave. The mistakes Walmart made in Germany were numerous. But one that caught my eye was the fact that Walmart's CEO, H. Lee Scott, and other high-level executives ignored the advice of the company's midlevel German managers regarding the intricacies of German laws and German corporate culture, including laws on opening hours and price setting. Although the German managers were of lower rank than Walmart senior management, they were clearly more experienced and more knowledgeable regarding the way "things get done" in Germany—yet their advice was ignored.[6]

Beyond the business world, we can also find stories of ignored advice that have had costly consequences in other spheres, including politics, medicine, and education, not to mention personal experience. At some point or another, most of us have probably ignored a doctor's advice—to stop smoking or start exercising, for example. Similarly, politicians in Washington, DC, regularly ignore sound advice to make tough budget decisions, cooperate with each other more, and so on.

Why do we so often ignore advice from others, even when it would lead to better decisions? One possibility is that it can be difficult to assess whether advice is good or bad. After the fact, it is easy to condemn Richard Syron and Ken Olsen for failing to listen to sound advice; at the time, however, it might have been difficult for them to assess the quality of the advice they received. A second possibility is worth further consideration: that we find the opinions of others to be less compelling and less convincing than our own, especially when we have invested time and effort in forming our opinions. As a result, it could be that we ignore advice we receive from others even when it is more accurate than our own perspective.

Do you think this is unlikely? I was not convinced myself, so I went to the laboratory to test these ideas on a group of college students from the University of North Carolina at Chapel Hill. I recruited about one hundred participants for a study examining how people reason through business problems. As a cover, the students were told that the study was part of a broader initiative to find ways to advise college students interested in applying for consulting jobs, which often use case analyses in the recruiting and selection process. The study employed business cases that students commonly face and are asked to reason through during interviews. In the first part of the study, participants were presented with the following business problem:

> *Your client is a company that makes specialized batteries for mobile homes (motor homes) in the USA. The battery is very powerful, long lasting, and of high quality. New industry conditions are occurring, and motor home dealers are starting to use a cheaper battery as the "factory standard" in an attempt to lower the overall price of motor homes. Your client's product is now only offered as an added feature for which the customer must pay an extra $500. In this case question, you are to discuss how your client should go about maintaining profits given these new market conditions.*

Study participants were given twenty minutes to read the problem and think about how they would answer the question asked in the case. They were allowed to take notes. Before they got to work on their answers, the experimenter informed them that MBA students with consulting experience had been presented with a similar case in an earlier session and had spent twice as much time (forty minutes) working through the case and preparing an answer for it. The undergraduate participants were given notes that the MBA students had prepared with their advice on how to successfully reason through the problem. Each participant received one page containing the notes of one MBA student.

Imagine you are one of our participants, sitting in a cubicle working through this business problem. You have practiced answering this type of problem before, as you prepared carefully for consulting interviews many times throughout college. You are confident in your ability to formulate a solid answer. Just to satisfy your curiosity, however, you read the notes left by one of the experienced MBA students. Do you think you would follow the advice?

Most of the study participants did not. About 60 percent of them completely ignored the advice, and the remaining 40 percent weighed it into their final answers but did not fully follow it. In fact, most participants reported believing they had better information for effectively solving the problem than their adviser did.

In general, when asked to justify their choice to ignore others' opinions, decision makers who discount advice from others typically reference the fact that they lack access to the adviser's internal thought processes, while having privileged access to the rationale behind their own opinions. From their perspective, weighing their opinions much more heavily than those of an external adviser makes a lot of sense. Yet they continue to unduly discount advisers' counsel even when the advisers clearly express why they hold certain opinions or consider certain information to be important.

So let's put aside this first explanation for discounting advice.

A second reason people might tend to ignore advice has to do with the perceptions they hold regarding their own intelligence and competence. For example, the college students in my study reported feeling more competent and capable than their advisers. They reported believing their own opinions and choices were superior to those of others, including their advisers and fellow study participants. These findings suggest that *our own perceptions* of how competent and capable we are can sidetrack our decisions. Whether we recognize it or not, our perceptions are often inaccurate.

Let's use a simple test to explore this issue in more detail. Grab a pen and a piece of paper. For each item in the following test, try to rate yourself, using percentiles, in comparison with the other people who decided to buy this book (as you imagine them to be). For example, for item 1, if you think your decision-making abilities are worse than those of all other readers of this book, enter "0" for the item. If you think your decision-making abilities fall in the middle, enter "50." If you think your decision-making abilities are superior to those of all other readers of this book, enter "100." All numbers between 0 and 100 are acceptable responses. Be open and honest: after all, you will be the only one who knows what you answered.

Ready? Here is the test:

1. Your decision-making abilities: _____

2. Your intelligence: _____

3. Your cooperativeness: _____

4. Your honesty: _____

5. Your physical attractiveness: _____

6. Your level of life experiences: _____

7. Your driving ability: _____

8. The refinement of your eating preferences: _____

9. Your aesthetic skills: _____

10. Your number of close friendships: _____

Now, let's see if this simple test can help you discover something new about yourself. Do you think you drive better than the average reader of this book? Do you believe you're more intelligent than most readers? Do you make better decisions than they do? I obviously cannot see your answers, but I bet most of the numbers you wrote down were higher than 50. In fact, when people are asked to answer this type of questions and compare themselves with others on a variety of socially desirable dimensions, they tend to report numbers that are in the seventieth or eightieth percentile.

One of my favorite examples of this human tendency comes from a survey conducted by *U.S. News and World Report* in 1997. The survey asked one thousand Americans the following question: "Who do you think is most likely to get into heaven?" Respondents indicated a 52 percent likelihood for then president Bill Clinton; they gave Michael Jordan a 65 percent chance (maybe partly because the Bulls had won the NBA championship that year); and they gave a 79 percent chance to Mother Teresa. But guess who received the highest likelihood for getting into heaven? It was the person completing the survey, with a score of 87 percent! Apparently, most of the respondents taking the survey thought, "Mother Teresa has a pretty good chance of getting into heaven. In fact, there is only one person I can think of who has a better chance than she does, and that's me."

We commonly think that we are luckier, better drivers, more capable, healthier, and better investors than our peers. Research in behavioral decision making and social psychology refers to these inflated perceptions as *better-than-average beliefs*, and they've been demonstrated in a wide range of contexts, including intelligence, performance on tasks and tests, and the possession of desirable characteristics (such as attractiveness and wealth) or personality traits (such as honesty and confidence).[7] Of course, it is impossible for a majority of respondents to do better than average across each desirable dimension in the test; someone, after all, needs to fall in the bottom 50 percent. The test demonstrates that our perceptions are inflated.

Now, there are certainly benefits to having a positive view of who we are and what we can accomplish thanks to our knowledge and IQ. This type of positive view can be helpful when we need to cope with stressful events or traumas such as life-threatening illnesses or serious accidents. In fact, the ability to develop or maintain positive beliefs in the face of these potential setbacks makes it easier for people to successfully cope with them and reduces their psychological distress. Holding a positive view of ourselves can also enhance our effort and persistence on tasks on which we may otherwise give up. If we believe we can achieve challenging goals, this belief fuels our energy and increases our productivity, thus spurring more progress than that we would achieve in the absence of such a positive view.

But having inflated beliefs can also lead to problems, including in many types of competitive decision-making contexts.[8] If entrepreneurs believe they are savvier than the competition, they are likely to make overly risky business decisions. If CEOs believe they're smarter than other executives at their level, they will plunge ahead with ill-advised mergers and acquisitions. And the frequency of strikes, lawsuits, and wars becomes more understandable when you know that most disputants believe they have a better case than their opponents do.

Getting back to the topic at hand, viewing ourselves as more capable and competent than others may also cause us to give more weight to our own ideas and carefully gathered information than to the ideas and information that others provide. Because of our inflated perceptions of how good we are, we may ignore the sound advice we often receive from others.

In addition to inflated perceptions of our own competence, another important element pushes us toward focusing on our own opinions and heavily discounting advice from others: our level of confidence. Another simple test demonstrates this point.[9] Grab your pen and paper again. For each of the following items, write down a range of values such that you are 90 percent sure the correct answer falls within the specified range. As an example, imagine you are supposed to indicate the air distance from London to Tokyo (in miles). You answer 5,500–6,000 miles as your range, indicating that you are 90 percent sure that the air distance from London to Tokyo falls within the range you specified. And, in fact, you are correct; the number of miles for that distance is 5,959.

Now here is your test:

1. Rank of the Coca-Cola company in the 2010 *Fortune* 500

2. Rank of United Parcel Services (UPS) in the 2010 *Fortune* 500

3. Revenue of CVS (pharmacy) in the 2010 *Fortune* 500

4. Revenue of Halliburton in the 2010 *Fortune* 500

5. Revenue of Gap (clothing store) in the 2010 *Fortune* 500

6. Market value of Verizon Communications as of March 26, 2010

7. Market value of Time Warner as of March 26, 2010

8. Projected number of bachelor's degrees that will be awarded to women in the 2009–2010 school year, according to a 2010 report by the National Center for Education Statistics

9. Number of grandparents in the United States, according to 2010 US Census Bureau Report

10. Number of animal species threatened with extinction in the United States as of May 2010, according to the US Fish and Wildlife Service

Not that easy, right? Here is how the scoring works. If the answer to a question falls within your range, you earn a point. If the answer falls out of your specified range, you do not get a point. Here are the answers:

1. 72

2. 43

3. $98,729 million (i.e., almost $99 billion)

4. $14,675 million

5. $14,197 million

6. $86,121 million

7. $36,232.3 million

8. 941,000

9. 80 million

10. 574

How many points did you get? Divide that number by ten to get a percentage. So, if your answers fell within the specified range six times out of ten, your score is 60 percent.

Since you were supposed to be 90 percent confident of your estimates, your final score should have been 90 percent. Is it? Although I cannot see your answers, I bet it is not.

When facing these types of general knowledge questions, people's answers typically show overconfidence. Their confidence intervals tend to be too narrow because they overestimate their ability to answer the questions correctly. In fact, for these types of questions, people who are asked to answer with 90 percent confidence answer only about 50 percent of the questions correctly. Paired with our self-centered perceptions of our own competence, overconfidence in the value of our opinions can easily lead us to ignore advice from others. The Kennedy administration's failure to consult the CIA or State Department when planning the Bay of Pigs invasion of Cuba (and its decision to just listen to military advisers), as well as the decision of NASA management to ignore outside advice about the dangers of the 1986 *Challenger* launch, illustrate the problems that can occur when people think they have more information than they actually do and when they are overly confident in their own judgments.

Once you realize how often inflated perceptions of competence and overconfidence make us unreceptive to advice, you might start thinking about what could protect you against these biases. Usually, when I pose this question to students in MBA or executive courses, their answers are similar: experience and leadership skills will help us critically weigh our own opinions and those of others when coming to a decision.

Together with my colleagues Leigh Tost (a professor at the University of Michigan) and Rick Larrick (a professor at Duke University), I conducted an experiment to find out whether this is true. One cold winter day in Pittsburgh, 107 undergraduate students from Carnegie Mellon University came to our lab to participate in a study for pay. The students sat in private computer cubicles and took part in what they believed to be two unrelated studies: a weight estimation study, which included two parts, and a vivid writing skills study. The task that participants completed for the weight estimation study was simple: in each of three rounds, they saw a picture of a person and estimated the person's weight. The closer their estimate was to the pictured person's real weight, the higher their payment for that round.

After they made their estimates, they were told they were moving on to the next study but that they would have the opportunity to see the same pictures again later. The vivid writing skills study had three conditions: high power, low power, and a control condition. Those in the high-power condition were asked to recall a situation in which they had power over other people; those in the low-power condition were asked to recall a situation in which other people had power over them; and those in the control condition were asked to recall their last visit to the grocery store.[10] After finishing the writing task, participants moved on to the second part of the weight estimation study, in which they were again asked to estimate the weight of the same people pictured in the photos they saw earlier. This time, however, they were given estimates that they could use in their decision-making process. According to the instructions, the estimates were chosen randomly from those that participants in a previous study had made when they were assigned to the role of adviser and were paid based on the accuracy of their estimates. The advice (which we actually came up with ourselves) was of good quality, falling within 5 percent of the true weight of the person in each photograph. Although the participants did not know how good the advice was, they could safely assume it was of good quality, given that their advisers had been paid according to the accuracy of their estimates. The advice definitely could have helped participants put more money in their pockets by the end of the study. However, we did not tell them this fact.

Imagine that you are a participant in this experiment. In the first weight-estimation task, you scrutinize each picture carefully and then provide your estimates: 184 pounds, 176 pounds, and 201 pounds. Upon moving on to the writing task, you are asked to think and write about a situation in which you had power over others. You start writing about the last time you led a project team and had the power to allocate resources to the members depending on their needs, requests, and performance. You clearly remember the strong sense of power you felt, since you had control over resources that team members depended on. Would you revise your estimates after having the opportunity to see another person's advice? Would you second-guess your initial judgments of the photos you saw previously?

It turns out that the extent to which participants listened to the advice they received from a previous participant depended on how powerful they felt after working on the writing task.

Participants in the high-power condition used the advice less than did those in the control condition and the low-power condition, and those in the low-power condition used advice more than those in the control condition. When participants gained a sense of power through their writing, they ignored the advice on almost 66 percent of their judgments. When they instead felt powerless, they ignored the advice on only about 26 percent of their judgments. (Those in the control condition were somewhere in the middle, at 34 percent.) The findings suggest that, contrary to intuition, power seems to *exacerbate* the tendency to ignore useful advice; even the subtle, temporary feelings of power induced by our writing task caused our participants to experience higher levels of optimism and overconfidence that in turn produced a disinclination to use others' advice. In this study, since the advice was good to start with, the accuracy of the final judgments of those who felt powerful was hindered and their payment ended up being lower.

It is not difficult to find recent examples of how a sense of power and resulting overconfidence may lead people in leadership positions to ignore good advice. Beginning in 2004, some economists began to warn that the housing bubble was unsustainable and headed for a crash. Alan Greenspan, the highly respected chairman of the US Federal Reserve since 1987, dismissed these warnings and brushed aside calls for greater regulation of subprime and other high-risk mortgages. After the financial crisis hit in 2007, it became apparent that Greenspan and his policy makers had placed too much confidence in their economic models when making key decisions. In his testimony before the House Committee on Oversight and Government Reform, Greenspan admitted that he had "found a flaw" in his ideology. "Those of us who have looked to the self-interest of lending institutions to protect shareholders' equity, myself included, are in a state of shocked disbelief," he said.[11] Like the participants in our study, Greenspan's overconfidence in his own opinions caused him to resist good advice.

If it is so challenging to see good advice when it presents itself, then when do we actually listen to it? It's not difficult to think of situations in which, if anything, we seem to have the opposite problem: we listen too much to advice. For instance, when it comes to selecting investments, people have been found to pay too much attention and too many fees to their financial advisers. Corporations, for their part, spend substantial amounts of money hiring management consultants to provide advice on their complex business problems. As a recent example, consider the decision of Facebook, which was exposed publicly in May 2011, to pay high fees to a well-known PR agency, Burson-Marsteller, for advice on how best to raise questions about Google's privacy policies. Facebook was looking to create some bad press against Google on this contentious issue. As part of its efforts, Burston-Marsteller asked blogger Chris Soghoian to write about whether one of Google's products violated user privacy. When the PR firm refused to tell Soghoian the name of its client, Soghoian posted the request on his blog, and Facebook ended up being the subject of bad press. In an interview with National Public Radio, communications expert Mary Spaeth of Spaeth Communications, Inc., commented, "Facebook probably ended up paying a small fortune for some horrible advice."[12]

Another example comes from my time working at one of the US *Fortune* 10 companies in the summer of 2010. To better understand one of the problems the company was facing, the team I was working with decided to design a survey to seek the opinion of a large number of the company's potential customers around the United States. The company allocated about $100,000 for the project. Having worked with various research software companies in the past, I contacted three of them and priced the survey effort at about $10,000. I reported the cost to my company team members, confident they would be pleased that I had found such a low quote. Instead, they told me to find another company that would charge more for the work. As one of the team members said, "Only when you have paid a lot of money can you be sure the opinions collected through the survey are convincing." That was a good opportunity for me to tell the team about the results of the study that I am about to describe.

In these examples, a person or organization spends money to acquire advice, and the advice has a strong impact on that person's or organization's subsequent decisions. I wondered if paying for advice and the price of the advice might affect how much weight we give to it.

On another snowy winter day in Pittsburgh a few years ago, I walked the halls of Carnegie Mellon University's business school, looking for students who might be interested in taking a little break from studying. By early afternoon, I had convinced thirty of them to answer a set of sixty questions regarding dates of specific events in US history, such as: "In what year was the National Labor Union formed?" and "In what year was the SEC (Securities and Exchange Commission) created?" I used the students' answers to screen out the most difficult questions and created a list of ten to use in my planned experiment. I chose questions that the students had intelligently estimated on the basis of some rough idea they had—even if it was not entirely accurate—about when the historical event occurred.

A couple of weeks later, armed with my list of questions, I recruited a group of 168 individuals (mostly college and graduate students) for my main study. As with my previous group of volunteers, I asked these participants to estimate the dates of ten specific events in US history (working individually). In this case, I also asked them to indicate a range of dates such that they were 90 percent sure the right answer fell within that range. To give them incentives to be as accurate as possible, I told them they would receive 50 cents every time their estimated answer to a certain question was within 1 percent of the correct date. Immediately after they finished the quiz, I gave them the very same quiz to repeat with the same financial incentives for accuracy. This time, however, the participants were given the option of receiving advice on the correct answers on all the questions. As the participants were informed, the advice came from another participant's best estimate when asked the same questions in a previous session, and it had been randomly selected from the pool of answers to those questions.

Now, imagine you are sitting in your cubicle reading these instructions to yourself. If you choose to receive the advice, then you will be advised on the possible correct answer for each of the questions of the trivia quiz. But there is a twist: if you choose to receive the advice, the experimenter will toss a coin. As the instructions indicate, if the result of the coin toss is tails, then you will receive the advice for free; if the result is heads, then you will have to pay for it. The cost of the advice will be subtracted from your final payoff, computed as the sum of the $4 show-up fee and a bonus based on your performance. The study included two conditions: a high-cost advice condition and a low-cost advice condition. For half of the participants, the cost of the advice was $2 (this was the high-cost advice condition). For the other half, it was $1 (the low-cost advice condition). What do you think you would do when presented with the choice of whether to buy advice? Would your answer differ depending on whether the advice cost $1 or $2?

As often occurs in my research, I was testing an interesting puzzle about human nature that I had observed across contexts, including at home when I was growing up. Before he retired, my dad was a very curious doctor. One of the many behaviors he noticed was that his patients seemed to be much more inclined to follow his recommendations on how to live a healthy life when they actually wrote him a check than when they received the exact same recommendations without spending a penny (when their health insurance took care of the cost). Does the price we pay for advice influence our view of how valuable it is? This was the question motivating the study I'm telling you about right now. So let's return to the laboratory and see what the participants in this study did.

Participants who chose to pay for advice were shown the advice for each of the ten questions and then were asked to provide their answers for the second time. To measure their perceptions of the quality of the advice, I also asked them to indicate for each question how accurate they believed the advice to be. Note that I used the coin toss so that it was clear to participants that costly and free advice had exactly the same quality.

So, what did participants do? Remember that half of the participants had been randomly assigned to the high-cost advice condition and half to the low-cost advice condition. In the high-cost advice condition, 43 percent of participants chose to receive advice. In the low-cost advice condition, 52 percent chose to receive advice. For those who chose advice, a coin toss determined whether they actually paid for it or received it for free. I was interested in comparing the receptivity to advice of these two groups of people: those who paid for the advice and those who did not.

I created a score that assessed the extent to which each participant used the advice. (For those of you who like math, here is how the score was computed. It was a ratio called *weight of advice*, or WOA. The numerator [the top part of the fraction] was computed as the absolute difference between the participant's final estimate and the participant's initial estimate. The denominator [the bottom part] was computed as the absolute difference between the advice the participant received and the participant's initial estimate.) Participants received a score of zero when they completely discounted the advice and a score of one when they followed the advice precisely. Participants' scores were significantly higher on this measure when the coin toss indicated they had to pay for the advice rather than receiving it for free. (The WOA was, on average, 36 percent higher when the advice was costly rather than free.) That is, paying for advice led people to listen to it. By contrast, receiving the exact same advice for free made people focus on their own opinions rather than those of another person. Whether participants thought the advice was of good quality or not did not affect whether they used the advice. The participants were also more likely to listen to the advice when they paid $2 for it rather than $1.

These results suggest a novel explanation of why paying for information makes it seem more convincing and credible. Our prior investments in a given plan cause us to continue to make investments, even when we receive information suggesting that we should cut our losses. Similar irrationalities characterized the behavior of many of my experiment's participants, who construed costly advice as a sunk cost that needed to be recouped. More generally, when people pay for advice, the sunk-cost effect kicks into gear: to avoid the regret of wasting money on unused advice, people justify their payment by using the information they received, whether or not it appears to be good.

You might argue that when you pay for advice, whether it's from a doctor, lawyer, or business consultant, you can be confident that you are accessing expert information. Yet my data shows that we are not especially focused on the quality of the advice for which we pay. Rather, the cost of the advice weighs more heavily in our decisions, even when free advice is of the same quality. As the experiment demonstrates, our minds are on the money, not the decision at hand. So, before acting on those premium-priced recommendations from your management consulting firm, you may want to ask yourself whether you would act on the same advice if you had gotten it for free.

Giving and receiving advice in a business environment is vastly more complex than how I modeled it in these experiments. For one thing, people seeking advice in a business setting try to gauge the quality of the information they receive based in part on how reliable the source has been in the past. In addition, it's a rare manager who makes an important decision without soliciting advice from multiple sources, including colleagues, superiors, or external experts—advice that often has a strong influence on final decisions. So far, the experiments I've discussed have asked people to complete simple problems, including a weight estimation task and a trivia quiz. But what happens when the situation is much more complex? The intricacy of real-life problems may affect how we weigh advice. In particular, it stands to reason that the more complex the issue is, the greater scrutiny we should give the advice we receive.

My colleague Don Moore (a professor at the University of California, Berkeley) and I studied this hypothesis in a series of experiments. In one study, we asked our participants to guess the weight of people in various pictures, just as the participants in the study I discussed earlier did. In this case, however, we varied the difficulty of the task by blurring some of the pictures. Half the participants received pictures that were in focus (making guessing easier) and half saw pictures that were blurry (complicating the guesswork).

For each picture they were presented with, participants guessed the individual's weight twice: the first time without advice, and the second time (as they were told) with input from another, randomly chosen participant. Would the complexity of the task affect participants' susceptibility to advice?

It did. When the pictures were in focus, we found that participants tended to discount the advice; apparently, they were confident in their ability to guess correctly. In fact, the accuracy of their estimates would have improved had they listened to the advice. When the pictures were blurry, however, they leaned heavily on the advice of others and seemed less sure about their initial opinions. The results suggest that when situations are complex, we blindly follow the recommendations of people who—as far as we know—are as knowledgeable (or ignorant) as we are. Thus, we overvalue advice when addressing a difficult problem and undervalue it when the problem is easy.

Why might we overvalue advice on difficult problems? As I explained earlier in this chapter, we routinely think we perform better than others on many desirable dimensions. Yet these beliefs hold only when we are facing simple tasks, such as answering a history quiz or estimating a person's weight from a sharp photograph. On such tasks, overconfidence leads us to believe we will perform better than others, and we have little reason to pay attention to others' advice. But on difficult tasks, we tend to assume we will perform worse than others. For example, if I were to ask you whether you are better than other readers of this book at juggling, riding a unicycle, or writing good poetry—that is, tasks that are rather difficult—you are likely to believe that you would perform worse than other readers. As a result, you are more likely to believe that others might have something useful to tell you on the subject, even if they aren't experts and, in fact, know as little about it as you do. This is why our study participants overvalued advice when they faced hard problems (blurry pictures) and undervalued it when they faced easy ones (clear pictures). Because they misjudged the value of the advice they received—consistently overvaluing or undervaluing it depending on the difficulty of the problem—they made suboptimal guesses overall. They would have done better if they'd considered the advice equally, and to a moderate degree, on both hard and easy tasks.

Now that you know about these quirks of human nature, be careful: when you think the solution to a problem is simple, and you find yourself waving off advice givers, think again. You may know a lot about the issue, but that doesn't mean you won't benefit from the opinions of others who know a lot, too. And when you're struggling with a challenging problem and receive advice that is at odds with your own impulses, ask yourself whether you're overvaluing that counsel. Beware of being too willing to listen to those who are no better informed than you are.

The studies I have discussed help us identify a first important factor that tends to influence our decisions for the worse: our own biased self-views and our overconfidence. Our biased perceptions of how competent and capable we are, as we have learned in this chapter, can get in the way of good decision making and lead us astray. For instance, they can make us too unwilling to listen to the opinions of others even when they are in fact valuable and could help us make better decisions. As I have discussed, whether we weigh information obtained from others into our final decisions depends on how confident we are in our own abilities and opinions, as well as whether subtle factors, such as how much the advice costs or the complexity of the problem we are facing, make us question our knowledge and competence. We would all benefit from considering the impact of these factors when giving and receiving advice, in addition to carefully examining the strength and validity of others' opinions.

This leads us to the first principle for avoiding getting sidetracked:

Raise your awareness.

In other words, become more aware of the subtle influences on your decisions. Think about the strategies you would use to lose weight, for example. You would exercise more frequently and start paying more attention to what you eat. You might go so far as to create a diary of your daily food intake to carefully examine how many calories you are consuming and compare it to how many you are actually burning. The ability to make good decisions requires the same type of exercise, attention to detail, and the same type of diary. Reflecting on the information that enters our minds as we consider different courses of action, and on how much of it we end up "consuming," is an important step toward making sure that our own opinions receive the appropriate weight in our decisions.

For the majority of us, the tendency toward positive self-views and confidence in our own information and opinions is difficult to avoid. Raising your awareness about the sources of this common tendency can help you challenge the assumptions behind your future decisions and take a more balanced view of the information available to you at the time of the decision. This principle can also help you be more open to others' perspectives and advice.

Applying this principle may involve reflecting on your own past experience with the goal of recognizing how your decisions were derailed by your biased perceptions of your own competence. The R&D team at pharmaceutical firm Eli Lilly and Company engaged in this type of activity, as I learned when my Harvard colleague Gary Pisano and I worked with them in 2004. The team had just introduced a new approach to the discussion of a key decision regarding development projects: should the project move on to the next phase of development or should it be killed? Over the years, the team came to realize that scientists sometimes made overly positive predictions regarding the future success of the drugs they were working on, since they were confident in their ability to produce breakthrough drugs. This confidence was at times driven by past successes and at times simply the result of having invested time and energy working on the drugs. Thus, instead of allowing the scientists to dominate decisions about investments, the R&D team added evaluations from experts who had no personal investment in the drugs being developed. These experts, who had access to data from past tests of the drugs, could provide a more neutral view to important decisions. By requiring this approach as part of the team's decision-making processes, and by recognizing the possible limits of scientists' evaluations, the R&D team nicely exemplified the principle of raising awareness of how biased perceptions of our own competence can sidetrack our decisions.

CHAPTER 2

The Unreliable Motorcycle Racer

Infectious Emotions

During their doctoral studies in the early 1990s, Jerry Yang and David Filo, PhD candidates in electrical engineering at Stanford University, would often get together to work on their class assignments. At one point, they decided to create an online system to keep track of their personal interests on the Internet. The website, which they called "Jerry's Guide to the World Wide Web," initially started as a hobby, but soon took up more and more of Yang and Filo's time. In fact, they started spending more time on the website than they did studying for their degrees. Eventually, their online record keeping became so unmanageable that they had to break it down into categories and, later on, subcategories. The two were trying to categorize content available on the Internet, and they were at the early stages of creating what would become known as a search engine. As their website grew, they decided to rename it "Yahoo!"—a word whose dictionary definition they liked: "rude, unsophisticated, uncouth."

Their system started gaining popularity, and within a few months of its conception, hundreds of people were accessing websites using

Yang and Filo's system. By autumn 1994, Yahoo! reached its first million-hit day.

Could their idea become a profitable company? Yang and Filo decided to find out. In March 1995, they began looking for investors. Just a month later, Sequoia Capital, a well-regarded investment company, agreed to fund Yahoo! with an initial investment of almost $2 million. Within months, Yang and Filo hired a management team and secured further funding from investors Reuters Ltd. and Softbank. In April 1996, Yang and Filo took Yahoo! public. At that time, the company had forty-nine employees.

For a few years, Yahoo! was the most popular search engine in the world. Through continuous growth, it became a leading global Internet communications, commerce, and media company. By the late 1990s, the company had more than three thousand employees.

But with the turn of the new century, Yahoo! began to face tough new competitors, such as Google. Yahoo! reported roughly $6.4 billion in revenue for 2006; Google reported about $10.6 billion. In the first quarter of 2007 alone, Google announced profits of $1 billion, while Yahoo! was down to $142 million.[1]

A once very successful company was now facing difficult times. In response, Yahoo!'s board of directors fired the company's CEO, Terry Semel; Yang soon took his place, in June 2007. His first year in the position was nothing but challenging, as Yahoo!'s stock price dropped steadily and its revenue growth slowed considerably.

During these difficult times, the company began to receive attention not only from the business press, but also from executives interested in buying the company. One of these executives was Microsoft CEO Steve Ballmer, who offered $45 billion for Yahoo! in early 2008. For Yang, this was no easy decision. As the business press speculated, it involved a complex, rational analysis, but emotions also played an important role. "The emotional part of Yang would rather do anything but sell to Microsoft," a source close to the situation told the *New York Post* on February 19, 2008. At the time, Yahoo!'s market value was approximately $39 billion.

Ultimately, Yang rejected the offer, reportedly deciding that it was too low. After all, how could he sell the once successful business he created with his peer Filo on the Stanford campus for "just" $45 billion? Yang was so attached to the company he had created with his friend that it was difficult for him to realize the offer was more than fair. This rejection was not well received by the market: Yahoo!'s stock price dropped significantly. The company's profits continued to shrink as well. Many speculated that Yang's judgment was clouded by his emotional attachment to the company. Many also believed that rejecting the Microsoft offer was not the right decision for Yahoo! As a result, within a few months, the company's board members pressured Yang to resign as Yahoo!'s CEO, which he did in November 2008. By mid-2009, Yahoo!'s market value had sunk to $22 billion.

As the story of Yahoo! and Yang demonstrates, allowing emotion to color decisions is common, especially when the decisions concern someone we care for or something we created. Think, for instance, about a time you were weighing a decision on behalf of your company or significant other, or a time when you were making an important purchase, such as a house, a financial investment, or an entire business. These decisions are inherently complex, and we often feel overwhelmed when working through the pros and cons of each choice in the decision process. Emotions may be useful in directing our attention and energy toward what we feel are the most important aspects of the decision. Yet overly intense emotions may lead us to make misguided decisions or outright disastrous ones, as in the case of Yang's rejection of an attractive offer from Microsoft.

A more amusing example of how emotions can unexpectedly derail our decisions comes from the 1991 movie *Defending Your Life*.

In the movie, Daniel Miller, played by Albert Brooks, must justify his lifelong lack of assertiveness after he dies and arrives in the afterlife. In one flashback scene, Daniel asks his wife to help him prepare for an upcoming salary negotiation with his boss. He wants to try out the tough bargaining strategy he is planning to use in the face-to-face negotiation that will take place the next day. By pretending to be his boss, his wife can push back and test Daniel's ability to get what he wants. The plan is clear, and thus the two start negotiating. His wife makes various salary offers, such as $55,000, and Daniel rejects every one of them, saying, "I cannot work here for a penny under $65,000," and "Let me make it plain to you: I cannot take the job for under $65,000, under no conditions." As Daniel refuses to budge from his $65,000 position, his wife starts to make him increasingly attractive offers. Daniel feels very prepared. The next scene in the movie is Daniel's negotiation with his boss. His boss opens the discussion by saying, "Daniel, I am prepared to offer you $49,000." Before he even finishes his sentence, Daniel replies: "I'll take it."

Daniel's goal for the negotiation was very clear, yet the anxiety he felt while sitting at the bargaining table with his boss took over and unexpectedly softened his position. Daniel's decision to be tough got derailed by a subtle factor he failed to anticipate: the anxiety triggered by sitting in front of his boss and negotiating with him.

Emotions triggered by one event can also spill over to affect another, unrelated situation. Imagine, for instance, that you hit heavy traffic while driving to work. That morning, you have an important meeting scheduled with a client who is interested in placing an order for the new product your company is launching. You initiated the product's development and oversaw its creation, so you have a lot at stake in this meeting, both financially and in terms of your reputation within your company. Because of an accident, several lanes have been closed on the highway, and you are now stuck in traffic. "Of all days, why did this have to happen today?" you keep asking yourself, feeling increasingly impatient and frustrated. By the time you reach the office, you are fuming with anger. You are forty-five minutes late to work, so you won't have time to enjoy your morning cup of coffee and review your notes before your meeting with your client. Do you think your anger would influence your discussion with the client, your receptivity to his suggestions, and the decisions you make during the meeting?

While the anger you felt as a result of being stuck in traffic has nothing to do with your client meeting, it is difficult to ignore. You should be able to put your anger aside, right? Let me tell you about a study I conducted with Maurice Schweitzer (a professor at the University of Pennsylvania) that was designed to examine this question.

In the fall of 2006, I intercepted students from Carnegie Mellon University as they were changing classes and asked them whether they would be willing to watch a short video clip on my laptop and answer a few questions about it. I told them I was interested in their reactions to the clip, which I would be using in an upcoming experiment. Since I was paying them a few bucks, it was not too difficult to convince forty-nine college students to sit down for less than ten minutes (even if this meant they probably would be late for their next class). The students watched one of two video clips, each of which lasted less than four minutes. One of the video clips came from a *National Geographic* special that portrayed fish at the Great Barrier Reef. The other clip, from the movie *My Bodyguard*, portrayed a young man being bullied. Immediately after viewing one of the clips, the students answered questions about the degree to which they were experiencing various emotions, including emotions related to anger (such as angry, furious, and mad) and those related to being in a neutral state (neutral, unemotional, indifferent). As I had hoped, the students who watched the clip from *National Geographic* felt neutral, while those who watched the clip from *My Bodyguard* felt angry.

Now that the materials for our emotion induction had been tested, it was time to conduct the main experiment. Maurice and

I recruited 103 students to participate in the study in exchange for course credit in their introductory business courses. They sat in private cubicles and engaged in what they believed to be a series of unrelated tasks. As in some of the experiments I discussed in chapter 1, students were first shown photos of three different people and asked to guess their weight. Next, the students answered a questionnaire that assessed their own emotional state. For each of nineteen different emotions, they indicated the extent to which they felt the emotion at that moment. After that, half of the participants watched the neutral *National Geographic* film clip, and the other half watched the clip from *My Bodyguard*. They were told that they would later be asked to reflect on the clip they watched.

Imagine that you have been randomly assigned to view the *My Bodyguard* clip.[2] You watch a boy who is new to school being bullied and blackmailed by a group of classmates. The boy is treated aggressively and unfairly, but instead of succumbing to his anger, he accepts his classmates' scorn. If you are like most people, this clip would make you feel angry on the boy's behalf.

But before you have much time to think about the clip, it is time for you to move on to the second part of the weight estimation task. Once again, you are asked to estimate the weight of the same people you saw earlier in the study. This time, though, you are also shown the estimates that another participant made for the same set of photos. You are told that this person had an incentive to make accurate estimates. Would you factor this information into your final estimates?

Most of our study participants did not. For the participants who saw the clip from *My Bodyguard*, the anger they experienced while watching the video clip carried over to this next, unrelated task. And because of these angry feelings, they largely distrusted and disregarded the other person's estimates, preferring to rely on their initial judgments as their final estimates. In fact, 74 percent of these participants did not attach any significance to the advice they received. By contrast, only 32 percent of participants who watched the neutral *National Geographic* clip disregarded the advice; the majority of this group accounted for the estimates they received in their final judgments. After completing this estimation task, we asked participants to think back to the video clip they watched and tell us how it made them feel. As we suspected, the *My Bodyguard* clip made participants feel angry, and the *National Geographic* clip made people feel neutral and indifferent—and those emotions played a significant role in how they were able to perform afterward. Angry participants made less accurate judgments compared to the neutral participants.

Incidental anger—anger triggered by a prior, unrelated experience that, from an objective perspective, should not influence our current judgments or decisions—can sidetrack our decisions by making us unreceptive to what others have to say. On a related note, in a recent series of studies, Scott Wiltermuth (of the University of Southern California) and Lara Tiedens (of Stanford University) examined whether incidental anger more generally affects how we evaluate others' ideas. Many jobs include the task of evaluating the ideas of others, including our colleagues, customers, employees, friends, and family members.

To address this question, Wiltermuth and Tiedens invited college and graduate students to their lab and asked them to engage in a series of tasks, beginning with a writing task. About a third of the participants spent six minutes writing about a time in their life when they felt extremely angry. Another third wrote about a time they felt extremely sad. The remaining participants wrote about how they spent the previous day; this group was the control condition, and the researchers wanted to induce them to be in a neutral emotional state. (Various scholars have successfully used such writing tasks to induce particular emotions—or a lack of emotion—in their study participants. They included a sadness condition to find out whether it was anger, rather than a more general negative mood, that affected the appeal of evaluating others' ideas.[3])

After completing their writing task, all of the participants were asked to indicate how appealing they would find two tasks to be: (1) listing ideas for businesses that could fill a space vacated by a failed restaurant on a university campus, and (2) rating the ideas other people came up with for uses for the vacated space. Participants who had been induced to feel angry found the task of evaluating others' ideas to be more appealing than did people who felt sad or who were in the neutral condition. Angry participants also found much more appeal in evaluating ideas than they did in creating them.

Wiltermuth and Tiedens hypothesized that anger increases the appeal of evaluating others because it instills the desire to strike out at them. In a second study, using the emotion inductions from their prior experiment, they induced half of the participants to feel angry and the other half to be in a neutral state. Next, all of the participants were told they would be evaluating ideas generated by others. Half of the participants were led to believe they would be judging high-quality ideas and likely be making positive evaluations. The other half believed instead that they would be judging low-quality ideas and probably be making negative evaluations.

The two manipulations—the anger induction and the type of ideas participants expected to evaluate—made a big difference. Those who were induced to feel angry found much more appeal in evaluating others' low-quality ideas than did participants in the control condition. They also found less appeal in evaluating others' high-quality ideas than did those in the control condition. Although most participants, whether angry or neutral, preferred to evaluate good ideas rather than bad ideas, those induced to feel angry much preferred to make negative judgments than did those in the control condition.

It seems that incidental anger can increase the appeal of criticizing others and their ideas. These findings should give us pause. The next time you feel angry, for whatever reason, you might try to avoid tasks such as evaluating the contributions of team members or providing performance feedback to colleagues or employees. Moreover, incidental anger may lead to problems not only in your professional life but also in your personal life. If you discover just before a first date that someone has scratched your new car, you will want to make sure the anger you feel does not transfer over to dinner. Or if you feel disappointed by the restaurant's service during dinner, you might want to avoid evaluating whether you enjoyed your date's company, lest you end up creating a score sheet of your date's pros and cons. An angry mood could generate a long list of cons that may not reflect reality. Finally, since we often can choose when to perform each of the many tasks required of us, we could choose to evaluate ideas when we are most capable of doing so objectively and thoroughly. For instance, an executive who is angry about receiving a speeding ticket could decide to wait to review proposals for new business plans until his anger has subsided and he can approach the task more objectively.

Emotions can dramatically affect how we perceive and evaluate the world around us, yet the ways in which emotions influence our decisions are very subtle. Anger triggered by circumstances unrelated to the decision at hand can end up encouraging us to attack others' weak ideas. Other negative emotions, such as sadness, and positive emotions, such as gratitude and happiness, can have other, equally subtle effects.

In the early 1980s, a study by psychologists Norbert Schwarz (of the University of Michigan) and Gerald Clore (of the University of Virginia) beautifully demonstrated how this misattribution process happens. The question the two scholars set out to investigate was simple: would people misattribute their emotions, such that thinking of a time they felt happy would lead them to report that they are happier overall than they would normally? To answer this question, Schwarz and Clore designed a clever study in which a female interviewer called up ninety-three people using telephone numbers randomly selected from the student directory of the University of Illinois at Urbana-Champaign. The interviewer made the calls either on a sunny or rainy weekday in the springtime. (Weather has been shown to influence our moods.[4])

Respondents were informed that the telephone survey concerned life satisfaction.

The two researchers used three types of priming: indirect, direct, or no priming. "Hello, I am Kristen," the interviewer said to start the conversation across all conditions. "We're doing research for the psychology department at Circle Campus in Chicago." Her follow-up varied depending on the priming condition. "By the way, how's the weather down there?" she asked in the indirect-priming condition. After hearing the respondent's answer, she continued, "Well, let's go back to our research. What we are interested in is people's moods. We randomly dial numbers to get a representative sample. Could you just answer four brief questions?" In the direct-priming condition, the interviewer used the same script but replaced the question about the weather with a statement that told the respondents that the study was measuring the effects of weather on mood. Finally, in the no-priming condition, the interviewer used her opening line and did not make any reference to the weather or to people's moods. Across all conditions, the interviewer then asked the respondents questions about their perceived quality of life and how they were currently feeling.

Not surprisingly, people felt happier on sunny days than rainy days. More interestingly, on rainy days, mentioning the weather or moods (whether indirectly or directly) influenced people's self-reported happiness, but the mention of weather or moods had no effect on sunny days. Specifically, on sunny days, respondents tended to report being happy and generally satisfied with their lives, independent of the script the interviewer used on the call. On rainy days, however, respondents reported being less happy and generally less satisfied with their lives when there was no priming (no reference to weather or mood) than when they were primed with references to the weather or mood. In short, the day's weather influenced respondents' moods and their judgments of happiness and life satisfaction. However, the negative feelings they experienced because of rainy weather were easily eliminated when priming occurred.

Why? Schwarz and Clore reasoned that if people unconsciously evaluate their overall life satisfaction and well-being based on their present emotions, then we can expect them to report greater satisfaction and well-being on sunny rather than rainy days. But when people are given a cue that links their mood to the weather, they recognize the basis of their judgments and adjust accordingly. When the link between weather and current emotions is made salient, they will tend to correctly discredit their mood as a reliable source of information regarding their general life satisfaction and well-being. But when the cue is not made salient or is absent, then people incorrectly misattribute their emotions. And this is exactly what happened.

Other research has shown that emotions triggered by the weather influence decisions such as how stocks are traded on Wall Street, how much we buy and consume, and how college students decide to enroll in certain programs.[5] Our emotions can also affect how we feel about ourselves overall and the extent to which we exert effort in our jobs.

Let me tell you about two studies I conducted with Adam Grant (a professor at the University of Pennsylvania) to explore the link between emotions and job performance in situations where working hard and performing well meant being more helpful toward others. The emotion we focused on in this joint project was gratitude. Specifically, we were interested in the impact that expressions of gratitude have on helpers. Adam and I wanted to test whether people who express gratitude after receiving help from another person make their helpers feel more socially valued. We also wanted to know whether this increased sense of self-worth would in turn motivate helpers to assist others in need.

We tested this idea by recruiting fifty-seven students for an online study on "writing and feedback" that would pay $10. The experimenter communicated with participants by e-mail throughout the entire study. In the first e-mail message she sent to participants, the experimenter explained that they would have to read a student's job application cover letter (which was attached) and then send their edits and comments directly to the student. The cover letter began like this:

> Dear Ms. Klein:
>
> My name is Eric Sorenson and I send you this letter inquiring about a receptionist position at your company office and tell you a little about my qualities. I believe I'm very able to contribute to your company's work labors.
>
> I have extensive clerical and computer skills, that have been sharpened during my year and a half of education in college. My computer usage exceeded five times daily. I also am proficient in Microsoft Word, Excel, Frontpage, Publisher and internet research.
>
> I would also like to mention having experienced working in an office setting. In high school I assisted the secretaries in the front office an hour a day for one semester. I made many friends there and gained a great deal of organizational skills. My time there taught me how to interact well with fellow co-workers and also to serve students in a timely and efficient way. I learned to use their computer software quickly proving that I learn fast and am good with technology.

Eric Sorenson needed some help! As specified by the study instructions, within twenty-four hours, all participants were asked to send their feedback to Eric. All of the participants sent their edits and, in many cases, some general comments, by the given deadline. After participants submitted their feedback, the experimenter, posing as Eric Sorenson, sent a reply from the alleged student's e-mail account. The message sent to half of the participants read:

> Dear [name],
>
> I just wanted to let you know that I received your feedback on my cover letter.

The other half of the participants received the following message:

> Dear [name],
>
> I just wanted to let you know that I received your feedback on my cover letter. Thank you so much! I am really grateful.

The first type of message was our control condition, and the second one was designed to be perceived as an expression of gratitude. The next day, the experimenter sent all participants a link to an online survey, which included a measure of social worth—the extent to which participants felt valued and appreciated by the student they helped. We also asked them whether they thought Eric's e-mail expressed gratitude. Not only did participants believe that the second e-mail expressed more appreciation than the first one, but they also reported feeling more valued when Eric expressed gratitude.

Now, you might not be particularly surprised that the beneficiary's expression of gratitude caused the helpers to feel good about themselves. But another result from this study was more surprising. One day after participants took their surveys, the experimenter sent all participants an e-mail message from the account of a different student, Steven Rogoff. The message read:

> Hi [name],
>
> I understand that you participated in a Career Center study to help students improve their job application cover letters. I was wondering if you could give me feedback on a cover letter I prepared. The cover letter is attached. Would you be willing to help me by sending me some comments in the next two days?

At this point, the study was over. The day before, participants had received their payment, and it was clear they had completed the study as asked. Now they were getting a request for help from someone else. Would they be willing to give Steven feedback on his letter?

Our motive for having a second student contact the participants was to determine if the participants who received an expression of gratitude from Eric two days before would be more helpful toward another student than participants who received only a neutral note would be. As it turned out, 25 percent of the participants who received the neutral note from Eric helped the second student, Steven, with his letter. This percentage *more than doubled* for participants who had received a note from Eric expressing gratitude: 55 percent of them voluntarily sent feedback to Steven. This higher level of helping was explained by the helpers' feelings of self-worth: the expression of gratitude participants received from the first student made them feel valued, and these feelings led them to offer help to a second beneficiary. So, a little thanks really does go a long way.

We decided to put this proverb to another test, this time in the field rather than in the lab. Our participants were forty-one fundraisers responsible for soliciting alumni donations to a public US university. In this case, an annual giving director expressed gratitude to half of the fundraisers in the study. The director visited the fundraisers in their office, telling them, "I am very grateful for your hard work. We sincerely appreciate your contributions to the university." The remaining half of the fundraisers (our control condition) were not visited by the director. Would the director's simple expression of gratitude impact the fundraisers' job performance? We obtained data regarding the number of voluntary calls each fundraiser made the week before and the week after the intervention, an objective measure that the university automatically recorded. (This measure can be used as an indicator of helping because the fundraisers received a fixed salary and were not compensated for their effort; any voluntary calls they made were purely meant to help the university.) The result? Gratitude increased the number of calls that the average fundraiser made in a single week by more than 50 percent. Fundraisers who received the expression of gratitude from the director showed an increase in helping, while those who did not performed about the same as they had the week before. Confirming the results of our online study, we also found that the gratitude expression increased calls by strengthening fundraisers' feelings of social worth.

Although we may not be aware of how emotions are pushing us toward a certain course of action, those around us often recognize the powerful effect of emotions on our decisions. This was made quite clear in a statement by Brad Brinegar, chair and CEO of McKinney, an independent advertising agency based in Durham, North Carolina, during a marketing conference in 2011: "I'm not sure that I really care about what people think about my brand because I know that most of the decisions [consumers] make have nothing to do with thinking. If you're not catching people emotionally, you're not going to catch them at all."[6] In some cases, costly mistakes lead us to a better understanding of how emotions influence decisions, as some of the companies I have studied can attest. Let me tell you about one of these companies: Ducati Corse, an Italian Ducati motorcycle racing team, which I have gotten to know quite well over the last decade.

Since my teenage years, I have been interested in engines. I started driving cars when I was only fourteen, thanks to friends who were courageous enough to let me get behind the wheel. In my family, I was always the one responsible for restarting our old Fiat 127 whenever the carburetor had trouble closing during the cold winters in Northern Italy. As soon as I was tall enough, I also started riding motorcycles. When I was offered the opportunity to do field research on motorcycle manufacturer Ducati back in 2004, I could not pass up the opportunity. I loved the design of Ducati's bikes, and this was a great way to learn more. Plus, I hoped that I would have a chance to drive one of the motorcycles on a racing circuit during a practice session.

The racing circuits in which Ducati Corse competes are intensely competitive; during the season, a dozen world-class teams battle each week for the top spots. Each of these racing teams represents a different commercial bike manufacturer (such as Honda or Yamaha) and has two riders competing in each race. Each week's race takes place in a different location, often in different countries across the world. For an organization like Ducati, winning matters, as track performance has a huge impact on brand equity and commercial bike sales. Ducati Corse had a long legacy of success in designing bikes for various racing formats (such as its "Superbike"), and in 2003 it entered the Grand Prix motorcycle racing circuit (or "MotoGP") for the first time.

My colleague Gary Pisano and I had the opportunity to study the decision-making process surrounding Ducati's entry in the MotoGP as well as the work of the designers and engineers involved in developing a racing bike for the circuit. We soon learned that developing racing bikes is a complex problem that requires, among many other steps, session after session of testing on the track before, during, and after every racing season. The team's bikes were fitted with sensors to capture telemetry data on twenty-eight different engine and bike performance parameters (such as temperature and horsepower). Riders were debriefed after every race for input on more subjective characteristics of the bike's performance, such as handling and responsiveness. In our interviews with the development team, riders were described as "the most expensive sensors" on the bike.

Motorcycle racing is a high-pressure context with little margin for error. In our interviews, we learned that costly errors are often attributed to emotions. In their debriefing sessions with Ducati engineers, riders sometimes recommended changes to a bike, when in fact an apparent malfunction actually reflected a subpar performance by a rider who had been in a bad mood that day. "The ideal world would be one where our simulation capabilities were so good that we did not need the riders' feedback to improve the bike," Ducati Corse's MotoGP team technical director, Corrado Cecchinelli, told us. "Our simulation would tell us everything we would need to know."[7] Cecchinelli recounted times when riders' feedback conflicted with analyses resulting from objective data collected through simulations and on the track. At first, the team listened to the riders and made costly changes to the bikes that, in the end, did not lead to improved performance on the track. Over time, the team learned how important it was to resolve these conflicts, specifically by determining how emotions weighed into the problem. By comparing riders' feedback to more objective data from sensors and simulations and then examining discrepancies between these two sources of information, the development team realized that the riders' emotions were sidetracking the riders' feedback. The development team learned to pay close attention to objective data and to discount riders' emotions in the debriefing sessions—an important first step in improving how the team made decisions.

People are surprisingly adept at identifying emotions from facial expressions, even when looking at pictures of complete strangers and members of different cultures. Through our recognition of another person's emotional state, we glean information about how that person feels and how he intends to behave. In addition to conveying emotional information, facial expressions elicit vicarious emotions in observers. That is, they lead to *emotional contagion*— the transfer of emotions from one person to another.

How do these expressed emotions impact recipients' feelings and subsequent decisions, if at all? This question motivated a research project I conducted with Maurice Schweitzer. We recruited eighty-seven college students to participate in a paid study and told them they would perform a recognition task. We also told them that when the recognition task had ended, they could volunteer to participate in a different study for no extra pay, namely a marketing study that would involve tasting and evaluating a beverage. We gave participants a folded, handwritten note, purportedly from another participant who had previously participated in the marketing study. (In reality, research assistants wrote these notes by hand in advance.) The participants were asked to read the note so they could make an informed decision. Each note read, "Hey, you should definitely participate in the study. Not that you asked for advice but . . . The drink is good, you should taste it!"

During the recognition task, we primed participants with subliminal expressions of emotions by having them view different photographs on the computer. In each of eight trials, participants viewed three photographs, in this order: (1) a cross shape, presented for fifty milliseconds (a type of image that is usually presented to participants to capture their attention on the screen before the subliminal prime); (2) a photograph of a person expressing an emotion, presented for sixteen milliseconds (our subliminal prime); and (3) a photograph of a person with a neutral facial expression, presented for four hundred milliseconds. In this procedure, participants do see the cross shape and the "neutral" photograph, but the photograph used as the subliminal prime passes by too quickly for them to consciously recognize it. At the end of each trial, the participants were asked to indicate the gender of the neutral face, which had been easily visible. We manipulated the subliminal prime by using a different photograph for the second photograph in each of the eight trials. In the angry condition, the second photograph always depicted someone angry. In the happy condition, the second photograph always depicted someone happy. And in the neutral condition, the second photograph always depicted someone with a neutral expression.

After the gender classification task, the experimenter informed participants that they had completed the study but reminded them that they could participate in a short marketing study if they wanted to. Next to the computer, the experimenter had placed an unlabeled, plastic bottle of iced tea and a plastic cup. Participants were told that if they chose to stay, they would be asked to taste the drink and suggest a retail price for it. We also told them they would be asked to write a short report on the drink and to come up with a possible slogan to advertise it. Although we were not directly interested in this data, we wanted to make sure that the effort required to complete this task was great enough that some people would refuse to participate. As they were reminded, they would not be paid extra money for completing this second task. In addition to recording whether or not participants agreed to complete the beverage study, the experimenter recorded, with an electronic scale, the amount of beverage each participant consumed.

How do these seemingly unrelated studies tie together? We found that the faces presented subliminally in the first study influenced participants' likelihood of following the advice to participate in the beverage study. Among those subliminally primed with angry faces, 24 percent decided to take part in the beverage study; 41 percent of those subliminally primed with neutral faces decided to participate; and 62 percent of those subliminally primed with happy faces decided to participate. Among the participants who agreed to complete the beverage study, the amount of drink they consumed varied depending on the subliminal stimuli they received. Those who saw happy faces consumed more (about ninety grams!) than both those who saw neutral faces (who drank about seventy-four grams) and those who saw angry faces (who drank about fifty-six grams).

These results suggest that even when others' emotional expressions are subliminal, and even when those expressions belong to strangers, they influence recipients' decisions through emotional contagion (in this case, the decision to follow advice). Subliminal happiness caused participants to be more receptive to advice from another person as compared to a control condition, and subliminal anger caused participants to be less receptive to another person's advice as compared to a control condition. These findings demonstrate that *subtle cues*, such as expressed emotions, can have significant effects on judgment and behavior. With little effort, we can become either more persuasive (for example, by smiling) or less persuasive (by expressing anger). This suggests that people who are self-aware of their expressed emotions and capable of regulating their emotions well may be particularly persuasive in such realms as negotiation, sales, and job interviews. That is, they should be able to use their emotions strategically to influence others in a desired direction.

In social interactions, emotional contagion commonly involves two stages. First, once a person publicly displays certain emotions, observers tend to unintentionally and automatically mimic these displays. For instance, if you begin to smile while talking to someone, it is very likely that she will subconsciously mimic your smile. Second, the very act of subconsciously mimicking another person's behavior (including facial expressions) leads us to experience the emotions associated with that behavior. For example, smiling evokes happiness, and a glare evokes anger.

By the time we reach this second stage of emotional contagion, we may be in trouble. As we have seen, our emotions (including those triggered by others' expressions) influence our judgments and decisions. Even when the emotions others express are imperceptible, they can greatly influence how we feel and behave.

All of us are affected by emotions triggered by events related to an impending decision—and, more importantly, by emotions that are unrelated to the decision at hand. As we have seen, these emotions can sidetrack our decisions across different contexts. That's a problem if new, often fleeting emotions set us off course from our carefully set plans. If emotions are so powerful, what can we do to avoid the problems they cause?

You might think that the best course is to try to dismiss or downplay emotions that could be interfering with your decisions. But emotions can provide important information, so it is more useful to acknowledge them than to dismiss them when they were triggered by the choice you are facing. Emotions can serve as signals about how you (and others) are feeling regarding a course of action and help you make important adjustments to existing plans. Some emotions, including incidental ones, may even provide a useful performance boost.

In a well-known study conducted by Alice Isen, a Cornell University psychologist, doctors were brought into the lab and presented with a familiar task: an assistant described a few unambiguous ailments that were plaguing him and, based on that information, the doctors were asked to reach a diagnosis.[8] Every time the assistant described a new symptom, the doctors had to give their diagnosis based on what they had heard up to that point. Half of the doctors had received a small gift (such as a notepad, a nail clipper, or a small bag of hard candies) before the experiment started, and the other half did not. By giving the doctors this small, unexpected gift, the experimenter wanted to raise the doctors' level of happiness. In this way, she could compare the behavior of doctors who felt happy and those who were in a "neutral" emotional state (i.e., those who had not received the gift).

As expected, the unexpected gift caught the recipients by surprise and boosted their happiness (in fact, it lifted their dopamine levels, which stimulate the brain to process information). As a result, it also increased their creativity. Compared with doctors who did not receive the small gift, those who did thought more creatively and reached the correct diagnosis in half as many steps. Clearly, the doctors did not realize that the unexpected gift had an impact on their thinking. Similar to the results of the studies I described earlier, where expressions of gratitude motivated participants to give extra help to a student in need, a triggered emotion had a positive impact on doctors' behavior. Emotions sometimes lead to good outcomes, including happy diversions from our initial plans.

This leads us to a second principle to avoid getting sidetracked:

Take your emotional temperature.

When you are in the midst of making an important decision, try to carefully consider your emotional state. By taking your emotional temperature before making a decision, you can reflect on the causes of your current feelings and determine whether they were triggered by an event unrelated to the decision at hand. You may discover you are dismissing the suggestions of a colleague or your spouse just because you are in a bad mood. Taking your emotional temperature may also enable you to better understand others' feelings going forward. For instance, over the years, Ducati Corse successfully learned how to take the emotional temperature of its riders, recognizing when their feedback was influenced by their emotions and their overall mood.

Although there are many situations in which our feelings about a decision we are facing tell us something about the decision itself, there are also many situations where irrelevant emotions—those caused by an event completely unrelated to the decision at hand—take us off track. Drinking a bitter cup of morning coffee or getting stuck in traffic on the way to work may carry over to influence our subsequent decisions for the worse, without our knowledge. Similarly, anxiety about a possible promotion could lead us to conform to others' ideas even when we planned to carefully follow our own analyses. By taking your emotional temperature, you can examine whether incidental emotions are clouding your decisions.

In addition, a better sense of your emotional temperature can improve your forecasts of how you will approach future decisions and, more specifically, how your emotions might affect them. This is probably what has motivated many people to purchase "Clocky," a special alarm clock that Gauri Nanda invented while a graduate student at the MIT Media Lab. Clocky is outfitted with wheels so that it can roll off a bedside table and hide when its owner presses the snooze button, thus forcing the owner to get up and look for it. If you know you will be grumpy and tired when your alarm goes off and consequently stay in bed too long, a little help from Clocky can prevent your emotions from ruining your original plan of waking up on time. As Clocky demonstrates, when you know that your emotions can derail your decisions, you can plan ahead to circumvent them.

CHAPTER 3

What the Cracked Pot Couldn't See

An Overly Narrow Focus

Not too long ago, I stumbled upon an ancient Chinese parable. It concerns an elderly Chinese woman who owns two large pots. The two pots are hung on the ends of a pole that the woman carries across her neck. Day after day, the woman engages in the same routine. She walks to a nearby stream, fills the two pots with water, and walks back to her house. By the time the elderly woman gets back home, one of the pots is still full of water, but the other is only half full. This second pot, in fact, has a crack in it, which is why some of the water is lost during the long walk home. Every day for more than two years, the woman brings home only one-and-a-half pots of water when she could have brought home two full pots.

The two pots had different reactions to this fact. (Yes, pots experience feelings and express thoughts in this parable.) The pot that had no crack felt proud of its accomplishments. After all, every day it ensured that a full pot of water reached home. The pot with the crack, instead, felt miserable: it was ashamed of its own imperfection and disappointed that it could do only half of what it had been made to do.

After two years, the cracked pot decided to share its feelings with the old woman. "I am ashamed of myself," it confessed, explaining that its crack, as she may have noted, caused water to leak out during her walk back to the house.

The old woman, well aware of the crack, smiled at the pot. She asked the pot whether it noticed that there were flowers on its side of the path but not on the other pot's side. Knowing about the crack, the woman had decided to plant flower seeds on that side of the path and water them every day while she walked back home. "For two years," the woman told the cracked pot, "I have been able to pick these beautiful flowers to decorate the table. Without you being just the way you are, this beauty would not grace my home."

By focusing too narrowly on its flaw, the cracked pot missed the fact that it was actually doing something of value. Or, in the common idiom, the cracked pot missed the forest for the trees: it was so focused on the details of its problem that it overlooked the bigger picture.

Being too narrowly focused is a trap to which most humans, like the pot in the parable, fall prey. Consider the case of one of South Korea's largest and most successful family-run conglomerates, Samsung Group, which was funded by Lee Byung-Chull in 1938. The company, which started in Seoul as a small trading company with forty employees, grew to become one of the largest multibillion-dollar corporations in the world. In particular, three businesses form the core of Samsung Group and reflect its name: electronics, shipbuilding, and construction; in Korean, *samsung* means "three stars." In addition to being a global force in these and other industries, the company also leads several domestically, including the financial, chemical, and entertainment industries.

For generations, the Samsung Group has been run by one of the world's wealthiest families and is currently managed by chairman Lee Kun-Hee, the third son of the company's founder. The company has quite an interesting history, filled with memorable milestones. To take one example, in 1992, Lee realized a long-cherished dream of his father's by announcing the group's entry into the car sector.[1] The chairman publicly declared that Samsung Motors would be among the world's ten largest car manufacturers by 2010.

Samsung managers, Korean government officials, and industry commentators all questioned the company's significant bet on the car industry. Senior managers within the company suggested a joint venture to test the waters before making a major commitment of resources, but the chairman was dead set on his decision to plunge into the automotive world. After all, the data on the company's success in other industries seemed to suggest that Samsung should not be afraid of entering a new business. The company dedicated large amounts of corporate resources to achieve success in its new venture. It also borrowed heavily to build a state-of-the-art research and design facility and a greenfield factory with clean-room production technology and cutting-edge robotics. The chairman redeployed several of Samsung's most seasoned executives from other divisions to lead the initiative.

Yet Lee Kun-Hee's plan failed to materialize. From the time the first car rolled off the assembly line in 1998, Samsung Auto suffered operating losses and significant interest charges on its loans. Within a few years, the company was forced to divest its car business for a fraction of its initial investment. Lee's narrow focus on Samsung's success in other contexts in the past, rather than on the complexities of the new industry, set the company up for failure on a grand scale.

How did such a thoughtful and accomplished executive overestimate the ability of his company to succeed in a new industry? Why did the cracked pot interpret its flaw as a problem and overlook the potential benefit? To answer these questions—and to further explore what they have in common—let's turn to some research findings in the realm of human cognition and attention.

Over a decade ago, psychologists Daniel Simons (of the University of Illinois at Urbana-Champaign) and Christopher Chabris (of Union College at Schenectady in New York) discovered that even when objects are in plain sight, we may completely fail to notice them if our attention is focused elsewhere, a phenomenon known as *inattentional blindness.* In an experiment that you may be familiar with, the two psychologists asked a group of participants to watch a short video clip in which two groups of people pass a basketball around.[2] One group of players is wearing black T-shirts, and the other is wearing white T-shirts. The instructions told participants to count the number of passes made by the team wearing the white T-shirts. Halfway through the clip, as the players are passing the basketball, a man wearing a gorilla suit walks across the screen. After watching the video, participants were asked if they had seen anything out of the ordinary take place onscreen. Over 50 percent of them reported not seeing the gorilla. Because of the clear instructions they had received, their attention was focused on counting the number of passes of the ball, and thus they failed to see the gorilla.[3] (The first time I watched the video, I missed the gorilla, too.) This common failure was so surprising to me that I started using this video every time I teach executive education, MBA, or undergraduate classes. Most of my students report not seeing the gorilla, and many claim that I am tricking them. Of course, when I play the clip for them again and ask them to look out for a gorilla, all of them easily notice him this time.

The results of Simons and Chabris's well-known study suggest that we do not see as much of the world around us as we think we do. These findings should make us think twice the next time we find ourselves multitasking—for example, talking on a cell phone while driving. The findings lead us to another, more important conclusion, which is supported by some of my past research: the way we process visual information is not very different from the way we process data when we make decisions. When we have a clear plan in mind, our plans may get sidetracked because of an overly narrow focus on the problem at hand. As a result, we miss information that could help us reach the effective decisions we were hoping to make.

In the spring of 2011, I conducted some field research on a complex, multiyear conflict among parties located in both Poland and the Netherlands.[4] At the heart of the conflict was the desire of Eureko, a large Dutch insurance company, to acquire a controlling stake in Poland's leading insurance group, Powszechny Zaklad Ubezpieczen S.A. (PZU). In 1999, Poland decided to privatize PZU. Under the terms of the share purchase agreement (SPA) entered into by the state treasury of Poland, Eureko acquired 30 percent of PZU shares for the equivalent of about $700 million. The SPA also signaled the state treasury's intent to hold an initial public offering (IPO) for all or part of the PZU shares it was holding—about 55 percent—by early 2001. Yet the treasury did not hold the IPO by this date, and this stalled privatization led to a heated conflict between the two major shareholders. After much litigation, Eureko and the Polish government agreed that Poland would sell another 21 percent of PZU shares to Eureko by the end of 2001 and hold the IPO in 2002.

Once again, however, Poland did not move to an IPO, nor did it sell Eureko the promised 21 percent stake. In 2003, Eureko filed an international arbitration case against Poland, seeking reimbursement of its $700 million purchase payment, plus damages for the privatization delay for a total of Polish zloty 36 billion (about $12.4 billion). The arbitration dragged on for five years.

In 2008, Gerard van Olphen signed on as Eureko's chief financial officer and as vice-chairman of its executive board. From van Olphen's perspective, Eureko's view of the arbitration was too narrowly focused. Convinced that Eureko would win the arbitration case, the company's upper management team had concentrated primarily on ensuring that the evaluation of damages would be accurate. Van Olphen agreed that Eureko would win in court, but felt his team was missing the point. He brought the team members together for a workshop in which he asked them to analyze what would happen if Eureko won the arbitration, pushing them to consider every possible option. By the end of the day, the entire team realized that even if they won, the Polish government would not pay Eureko, either because it did not have enough money or because it would avoid paying based on the history of the conflict. (As van Olphen realized, the Polish government had so far avoided adhering to international treaties.) Moreover, Eureko would not be able to receive its payment in any other way since any arbitration claims would not be enforceable. Up to that point, the members had a clear plan in mind: winning and claiming damages from the Polish government. But, as they realized during the workshop, they were too narrowly focused on the court case as their best option for resolving the conflict, and missed the fact that winning the arbitration would not be a beneficial outcome. As a result, they decided to enter into negotiations with the Polish government and be more open about discussions related to the size of the damages. In the end, the two parties reached a deal, and Eureko ended up getting €4.2 billion.

As this story illustrates, a narrowed focus of attention can hide important facts. Focusing solely on how they would use their money blinded the executives to the fact that they were unlikely to ever see it. Another interesting phenomenon that seems to impact both our vision and our decisions is *change blindness*. In the case of attention and vision, here is how this phenomenon might occur. Imagine that you are walking around your town on a sunny afternoon to stretch your legs and enjoy the nice weather. As you're walking through the town center, a person stops you and says, "Excuse me, do you mind helping me out?" He tells you that he is looking for a particular ice cream parlor, gives you the address, and shows you where the shop is supposed to be on his map. Since you are a nice person and know the town quite well, you start giving the stranger directions by showing him which route he should take to easily get to the ice cream parlor. How closely do you think you are observing the man you are talking to? How much of his physical appearance do you think you are noticing?

In the late 1990s, Daniel Simons and his colleague Daniel Levin of Vanderbilt University conducted a field experiment that followed this format in order to test people's attention to their environment.[5] In their study, a confederate stopped passersby on a college campus to ask for directions. As some point during each conversation, two men carrying a large board passed between the confederate and the person he approached. As the board passed by, obstructing the person's view, the confederate slipped away and was replaced by another confederate of the same gender. The two confederates were clearly different people, yet most individuals faced with this change failed to detect it. They continued to give directions, oblivious that they were suddenly talking to a different person.

You might think that you would notice such an obvious change. Odds are, however, that you would not. As this study demonstrates, we can be blind to changes that happen in the world around us if our attention is not drawn directly to these changes when they happen. Small distractions (such as a board passing by) and a narrow focus (concentrating on giving accurate directions) can make a change invisible to us. And even information as seemingly critical as our memory of the face of the person to whom we are actively talking seems to be susceptible to change blindness. In their research on visual perception, Simons and his colleagues have found that people frequently fail to notice gradual changes that occur right before their eyes. However, if the second confederate were a woman, you and others likely would notice such a change. (As a side note, given the failures that characterize our vision, we should likely reexamine the faith we give to the accuracy of eyewitness testimony in crimes and accidents.)

In Simons's research, the information people miss is visual, and the mental processes that might explain the failure to notice changes are perceptual. My Harvard colleague Max Bazerman and I demonstrated that similar mechanisms operate for information processing more generally. In one of our projects, we applied this idea to the case of ethical decision making and examined how individuals fail to see wrongdoing that occurs in front of their eyes, especially when ethical erosion occurs on a slippery slope.

Consider the case of an accountant working at a large auditing firm. The accountant is responsible for conducting an audit of a large company that has a good reputation in the market. For a few consecutive years, this company's financial statements have been impeccable—nothing seemed incorrect or unethical about them. Given the high quality of the client's statements, the accountant approved them with no trepidation; meanwhile, he built a strong relationship with the company. This year, however, something seems to be different. The client clearly committed some legal transgressions in its preparation of the financial statements. Despite his strong relationship with the client, the accountant in this situation is likely to notice the fact that the company broke the law. As a result, he is likely to refuse to certify that the financial statements were consistent with government regulations.

But what would happen if, instead, the corporation stretched the law in just one area, by a small amount? The auditor might not notice the transgression, or at least he probably would be less likely to notice it than he would in the previous situation. If, in the following years, the firm's transgressions are equally imperceptible, the auditor may fail to notice them again. Max and I theorized that by year six, the cumulative violations might be as large as those described in the first case, but since they built up slowly, year after year, they might go unnoticed.

With this question in mind, Max and I invited seventy-six individuals from the Cambridge and Boston areas to our lab. In the first stage of the experiment, participants played the role of "estimator." In the next stage, they played the role of "approver." As estimators, in each of sixteen rounds, they saw a picture on their computer screen of a jar containing American pennies and were asked to estimate the amount of money in the jar. As approvers, in each round they saw a picture of the jar as well as an estimate of the amount of money it contained; they were told that the estimate had been made in the previous stage by another participant in the same experiment. (We actually predetermined these estimates ourselves.) The approvers had to decide whether to accept or reject the estimate based on their examination of the jar. If they wanted to accept the estimate, they first had to virtually sign a document stating that they honestly believed it was accurate within a range of 10 percent. (We used this signing process to make the ethicality of participants' approval more vivid to them.)

In this second stage, when participants were in the role of approvers, we introduced our manipulation. In our "abrupt-change" condition, half of the participants received estimates equal to the true value of the money in the jar plus some random error for the first ten rounds; in round eleven, they received an estimate that was about $4 higher; and the estimates over the remaining five rounds were similar to the estimate in round eleven. The other half of the participants received estimates that increased by 40 cents every round, from round two through round ten; for rounds eleven through sixteen, the estimates were the same as in the other condition. In other words, in this second condition—which we called the "slippery-slope" condition—from round eleven on, participants evaluated the same estimates in both conditions; what varied was the series of estimates they received up to that point.

For you to fully appreciate the results of the study, I need to tell you about the payment scheme we set up. First, estimators had a financial incentive to behave unethically by providing a high estimate in the first stage of the study; they received 8 percent of each estimate the approver accepted and no payment if the approver rejected the estimate. Second, approvers were paid more when they allowed inflated estimates, but at the risk of a potential penalty for approving egregiously exaggerated estimates. (Approvers received 4 percent of the estimates they approved and no payment for estimates they rejected, but, as they were told, the computer would randomly double-check estimates 10 percent of the time and fine approvers $5 for each estimate that was not within 10 percent of the true value.)

As you may have noticed, this payoff scheme roughly parallels the payoffs faced by auditors charged with verifying that organizations report truthful information to the public. Auditors face a conflict of interest: because they have a financial incentive to please those they are supposed to be monitoring, they may be motivated to turn a blind eye to small infractions. However, they usually face a substantial penalty if they are caught allowing a great deal of cheating.

As we predicted, the percentage of participants approving estimators' estimates was significantly higher when those estimates increased slowly, round after round, rather than abruptly. When the changes occurred slowly, approvers failed to "see" them. Namely, in the slippery-slope condition, over rounds eleven through sixteen, the rate of approval was 52 percent on average; by contrast, the rate of approval was only 24 percent in the abrupt-change condition. That is, our participants were more likely to accept the unethical behavior of others when it developed gradually than when it occurred abruptly.

Could our results be attributed to differences in approvers' intentional search for a strategy that would maximize their own payoffs? In follow-up studies, Max and I added a condition in which participants did not have incentives to approve inflated estimates. We replicated our results: the rate of approval of inflated estimates was still higher in the slippery-slope condition than in the abrupt-change condition, suggesting that individuals perceive gradual changes in others' unethical behavior as acceptable.

As in the case of change blindness, participants did not seem to notice small changes in the information that was presented to them. Narrowly focused on the task at hand, they noticed only changes that were large and abrupt.

The types of "focusing failures" in information processing and decision making that I've described are pervasive in organizations, as I have had the opportunity to observe when working with companies in different industries. One of these companies, Teradyne, is a leading manufacturer of highly sophisticated electronics production equipment. Like many companies, Teradyne struggled with time delays in product-development projects. Projects scheduled to take three years were routinely completed in four years or more. As the market became more competitive and customers more demanding, Teradyne's senior management launched a systematic effort to improve its product-development performance through rigorous, up-front planning of projects, a well-defined development process, clear milestones for project reviews, cross-functional project teams with strong project leaders, and thorough post-project reviews to glean lessons learned. As Gary Pisano and I learned when conducting field research at Teradyne in 2006, the company's senior executives were strongly committed to these efforts, and some of the company's most experienced leaders were actively involved in driving the implementation.[6]

While the new system did improve the timeliness of newly launched products, the company's experience on a major project proved to be sobering. The project, known internally as the "Jaguar Project," centered on new-generation equipment for testing semi-conductors that involved significant hardware and software design. The project used rigorous methods to estimate development timelines, formulate schedules based on careful analysis of "critical paths," and track progress. A sophisticated, Web-based scheduling tool provided daily updates on project progress and early warnings about potential slip-ups. The team was given thorough training in these tools, and core team leadership was highly committed to their use and believed in their effectiveness. The team even received extra resources in the form of dedicated project coordinators charged with collecting the appropriate information, running the analyses, and providing them to the team. (The team met weekly, but team members often spoke to one another daily.)

The results of the project were a veritable "tale of two cities." For parts of the project involving hardware (such as mechanical and electronics design), the project ran like clockwork. Moreover, the project management tools worked exactly as expected. If a particular activity was delayed, the master schedule immediately showed the impact of the delay, and resources were redeployed or activities shifted to minimize the impact. Project leadership credited the early-warning system as a way to head off major problems that could have delayed the entire project.

Meanwhile, the software development effort was a very different story. From the very beginning, the effort began to lag behind, and it never caught up. Even worse, the project's timeline was compressed, exacerbating the software team's problems. To make up for lost time, the team cut back on testing, but this decision led to more bugs in the code, which further delayed the effort. As the project wore on, deadlines passed, and significant software resources were added. The software was completed about six months behind schedule, causing a delay in the shipment of the first commercial systems.

In any complex, multicomponent development project, it is not unusual for some parts of the project to run considerably better than others. In this case, differences in organizational capabilities, the complexity of technical requirements, and luck may explain why the hardware performed according to expectations and the software did not. What *is* puzzling, however, is that the project management tools put in place were designed to give the project team early warnings to which they could respond. By virtually all indications, the project tools performed this function equally well for both the hardware and software teams. Interestingly, when reflecting on the impact of the tools on hardware development, managers credited them with providing "visibility" into critical problems and enabling the team to respond. Weekly project reviews often resulted in changes to hardware development to optimize the critical path. Rather than making the team rigid, the tools were credited with providing the information needed for the team to respond rapidly to external changes (such as one customer's demand that a version of the product be shipped much sooner than scheduled).

Though functioning in much the same way, the tools did not have the same impact on the behavior of the software team. Several managers noted that the problems with software were evident from the beginning, but the organization did not react. The project leader reflected: "Our problem was not lack of data . . . it was data staring at us, and us not responding." Another reflected, "We let the data lie to us." The person on the software side who was in charge of using the new tools recognized that he and the rest of the team were too narrowly focused. They devoted energy to making sure the tools were used, but failed to focus on the information the tools actually made available to them.

In our modern world, being able to focus on a task is usually a pro rather than a con. Thanks to recent technological developments, information is available to us in all sorts of shapes and forms whenever we need it. While attending a business meeting, we can listen to the agenda items being discussed while checking our laptop for updates to the company website or reviewing e-mail messages on our phone. While on a conference call, we can work on a report and surf the Web for news.

Being able to focus helps us juggle tasks and sort through all the information available to us. But the evidence I have discussed so far in this chapter suggests that when our focus is too narrow, it can lead us to miss the big picture. A wider scope would help us capture and integrate important details into our decisions.

In addition to potentially missing the bigger picture, there are two other consequences of having a narrow focus that I want to share with you. Both have to do with how we use the information that is available to us to make predictions about the thoughts and decisions of others.

I'd like you to try a simple exercise, just to stretch your mental muscles. Think of a well-known song you really like. Depending on where you are right now, if possible, recruit someone—whether an acquaintance, your significant other, or even a stranger—to be your listener for a minute or two. If you are sitting by yourself in your favorite comfy chair, sipping wine, just imagine a listener is close to you. Ready? Now, start tapping out the rhythm with your fingertips. Don't stop until you are well into the song.

Now that you've had the chance to express your musical ability, consider the following question: how likely is it that your listener (whether imaginary or real) can correctly identify the song?

Although I can't be present to observe the results of this live experiment, I bet your prediction is far from accurate. Inside your head, the song unfolded very smoothly. So, you probably assumed that your listener would have an easy time guessing the title of the song. In fact, I predict that it is extremely unlikely that your listener guessed it.

The experiment you just conducted imitates the original tapping study that Elizabeth Newton performed as part of her graduate dissertation in 1990.[7] Participants in her study received instructions similar to those I gave you: they were asked to tap out the rhythm of a well-known song for a listener and then estimate the likelihood that the listener would correctly identify the song. The results were striking: tappers estimated that about 50 percent of listeners would correctly identify the song, but the actual accuracy rate was much lower—less than 3 percent of the listeners correctly identified the song.

A few years later, another well-known psychologist, Lee Ross of Stanford University, conducted a similar study with one of his colleagues to understand the perspective of tappers and listeners. The experience of the people placed in either role was very different. Tappers reported that they could "hear" the tune and even the words to the song they were tapping; some even reported hearing a "full orchestration, complete with rich harmonies between string, winds, brass, and human voice," according to Ross. Meanwhile, limited to "an aperiodic series of taps," the listeners found it difficult to even tell "whether the brief, irregular moments of silence between taps should be construed as sustained notes, as musical 'rests' between notes, or as mere interruptions as the tapper contemplates the 'music' to come next."[8] The experience of the tappers was so rich that they had a hard time setting it aside when assessing the objective stimuli that were available to listeners. As a result, tappers assumed that what was obvious to them (the identity of the song) would be obvious to their audience.

This basic lesson from Newton's and Ross's studies has a wide range of applications beyond the context of tapping out songs. One is particularly interesting given the changing nature of our everyday communication: away from face-to-face discussions and toward electronic mail and other forms of technology-mediated communication. E-mail was a great invention, wasn't it? It allows us to communicate efficiently and conveniently, no matter how far away in location and time we are from each other. But as a communication medium, e-mail comes with some costs: it does not allow us to add nonverbal cues to the information we are communicating. As it turns out, nonverbal cues, such as facial expressions and hand gestures, often play a crucial role in helping others understand what we are trying to say. Yet we often forget this when typing messages on our computers.

In a cleverly designed experiment, Nicholas Epley (a professor at the University of Chicago) recruited a team of colleagues to study how e-mail communication failures can occur. Participants were invited to the laboratory for a study investigating how people communicate humor. They were given ten jokes, asked to choose the funniest five among them, and told they would be e-mailing them to another study participant. As examples, here are two of the jokes that vary in terms of how humorous they are (both from the book *Deep Thoughts* by Jack Handey):[9]

1. *Question:* What is as big as a man, but weighs nothing? *Answer:* His shadow.

2. If a kid asks where rain comes from, I think a cute thing to tell him is, "God is crying." And if he asks why God is

crying, another cute thing to tell him is, "Probably because of something you did."

After selecting the five funniest jokes among the ten they were given, participants were randomly assigned to one of two conditions. Half of them were simply told to reread their chosen jokes carefully and informed that they would soon e-mail these jokes to another study participant. The other half first watched a videotape of their chosen jokes being read on the TV show *Saturday Night Live*.

Before actually sending their e-mail messages, participants in both conditions had to rate how funny they thought each joke was as well as how funny they thought the person receiving the e-mail would think it was. Then, the jokes each participant had chosen were e-mailed to a different participant. The recipients' task was simple: they had to read the jokes and rate how funny they thought they were.

Epley and his colleagues had two main predictions. First, they expected participants to think the jokes were funnier when they watched the videotape than when they read the jokes themselves. After all, the nuances of timing and delivery are part of what makes a joke funny. Second, the scholars expected participants to fail to take this detail into account in their predictions. As a result, they expected participants in the videotape condition to believe that others would find the jokes funnier than would those in the control condition (those who didn't watch the video). That is, the scholars hypothesized that participants would have difficulty distinguishing their subjective experience of the delivered joke from the objective properties of the joke.

Consistent with their predictions, the recipients found the jokes to be equally funny (or not funny) across conditions. But the participants overestimated how funny their e-mail recipients would find the jokes, and those participants who watched the videotape of the jokes being read made the greatest overestimations. If you are curious about the exact numbers, I reported the means across conditions in table 3-1 (note that the humor ratings were on a scale

TABLE 3-1

Mean results across conditions for Epley's e-mail communication experiment

	Videotape condition	Control condition
Own rating	8.15	5.64
Predicted audience rating	7.27	5.08
Actual audience rating	3.55	3.40

ranging from 1 [not at all funny] to 11 [very funny]). The study suggests that people tend to believe they can communicate over e-mail much more effectively than they actually can.

Of course, miscommunication does not happen only over e-mail. You might be able to think of a time when you used a joke or sarcastic expression to try to amuse someone but ended up hurting that person's feelings instead. As was the case in Epley's study, being overly focused on how funny a joke seems to us causes us to mispredict how others will react to it—a mistake that can have costly consequences.

Beyond humor, think of a time when you gave a presentation to your team, made a sales pitch to a customer, or tried to explain your point of view to a friend or significant other. You may have found yourself wondering why your audience just didn't seem to be getting it. While it is certainly possible you were being crystal clear, it is also possible you assumed that what was obvious to you (the meaning of your slides during the presentation) would also be obvious to your audience.

These examples and the results of the last few experiments I described highlight an important consequence of a narrow focus: we tend to overestimate the extent to which private information is available to others. We focus so much on what we know that we forget others do not have access to the same information. More generally, as human beings, we tend to be egocentric: we find it difficult to move beyond our subjective experience of a stimulus and imagine how someone who cannot read our mind and who does not share our privileged perspective might evaluate it. When executing our plans involves making assessments about how much others know, then our decisions can easily be derailed by our tendency to focus too much on ourselves.

There is another interesting consequence of being too narrowly focused: we tend to underestimate the extent to which our own constraints influence the actions of others. My colleague Don Moore and I examined this tendency in the context of negotiations. We recruited 320 students (mostly undergraduates) from Carnegie Mellon University for an experiment in which they would engage in a two-person negotiation over the sale of a used car. At the beginning of the experiment, we randomly assigned participants to the role of buyer or seller. Buyers and sellers were paired up, and they negotiated using a live-chat program. The instructions on the computer screen informed them, "You will be negotiating against a partner who will be seated at another computer, and who will remain anonymous. You will communicate via written messages sent via computerized 'chat.' In the negotiation, you will be negotiating over the sale of a used car."

The negotiation involved three main issues that the buyer and seller had to discuss: the car's price, which one of them would fix the car's broken alternator, and who would replace its tires. Their agreement on each of these issues affected their payoffs in the negotiation. Failure to reach an overall agreement (that is, a sale) resulted in zero payoffs for both sides of the negotiation—so, each party had an incentive to come to an agreement.

We included three manipulations in the experiment. First, we varied the amount of power the parties had in the negotiation. Half of the pairs had one party with less power than the other, as reflected in their alternatives to the current negotiation; the other half had parties with the same level of power (either low or high). Second, we varied whether one of the parties had a deadline in the negotiation: in a third of the groups, the high-power party had a deadline; in another third, the low-power party had a deadline; and in the remaining third, neither party had a deadline. Having a deadline meant having only five minutes to reach an agreement with the other party. Although it was possible for parties to reach an agreement in this time frame, it certainly created pressure. Participants without a deadline knew that they could negotiate for up to fifteen minutes. Finally, as our third manipulation, we varied whether participants who had deadlines had to reveal the deadline to the other party. Half of the participants in each role had to reveal the deadline as soon as they started negotiating. The other half were instructed not to inform their counterparts about the deadline.

Now, let's take a step back for a minute. Let's imagine you are in fact at the bargaining table and have a real deadline: you have accepted a new job in Europe and have decided to sell your car before leaving the States. Your plane ticket has a firm date on it, which imposes a final deadline on any potential negotiation regarding the sale of your car. Somebody stopped by to look at the car earlier today, and this person seemed interested in buying it. Would you tell her you have a deadline?

I am guessing that you, like most people in this situation, would choose not to reveal your deadline, reasoning that it is a weakness that reduces your freedom and puts pressure on you to reach an agreement quickly. But let's go back to the experiment and see what our participants actually did. Remember that they were instructed either to reveal their final deadline (if they had one) or keep it secret. Contrary to what participants believed, revealing final deadlines was beneficial. First, it decreased the rate of impasse, from 37 percent for pairs with secret deadlines to 23 percent for pairs where deadlines were revealed. Among the pairs with a final deadline who did reach agreement, the party with the deadline did better in the negotiation when he or she revealed the deadlines than when he or she did not. Interestingly, the benefits of revealing final deadlines did not depend on whether the party with the deadline was more or less powerful than his or her counterpart (as reflected in the number of outside alternatives to the current negotiation).

Together, these results indicate that participants were better at anticipating the effect of situational constraints (in this case, final deadlines) on their own behavior than on the behavior of others. They failed to predict that a deadline would affect a counterpart as much as the deadline affected them personally. Putting yourself back in this situation, if you thought that revealing your deadline would hurt you in the negotiation, you probably forgot to consider that the same deadline also ends talks for your negotiating partner. If you leave the country without reaching a deal for the sale of your car, your counterpart also would be left without an agreement. Final deadlines that seem one-sided are, in fact, symmetric because the time pressure influences both parties. Our narrow focus on ourselves prevents us from recognizing that the time pressure will affect the other party in a similar way. Here again, an overly narrow focus can derail our plans, if it keeps us from reaching a beneficial agreement.

The evidence I presented in this chapter highlights a third important factor that sidetracks our decisions: our narrow self-focus. Even when we have very detailed plans, the way we recruit and evaluate information as we follow through on our plans is often too narrow. This tendency has three main consequences that, as I discussed, can derail our decisions. First, we may miss the bigger picture, ignoring information that would improve our decisions as we try to execute our plans. Second, we may overestimate the extent to which other people have access to our private information. Focusing too much on what we know, we forget that others lack this data and will reach different conclusions as a consequence. Third, we may underestimate the extent to which constraints that influence our behavior, such as deadlines, also affect the behavior of others.

How can we best counteract the effects of narrow focus on our decisions? The answer leads to the third principle to avoid getting sidetracked:

Zoom out.

In other words, get a sense of the bigger picture and the role other people play in it. Zooming out involves widening our focus when considering information to include in our decision-making processes so that we don't miss important details. Think back to the PZU example, in which the Eureko team was focused on maximizing its results from the arbitration. By bringing more information to the table, CEO Gerard van Olphen encouraged his team to abandon its narrow focus and reach a broader understanding of the conflict.

Zooming out involves taking a step back when making decisions and asking questions that reflect the bigger picture. Such questions might include: "Why did I choose the information that I did?" "What information am I missing?" "What was my initial plan?" and "Why did I embark on this course of action, and am I still on track?"

Let's see if a simple metaphor can clarify this point. Have you ever seen paintings by the artist Georges-Pierre Seurat? If you haven't, you can easily find pictures of his work on the Internet, such as *Sunday Afternoon on the Island of La Grande Jatte* or *The Circus*. (If you are more adventurous, you can visit the Art Institute of Chicago or the National Gallery in London.) In Seurat's painting technique, known as pointillism, small dots of pure color are applied in patterns to form an image. Pointillism relies on the ability of the viewer's eye and mind to blend the individual dots of color into a fuller range of tones. Whether you are looking at one of Seurat's paintings or imagining it in your mind, consider the different ways you might view it. Stand too close to the painting, and you won't fully appreciate the artist's work. You would probably admire the brightness of the color and the precision of the small, distinct dots, but you wouldn't necessarily know what you were looking at. But if you were to step back and look at the painting from a distance, you would gain a better understanding and appreciation of the entire image, in addition to its details. In the same way, when you "stand too close" to a decision-making problem, absorbed by your own information and constraints, you may overlook how they affect others.

PART II

Forces from Our Relationships

CHAPTER 4

How to Draw an *E* on Your Forehead

Lack of Perspective Taking

Let's play a simple game. It will take only a few seconds. Extend your right forefinger (or your left forefinger if you are left-handed). Ready? Now draw a capital letter *E* on your forehead with your finger.

Once you are done, think back to your drawing. Did you draw the letter so that it faced you or in such a way that a viewer could read it? In other words: did you draw an *E* that looked like E or like Ǝ? There is no right or wrong answer to this question. But the direction of the letter you just drew may tell you something about your own disposition. In fact, this seemingly innocent game is actually a method social scientists commonly use to measure *perspective taking*—the ability to step outside one's own shoes and see the world from someone else's point of view.[1]

Depending on how you drew the *E*, you can conclude whether you tend to be a person who naturally takes the perspective of other people or not. People who draw the *E* so that they can read it themselves—making it backward for others—have not considered others' point of view. Those who draw the *E* so that it is backward to themselves but legible to viewers have instead taken the perspective of another person.

Although perspective taking is a dispositional trait, it is also a quality we can all make an effort to develop and use in our lives. As adults, we have the mental capability necessary to adopt someone else's perspective and consider that person's thoughts and feelings as we make decisions. This may happen, for example, when you are trying to understand how a colleague could possibly believe her idea is a good one or why your significant other chose a particular movie for your evening out. By taking the perspective of others, we can try to make sense of *their* decisions or at least understand them better.

It's one thing to possess the ability to take another person's perspective; it's a different matter to use this skill when it would be appropriate or helpful. Perspective taking, in fact, requires some effort, since we typically focus automatically on our own point of view when facing a decision or interacting with others. Why is perspective taking worth the effort? Let me tell you a couple of stories that answer this question.

On September 20, 2010, Telecom Italia's mobile phone brand, TIM, launched its new advertising campaign. Telecom Italia invests hundreds of millions of euros every year in advertising. Competition for mobile phone services is fierce in Italy, where customers often view the different companies that offer these services (including TIM, Vodafone, Wind, and 3) as indistinguishable. To win customers over, companies need to design advertising campaigns with particular care, since their marketing efforts can make a real impact.

Hoping to win over customers from other mobile phone companies in Italy, TIM hired Belén Rodriguez, a young Argentinean "showgirl" and model who was having quite a bit of success on Italian television. Because she seemed so well liked by the Italian audience, TIM's marketing team believed she would be the perfect candidate for the company's new advertising campaign. The new TV spots depicted her as a sexy teacher talking to a student's father (played by a famous Italian actor, Christian De Sica).

The company's excitement about the new campaign was short-lived. Many consumers, especially those with children, felt the ads were too racy and Rodriguez "too sexy." The advertising campaign also received negative attention from the press. By the end of 2010, TIM's senior management team realized that the new advertisements not only failed to produce the sales increase that the company expected, but also caused the company to *lose* sales: a significant percentage of TIM clients were so disappointed by the campaign and upset by its new brand image that they decided to switch to a different phone provider. It seemed that TIM customers across Italy felt the company's new image represented something inauthentic. As a result, TIM lost market share and experienced a 10 percent decrease in profit (almost €700 million less than the previous year). In addition, the company's upper management fired Fabrizio Bona, the manager responsible for consumer engagement and the brains behind the advertising campaign.[2] As various journalists in Italian newspapers and business magazines noted, Bona was unable to take the perspective of typical TIM consumers and failed to understand the types of images that would please them. In the end, this inability to take the customer's perspective cost the company quite a bit of money.

In business, the failure to take customers' perspective and understand their needs is not uncommon and has resulted in some notable product and project flops. For example, as you may recall, the Coca-Cola Company took drastic measures in 1985 to stop its flagship soft drink, Coca-Cola, from losing the cola war to Pepsi.[3] For fifteen years, sales of Coke had remained flat, while Pepsi steadily gained ground. In a risky attempt to reverse this trend, Coca-Cola reformulated Coke into what came to be known as "New Coke." In focus groups before the product launch, most people approved of the new taste, but a vocal minority responded quite negatively and influenced other focus group members to adopt their point of view. Similarly, when New Coke was launched, consumers responded relatively well to it in the northeastern United States. But some Coke drinkers in the South, where Coca-Cola is head-quartered, loudly protested the change, some even suggesting that it opened wounds from the Civil War and marked a new capitula-tion to the North.

A groundswell of criticism grew across the country, with many Coke drinkers coming to view the reformulation as a betrayal of their loyalty as consumers. Boycotts and protests took place; Coca-Cola received more than four hundred thousand calls and let-ters of complaint. As sales of Coke began to level off, Coca-Cola abruptly reversed course and announced the return of the soft drink's classic formula on July 10, less than three months after New Coke's introduction. "The passion for original Coca-Cola—and that is the word for it, *passion*—was something that caught us by surprise," Coca-Cola Chairman Robert Goizueta said at a press conference announcing the reversal. Sales of "Coke Classic" surged, and sales of New Coke (as it was now officially marketed) plummeted. Clearly, the company had failed to understand con-sumers' emotional attachment to their favorite soft drink and the Coca-Cola brand.

In the business world, the failure to take the perspective of others occurs not only in relationships with consumers, but also internally, across units or divisions of the same organization, and in negotiations with outside partners. A case I often discuss in my negotiation classes nicely illustrates how costly perspective-taking failures can be at the bargaining table. In the late 1980s, Endesa (Empresa Nacional de Electricidad S.A.), the largest publicly held utility company in Latin America, decided to build a series of elec-tric plants on the Biobío River in Southern Chile.[4] Endesa was privatized in 1989 and became a subsidiary of the Spanish Enersis Group. In 1994, Endesa announced its plans for the second of six dams to be built on the river, a project named Ralco. The Ralco project required the relocation of about 675 native people, the Pehuenches, who were emotionally attached to the land because of their long history in the region and its natural resources. The families were asked to leave the land on which their ancestors were buried in exchange for financial compensation.

Endesa believed it had the legal right to build the dam. The company's independent legal studies had concluded that Chile's electric law, which allowed the government to enforce eminent domain to bring electric capacity online, took precedence over a new indigenous law protecting the rights and land of native peoples. The Spanish-owned company viewed its negotiation with the Pehuenches, a relatively powerless opponent, as a price transaction involving the exchange of land for compensation. The Pehuenches had a different view. For them, the negotiation involved issues bigger than land and money: it was about their identity, their culture, and mutual respect.

This difference in perspective led to a conflict that lasted nearly a decade, finally ending with an agreement in September 2003. In accordance with the agreement, all of the Pehuenches (including those who were most strongly opposed to doing so) left their land in exchange for financial compensation, and Endesa donated money toward new schools for the Pehuenches and promised to provide lifetime pensions to some of the claimants. Overall, Endesa spent $20 million on the settlement, about twice the amount it had budgeted. The agreement allowed Endesa to finish the project, but the company's perspective-taking failure was costly to all parties involved. Some of the Pehuenches continued to live by the dam (a short distance from where they used to live), on portions of the land that were not flooded, to tend to "their" territory. As for the company, the uproar from the local population prevented it from building any of the other dams it had planned. To this day, the city of Santiago has serious energy problems.

As these stories suggest, failing to take another person or group's perspective can be costly. Let me tell you about a cleverly designed experiment that reveals just how difficult it can be to see the world through someone else's eyes. A few years ago, University of Chicago psychologist Boaz Keysar and his colleagues recruited a group of participants from the Chicago area and told them that they would be playing a communication game with another participant in the same experiment.[5] In reality, this other person was a confederate—someone trained by the experimenters to talk and behave a certain way. The experimenter assigned roles ostensibly at random, but in fact the actual participants were always in the role of the "addressee," and the confederate was always in the role of the "director."

The participant and the confederate were asked to sit facing each other at a table. In the middle of the table, the experimenter had placed a four-by-four grid with different objects in each of its sixteen slots (kind of like an old-fashioned message box behind a hotel desk, or like the grid in the *Hollywood Squares* game with a few added slots). Some of the objects in the grid (such as a toy car) were visible to both the confederate and the participant. Others were blocked from the confederate's view with cardboard on one side; only the participant could see them, and this was obvious to the participant.

In each trial, one of the objects visible to both the confederate and the participant was a cassette tape. Let's call it the target. Here's the experimental plot twist: the experimenter also included an object that could be referred to by the same name as the target but that was different from it. In this particular case, this additional object was a roll of tape. That is, both a cassette tape and a roll of tape can be referred to as "tape." The roll of tape was placed in a bag that was shown to the participant, but not the confederate, and then the bag containing the roll of tape was placed in one of the grid slots. Thus, the participant knew about the presence of the object in the grid, but the confederate did not, and the participant was also aware that the confederate did not know about the object's presence. In each different trial of this game, the target and the object in the bag changed.

The game was not too difficult: in each trial, the director (the confederate) received a picture indicating where the objects should be moved and in what order. The director had to instruct her communication partner (the real participant) to rearrange the objects as specified in the picture. So the director would provide verbal instructions, and the participant would move the objects. Importantly, the picture the confederate received showed her perspective: it showed only mutually visible objects, indicating that the objects in occluded slots were not part of the game.

Imagine that you are taking part in this experiment. At one point, the confederate looks at you and asks, "Move the tape to the right." What would you do? More specifically, which object do you think you would move based on the confederate's instructions: the tape . . . or the tape?

If you are naturally good at perspective taking, then you likely would ignore the roll of tape. For you, the picture would be quite clear: the other participant has no idea what is in the bag, you would think, so there is no reason she'd ask you to move it. Therefore, you would conclude that she must be talking about the cassette tape, and you would move it as specified by her instructions. But if perspective taking is not your strong suit, then you might not think about what the other person does or does not know and would be equally likely to move either the roll of tape or the cassette tape.

The results showed that most participants failed to take the confederate's perspective. In fact, across the four critical trials, 71 percent attempted to move the bag at least once, and 46 percent moved it at least half the time. These participants assumed that the other participant shared their perspective. The results are quite clear: people are not very good at taking the perspective of another person.

Here is another demonstration of this human tendency. Think back to the last time you engaged in a group activity, such as a team assignment at work or a home-improvement project with your family. What percentage of the total amount of work did you contribute to the effort? In the late 1970s, two well-known psychologists, Michael Ross and Fiore Sicoly, posed a similar question to married couples. In particular, they asked husbands and wives separately to estimate their responsibility for a number of joint activities, such as making breakfast, cleaning the house, or avoiding being the cause of conflicts. After collecting the data, the two scholars added up the proportions each pair of respondents claimed for themselves.[6] Of course, if the couples made accurate assessments of their contributions, their combined estimates should have totaled 100 percent. Instead, the data showed that the couples tended to claim more than the maximum 100 percent for most of their joint activities. In fact, the percentages in this type of study are often around 140 to 150 percent. Each individual failed to take his or her spouse's perspective and failed to properly account for his or her contributions.

The moral of these experiments: perspective taking is no easy task, even in simple situations and under the best of circumstances.

Failures of perspective taking can take many different forms. They may cause us to overestimate the extent to which others share our attitudes and feelings, to believe that others have more access to our internal states than they actually do, to use ourselves as a standard when evaluating others, and to draw on our own experiences when anticipating how others will evaluate us. Yet another form of perspective-taking failure also regularly gets us into trouble: using our own knowledge as a guide to others' knowledge. We all have a hard time remembering that others do not have access to the information and knowledge that we have. This form of perspective taking is often referred to as the "curse of knowledge": once we have become an expert in a particular subject, it is hard to imagine not having this knowledge and difficult to accept that other people may not have the same level of knowledge.[7]

Think about the last time you had an in-depth talk with your financial adviser, lawyer, or doctor. Halfway through the conversation, you may have begun to wonder why the discussion was so abstract and why you were so confused. You might have assumed that you weren't paying good enough attention and that you were to blame for not following the conversation. In fact, it is quite possible that these experts spoke too quickly and used terms and abstract knowledge from their fields, forgetting in the process that you did not have access to their privileged information.

George Loewenstein, Don Moore, and Roberto Weber, who were colleagues at Carnegie Mellon University at the time of the study I am about to describe, presented business students at CMU with pairs of images that differed in one important detail.[8] Participants were assigned to one of three conditions. In the first condition, participants received no information about the images (uninformed condition). In the second condition, participants were told the difference between the images before they had the chance to look for it (informed condition). Finally, in the third condition, participants could choose to learn the difference for a fee (choice condition). This third condition was included to test whether participants would spend real dollars acquiring information that might or might not help them. In all conditions, participants were asked to guess the percentage of participants in the uninformed condition who would correctly identify the difference, and they were paid for the accuracy of their predictions. What do you think the results showed?

Only about 20 percent of the participants in the uninformed condition correctly identified the difference between the two images. More interestingly, informed participants greatly overestimated this percentage relative to those who were uninformed. In fact, informed participants thought that about 58 percent of the uninformed participants would correctly identify the difference, while uninformed participants thought that this percentage would be about 30 percent. The study also had another noteworthy finding: 29 percent of participants in the choice condition paid to learn the difference, and paying for this information made their estimates less accurate. They estimated that about 55 percent of the uninformed participants would correctly identify the difference; those who chose not to acquire the information predicted the percentage would be about 35 percent. In this experiment, then, participants not only projected their privileged information onto others who did not possess it, but also paid for information that biased their judgments and systematically lowered their earnings. As in the experiments on costly advice I described in chapter 1, participants listened too much to the information they had paid for, probably as a way to justify the fact that they had spent money to acquire it.

The various forms of perspective-taking failures that I have discussed so far regularly affect not only our professional lives, but our personal lives as well.

Here's one from my own experience. Like many Italians, I enjoy cooking and having friends over for dinner. Back when my husband and I lived in North Carolina, we had a chef-designed kitchen that matched my love of cooking. On multiple occasions, Greg and I invited people over and then got invited back. Among the many dinner parties we had at our place, one was particularly memorable. Interestingly, it was not because of the food or the company. It was because of the wine.

One of our friends—I'll call him Gavan—has a passion for wine. In fact, he has a fully stocked cellar full of his favorites. He has divided the bottles into categories and stores them on different shelves for different types of occasions and meals. His wine cellar also has a section of bottles that might be labeled "missed gifts": bottles that Gavan received from guests and that he actually did not appreciate. Just by looking at the labels on these bottles, he knew the wine would not satisfy his palate.

When Gavan invited us over for dinner one time, I brought a bottle of Italian wine that I had not seen in his cellar. I enjoy this wine, so I assumed Gavan would too. As always, dinner was delicious. We drank a few bottles of wine, but the one that Greg and I brought for the evening remained unopened.

A few weeks later, Greg and I invited Gavan and his wife over for dinner at our place. They arrived, and Gavan handed us a bottle of wine. "Here's what we brought to celebrate your Italian roots—some red wine from Italy!" he exclaimed. "Should we open it?" As soon as I saw the bottle, I burst out laughing: Gavan had "regifted" us the bottle we bought for them a few weeks earlier!

As it turns out, regifting is a common practice. A recent survey by the National Retail Federation found that about half of all Americans expect to return at least one holiday gift every year, and a third of respondents in an American Express survey had regifted presents. Gift-giving failures may reflect a problem of perspective taking. But what is interesting about this context is that all of us have been on both sides of this common social exchange. We have all been both recipients and givers in a gift-exchange relationship at some point in the past. Yet, despite our years of experience, we still have difficulty choosing gifts that others appreciate.

One method people use to maximize the success of a gift exchange is to explicitly tell others what gifts they would like. To this end, when approaching a significant milestone in their lives, such as a wedding, a birthday, or the birth of a child, people increasingly set up "wish lists" and gift registries for themselves that recommend items for their friends and family members to purchase. Is this type of transparency effective?

Francis Flynn (a professor at Stanford University) and I discussed this question over coffee a while back. We talked about our own experience receiving gifts that we sold on eBay or regifted to others. We also recalled times when we, as well as others we knew, had prepared wish lists (on Amazon.com, for example) or registries that included all the gifts we truly wanted. Yet gift givers often chose to stray from these lists, and then seemed surprised if we (or our friends or colleagues) did not seem adequately excited about the gifts they had chosen. Finally, we both could think of times when we ourselves diverged from a friend's gift registry, thinking we were choosing the perfect, unique gift for the recipient—only to be disappointed when he or she seemed underwhelmed.

Intrigued by the commonalities among our experiences as both gift givers and recipients, Frank and I decided to test some of our ideas in a series of experiments. Specifically, we decided to test which kinds of gifts recipients would appreciate more: gifts that givers chose from a wish list, or "off-list" gifts that givers chose spontaneously.

We recruited ninety students and staff members at the University of North Carolina at Chapel Hill. To increase their engagement in the study, we told participants that, in addition to being paid a $10 gift certificate, they also had the opportunity to win a real gift from their own wish list, which they would create during the study, at the end of the experiment (based on a random draw). The study was conducted online, and participants received instructions via e-mail directly from the experimenter during the three parts of the study.

Half of the participants took on the role of gift recipients; the other half played the role of gift givers. The experiment also included a second manipulation: the gift being exchanged was either a requested or an unrequested gift. A requested gift was one chosen from the wish list each recipient generated, and the unre-quested gift was a spontaneous gift selected by the giver that was not on the recipient's wish list.

In the first part of the study, gift recipients had twenty-four hours to create an Amazon.com wish list containing ten products, all within a given price range ($20–$30). In the second part of the study, givers received their recipient's wish list and had to select a gift for this person. Givers did not receive any other information about the recipient other than the wish list. In the requested-gift condition, givers had to choose the gift from among those included in the wish list. In the unrequested-gift condition, they had to generate a gift idea for the recipient in the $20–$30 price range from the Amazon.com site that was not on the recipient's wish list. In the third part of the study, recipients received information about the gift their givers chose for them. Then, all the participants answered an online questionnaire that measured the recipient's appreciation, the gift giver's thoughtfulness, and the extent to which the gift was or was not impersonal.

Despite the fact that the gifts chosen in the unrequested-gift condition were similar in price to the items the recipient had explicitly requested, and although selecting these items required more effort from the gift giver, gift recipients nevertheless appreciated the gifts they requested more than the gifts they did not request. They also rated requested gifts as more thoughtful and personal as compared with those that givers chose spontaneously. However, gift givers did not accurately predict this preference.

These results, which were consistent with our own experiences, demonstrated that even in gift-giving relationships, where we have a great deal of experience on both sides of the exchange, perspective-taking failures are common. We next set out to investigate a second, related question: whether requesting money instead of a gift item would lead to a different pattern of results. Money, we theorized, might belong to a special category of gifts. Although recipients may not feel comfortable asking for it, they may appreciate receiving money, as it allows them to buy what they really want. At the same time, gift givers may consider money to be impersonal and not very thoughtful. As a result, they may believe that recipients will appreciate money less than a requested item.

We used a study similar to the one I just described to test this hypothesis. This time, we invited 107 students and staff members from UNC to participate in the study. We assigned half of the participants to the role of gift givers and the other half to the role of recipients. We also varied whether recipients received a gift they requested or a gift they did not request. The requested gift was chosen from a wish list each recipient generated (which included gifts costing about $15), and the unrequested gift was an amount of money that matched the value of the average gift on the recipient's wish list (i.e., $15).

Imagine that you are a participant playing the role of recipient. You spent time surfing the Amazon website and choosing products from various categories that you would like to receive as a gift. Then you learn that the giver with whom you were paired has chosen to give you $15. How would you interpret this gift? Would you feel happy about it, or would you wish you had received one of the items on your wish list?

In all likelihood, you recognize that the monetary gift is fungible: you can use the $15 to buy any of the items you chose earlier. In fact, the participants in the role of recipients reported appreciating money more than a requested gift. What about the givers? As in the previous study, they failed to take the perspective of their recipients; they predicted that recipients would appreciate any of the requested gifts more than the money.

Sticking with the domain of gift giving for another moment, let's examine how the nature of our social bonds can influence our ability to take the perspective of another person. Despite the current economic downturn, Americans still spent approximately $14 billion on Mother's Day and more than $9 billion on Father's Day in 2010, according to recent estimates from the National Retail Federation. An increasing number of gift givers are turning to "gifts that give twice"—gifts that support a worthy cause. These presents can come in the form of a charitable donation in someone else's name or the purchase of a product that will support an underprivileged group. Such gifts are often motivated by the desire to be socially responsible. In fact, however, doing good can actually be bad for gift givers.

Imagine that your birthday is coming up. You know that both your spouse and your child (be they real or imaginary) are looking around for a good present to buy for you. Let's imagine they both decided to spend $75 and are considering the following two options: either a massage gift certificate or a donation given on your behalf to Oxfam. What would you prefer as a gift from each of them?

Lisa Cavanaugh (a professor at the University of Southern California), Gavan Fitzsimons (a professor at Duke University—and, yes, he is the same Gavan from the story above . . .), and I asked a similar question of a group of married adults who have children. In our study, we varied whether the participants were told to imagine receiving the gift from their spouse or from their child, and then to imagine whether the gift the giver chose was the donation or the massage gift certificate.

We were interested in finding out whether recipients would react to socially responsible gifts differently depending on who the giver was, even when they greatly cared about being socially responsible. Our results demonstrated that this was in fact the case. Both men and women appreciated socially responsible gifts when they received them from their children but not when they received them from their spouses. We asked the participants to describe their thoughts and feelings about the gift they received. Their responses were illuminating. They interpreted a socially responsible gift from one of their children as a sign of caring and as an endorsement of their parenting (an affirmation "that I raised him to be kind and generous and always think of others," as one person wrote). But when they received the same socially responsible gift from their spouses, they interpreted it as a sign of lack of caring, love, and commitment to the relationship (for example, "I think if my spouse bought me this gift it'd be a sign he does not care about me").

In addition, we were interested in examining whether givers would accurately predict these reactions. Did they? Similar to the results of the previous studies we discussed, they did not. When givers were asked to predict how their recipients would react to the gift, they were unable to put themselves in the recipients' shoes. Children believed that their parents would in fact appreciate the tangible gift more than the socially responsible one, and adults believed that their spouses would appreciate the socially responsible gift more than the tangible one.

These may seem like lighthearted examples and decisions, but they highlight a deeper point: even in situations where it may be natural to ask ourselves questions about the other person's perspective, we fail to do so.

There is one more type of perspective-taking failure that I would like to discuss, since it is common in various contexts. As an example, my dad, who used to work as a doctor, often told me stories about his days at the hospital. One theme that ran through his stories was the fact that junior colleagues often made mistakes (at times with costly consequences to their patients) because they did not ask more senior colleagues for advice or clarification on the right procedures to use. The same tendency is common in the business world. Because new hires and experienced managers alike are often afraid of what others will think of them if they ask too many questions or seek advice, they keep quiet, and often make poor decisions as a result. I have noticed that employees often think that asking others for help will cause them to seem incompetent or weak. In fact, the people being consulted typically feel flattered to be asked and, as a result, feel more committed to the employee. Having seen this tendency in so many different contexts, I wanted to study it in greater detail.

With this goal in mind, Alison Wood Brooks (a PhD student at the University of Pennsylvania), Maurice Schweitzer, and I invited 170 Wharton students to participate in an experiment in which they would interact with another person through the computer. In reality, this "other person" was a computer-simulated partner. Half of the participants were paired with computer-simulated partners that asked them for advice at some point in the study (this was the advice condition). The other half were paired with partners who did not ask for advice (control condition).

As a cover story, we informed participants that we were studying the effects of instant messaging on performance on a difficult brain teaser and that they would be matched with an anonymous partner in the room. (The participants were sitting at individual computer carrels in a large room.) We told them that they would complete the brain teaser first and that their partner would complete it later in the study. Participants were informed they would be paid based on their brain teaser performance, thus giving them an incentive to solve it correctly.

At the beginning of the study, the computer-simulated partner sent the following message: "Hey, good luck." Then, after the participants completed the brain teaser, the partner sent one of the following two messages: "I hope it went well. Do you have any advice?" in the advice condition, or "I hope it went well" in the control condition. At the end of the experiment, even though participants did not have a lot of information about their partners, they were asked to evaluate them on a series of dimensions, including their level of competence.

Think back to your own experience for a moment, and try to remember a time a colleague asked you for your advice on a difficult matter he or she was facing. How did you feel about being sought out for guidance? What did you think about your colleague as a result?

If you are like the participants in our study, then you may have felt flattered to have been asked for advice. And, as a result, you may have also thought positively of your colleague. In fact, participants in the advice condition rated their partner higher on ability than did participants in the control condition, and they reported being more likely to ask their partner for advice on a similar problem-solving task in the future.

Now, let's switch roles: instead of being the person who was consulted for advice, you are the person asking for it. How would you feel about asking for advice? How do you think your colleague would evaluate you for consulting him?

We conducted another study to answer these questions, and reversed the role participants played. At this point in the chapter, the result may not surprise you: participants believed they would be penalized for asking for advice and failed to anticipate that they would in fact receive higher competence ratings from their counterparts.

Perspective taking is not a skill that switches on automatically once we turn five and remains active thereafter. Instead, it is more like a car engine that must be started every time it is needed. Failing to turn on our perspective-taking ability when needed—perhaps because of a lack of attention, time, or motivation—can easily cause our reasoning to stall. To move toward a better understanding of others' viewpoints, we need to actively turn on our perspective-taking skills.

This leads to a fourth principle to avoid getting sidetracked:

Take the other party's point of view.

When you are facing a decision that involves others, try to carefully analyze it from their perspective. Given that we are social beings, our plans are likely to involve others, in one way or another. So, the decisions we make when following through on our plans can easily be derailed by the failure to take others' perspective. The ability of Person A to predict how Person B will react to what Person A says and does is critical to predicting the success of many relationships. To execute the common plan of generating sales, companies need to understand the likely responses of their customers to advertising campaigns, promotions, and product launches. To stick to their plan of achieving satisfactory outcomes, negotiators need to predict how their counterparts will react to concessions. And anyone interested in following through on strengthening a social bond through a gift purchase must acknowledge the intended recipient's preferences and desires.

Of course, the operative question is, how? Psychologist Kenneth Savitsky (of Williams College) and his colleagues investigated ways to trigger perspective taking by making other relevant people salient. In a series of experiments, they asked participants to indicate the percentage they personally contributed to a variety of group tasks.[9] As we learned earlier in this chapter, people seem to think far more about their own contributions than others' to group efforts, and thus claim that they personally contributed far more than is logically possible. This tendency to "overclaim" also emerged in the control conditions of Savitsky's experiments: each group member's self-reported contribution added up to more than 100 percent. But when participants were explicitly asked to think about others' contributions by first reporting the percentage that others contributed to the group task, or when they were implicitly asked to think about others' contributions simply by listing the initials of each of their other group members, the tendency to overclaim almost disappeared. (In one experiment, the sum of the contributions decreased from 155 percent to 106 percent.) These results suggest that by making the "other" more salient, it is possible to enhance our perspective-taking skills.

Some companies have succeeded at tackling perspective-taking failures among their employees. For instance, *a/b testing* is a method companies employ to improve website design by presenting two different versions of the same site simultaneously and then measuring the effective conversion rate of users. (This method was initially used as a direct mail strategy for understanding customers' preferences.) This method springs from the knowledge that users view websites in unanticipated ways, though the site's owners generally understand the goals of a page or group of pages very clearly. The goal of a/b testing is to measure the reactions of a population of users against an identified goal—say, clicking a "Subscribe" or "Checkout" button. Often, it is unclear how a particular population will react to a small change in a website. By measuring users' reactions, companies can apply a change to dramatically impact the site's effectiveness.

Another good example of effective perspective taking comes from a start-up called Vitality, Inc., based in Cambridge, Massachusetts. In 2009, the company developed a pill-bottle system called GlowCaps to solve a big problem in medicine—that people do not consistently take the drugs they are prescribed. This problem costs the United States about $290 billion in added medical expenses each year, and it also costs lives: patients with diabetes and heart disease are twice as likely to die of their disease when they do not take their pills properly. Vitality's GlowCap works like this: when a pill-bottle cap is opened, a close-range wireless signal relays this information to a base station in the home that, in turn, can send messages through a phone network (similar to how a cell phone works).[10] This system is used to send reminders to the patient. In particular, if the bottle is not opened at the appointed time, the cap starts blinking to remind the patient to take the medication. If that does not serve as enough of a hint, a jingling sound follows, making the reminder even more salient. If the bottle still is not opened, the system sends a message that triggers an automated phone call or a text message with a reminder. What I particularly like about this innovative product is that it indicates effective perspective taking: Vitality realized that patients often do not take their medicine and thus developed a system to help them stick to the plan. Managers at Vitality successfully took their customers' point of view.

Both a/b testing and GlowCaps highlight the financial and other benefits of perspective taking at the time you make an important decision as well as later, when you are trying to follow through on your plan. In the same way that good dancers are able to put themselves in their partners' shoes and predict where their feet will go next, we all need to take the point of view of the parties involved in our decisions and to figure out how to avoid stepping on their feet. We can do so by asking questions about their views and opinions and by examining decisions from their perspective in addition to our own.

CHAPTER 5

The Curse of the Gray T-Shirt

Insidious Social Bonds

On the chilly afternoon of November 23, 1951, the Princeton University football team hosted a fierce competitor, Dartmouth. This was an important game for both teams for several reasons. First, it was the final game of the season, and each team was eager to end on a high note. Second, the Princeton team was enjoying an undefeated season and wanted to continue its winning streak. Finally, it was the last game for an All-American on the Princeton team, Dick Kazmaier.

This game is still vivid in the minds of fans and then-students of Princeton and Dartmouth because of how it unfolded. Just a few minutes after the opening kick-off, it became clear that the players were going to fight the game to the bitter end. In the second quarter, Kazmaier's nose was broken, and he had to leave the game. The next quarter, one of Dartmouth's players was carried off the field with a broken leg. Throughout the game, the referees stayed busy handing out penalties to both teams and keeping the players' tempers and violence in check.

In the end, Princeton won, 13–0, sealing its undefeated season. But bitterness lingered on both sides after the game ended. For several weeks, students, players, coaches, newspapers, and administrators at both schools blamed their competition for the game's rough play and rule violations. In fact, each side told a very different story about what had happened. For instance, just a few days after the game, a reporter for the *Daily Princetonian* reported:

> *The observer has never seen quite such a disgusting exhibition of so-called "sport." Both teams were guilty but the blame must be laid primarily on Dartmouth's doorstep. Princeton, obviously the better team, had no reason to rough up Dartmouth. Looking at the situation rationally, we don't see why the Indians should make a deliberate attempt to cripple Dick Kazmaier or any other Princeton player. The Dartmouth psychology, however, is not rational itself.*[1]

In contrast, the *Dartmouth* daily newspaper described the game as follows:

> *[T]he Dartmouth-Princeton game set the stage for . . . dirty football. A type which may be termed as an unjustifiable accusation.*
>
> *Dick Kazmaier was injured early in the game. Kazmaier was the star, an All-American. Other stars have been injured before, but Kazmaier had been built to represent a Princeton idol. When an idol is hurt there is only one recourse—the tag of dirty football. So what did the [Princeton] Tiger Coach Charley Caldwell do? He announced to the world that the Big Green had been out to extinguish the Princeton star. His purpose was achieved.*
>
> *After this incident, Caldwell instilled the old see-what-they-did-go-get-them attitude into his players. His talk got results. Gene Howard and Jim Miller were both injured. Both had dropped back to pass, had passed,*

and were standing unprotected in the backfield. Result: one
bad leg and one leg broken.[2]

Because of their allegiance to their schools, journalists and fans on each side recounted what happened quite differently.

Not too long after the game, Dartmouth professor Albert Hastorf and Princeton professor Hadley Cantril, both psychologists, decided to examine these differences in perspective. They invited students at both schools to participate in a study in which they would watch a film of the game and then answer a few questions about it. The scholars were interested in examining whether the students would interpret the game differently because of their connection to one of the two schools. And they did: Princeton students counted twice as many infractions by Dartmouth players as among Princeton players. Dartmouth students, instead, reported seeing only half as many infractions committed by the players of their team as did the Princeton students. The psychological bond the students felt to their team actually influenced what their eyes saw.

A feeling of connection to another person, a group, an organization, or even a country can come from many sources: a shared history or experience, shared preferences (such as liking Italian food) or characteristics (such as being from Italy), or a direct relationship.

In both our personal and professional lives, such connections are important. In the business world, a close friendship or a sense of rapport is often cited as the motivation behind starting a company. Microsoft, Apple, Google, Yahoo!, and Boston Scientific all began when friends started working together on a business idea. Yet mixing business and friendship can lead to problems. Consider the case of PubSub, a search engine for blogs, press releases, and other types of information on the Internet.[3] In 2002, Bob Wyman and Salim Ismail were roommates who had been living on Manhattan's Upper West Side for more than a year. Wyman was part of a design team for the Lotus Notes spreadsheet program (currently owned by IBM), and Ismail was a midlevel technology consultant. Eager to exercise his entrepreneurial spirit, Ismail convinced Wyman to start Pub-Sub with him. The major selling point of the business idea behind PubSub was its immediacy. Similar search engines, such as Google Alerts, ran periodic checks for new related content and then sent a message to their users. By contrast, PubSub notified users immediately after a reference appeared, thus providing value to users interested in real-time updates.

Wyman and Ismail's friendship and entrepreneurial insight got PubSub off to a good start, and the company soon raised about $4 million. The technology was working as planned. However, ad sales lagged, and the two entrepreneurs burned through cash rather quickly. This difficult financial situation led to a heated conflict between Wyman and Ismail, who disagreed about what to do next. The conflict became particularly heated when KnowNow, a well-funded company selling information-tracking services, showed interest in a potential merger. Ismail was against the merger; Wyman was in favor. In the end, the company's board rejected the merger, and Wyman reacted with bitterness. PubSub was so broke it could not even afford to file for bankruptcy. Soon after, Ismail resigned from PubSub's board and started looking for another job. Wyman, who tried in vain to keep the company alive, reflected on the experience of doing business with a friend: "This is one of the most painful experiences I've gone through in my life, second only to my divorce."[4]

In cases like this one, a sense of closeness or friendship can convince people it will be easy for them to do business together, such that they discount the potential risks of mixing friendship with business. Entrepreneurship is not the only business context where close relationships drive decisions. You've probably heard many stories of companies relying on their relationships and networks to find good hires. For most managers, the rationale behind this preference toward hiring people in their close networks is that they have information about them and know what contributions they can make. But, as we learned from the initial example of the rough football game between Dartmouth and Princeton, our social bonds can influence how we interpret "facts." Social ties are undoubtedly important, as they allow us to obtain what we want and need. But they can also influence our decisions and our plans in unexpected and sometimes harmful ways.

In the late summer of 2007, I walked around the Drama Department at Carnegie Mellon University looking for good spots to leave my casting call:

> *Interested in learning more about decision-making research by contributing to it? Practice your acting skills while earning some money by helping us conduct our studies.*

It did not take long for e-mail messages to start appearing in my inbox. It was time to hold my auditions. As I explained to interested candidates, if they were hired, their job would be to act as "confederates" in research studies on social influence and individual decision making. They would need to learn a script and execute it flawlessly—so well that our actual study participants wouldn't realize that they were actors.

Among the skillful actors I interviewed, one in particular stood out. His name was David. After he showed me his chops with a short interpretation of his favorite Shakespearean act, I asked him to tell me why he thought he'd be good for the job. "When I was little," he said, "I was diagnosed as a compulsive liar." Perfect! I was looking for a person who would be willing to lie in public, and I had clearly found the right man. David would be participating in an experiment that looked at how feeling similar to others leads us to imitate their behavior. The context we chose was dishonesty. Would people be influenced by the unethical behavior of others? Would another person's dishonest behavior lead others to be dishonest themselves?

To answer these questions, my colleagues Shahar Ayal (a professor at IDC Herzliya in Israel), Dan Ariely, and I conducted an experiment in which we asked participants to complete an ability-based task under time pressure. All participants in the study were students from Carnegie Mellon University, a detail you should remember because it will become important later on. The task they completed was the same one we discussed in the introduction: they had four minutes to solve twenty math puzzles like the one depicted in figure 5-1 (reproduced from the introduction). For each puzzle, they had to find the two numbers that add up to ten.

If you remember, this task looks easier than it actually is—especially when you are asked to solve the twenty math puzzles under time pressure. In four minutes, most people solve about six or seven puzzles. Participants were motivated to perform well on this task, as they received 50 cents for each correctly solved puzzle.

For each session, we invited eight to fourteen participants to the laboratory and asked each of them to sit at an individual desk. Sitting on each desk was an envelope containing nine one-dollar bills and four quarters, as well as the study materials. Participants would pay themselves from the envelope at the end of the study based on their performance on the math task.

We conducted several sessions for this experiment and randomly assigned each session to one of four conditions. In the first condition (control), participants were given four minutes to work on the task. Once the time was up, they were asked to report their performance on the task using a collection slip, pay themselves,

FIGURE 5-1

Sample math puzzle matrix for social bonds experiment

8.19	6.46	1.62
8.29	2.91	2.03
2.73	7.89	9.86
6.21	3.54	3.18

and then bring their completed test sheet and collection slip to the experimenter so that she could check their performance. Thus, participants' performance in this condition served as our baseline since they could not cheat; they did not have the opportunity to misreport their performance on the math task. In the second condition (the "shredder" condition), we followed a similar procedure, but this time participants were asked to shred their test sheet after reporting their performance on the collection slip.

Let's consider these two conditions before I tell you about the other two conditions. Imagine being a participant in this experiment. Unbeknownst to you, you have been randomly assigned to the shredder condition. The experimenter just announced that time is up and told you to report your performance on the collection slip, shred the test sheet, pay yourself, and then leave. You did not write down your name anywhere, but simply used a lab ID number. As far as you can tell, the experimenter has no way to tell whether your actual performance on the task matches the performance you self-reported. What would you do?

Maybe you would be honest and report your actual performance on the collection slip. But most participants who face this decision do not. They feel tempted to inflate their numbers and thus cheat on the task so that they can walk away with a greater payment. In fact, participants in the control condition accurately reported solving, on average, seven matrices, while those in the shredder condition reported solving about twelve matrices. As these numbers suggest, the reported performance on the collection slip in the shredder condition was about 50 percent greater than the performance in the control condition. Although participants really did shred their tests in the shredder condition, making it impossible for us to know who cheated and by how much, the difference in reported performance suggests that participants cheated when the task was self-scored. Even if you think you wouldn't cheat on this task, you may not be surprised by our results. In the shredder condition, participants had full anonymity, thus giving them leeway to easily justify their cheating.

Now consider the other two conditions we included in the same experiment. Both conditions were similar to our shredder condition, except that David, our confederate, was posing as a participant. We instructed David to stand up about sixty seconds into the math task and state loudly: "I've solved everything. What should I do?" The experimenter then reminded him about the procedure he was supposed to follow. When David finished shredding his test sheet, he loudly said: "I solved everything. My envelope for the unearned money is empty. What should I do with it?" The experimenter replied: "If you don't have money to return, you have finished and are free to go." David then said, "I want to thank you. I wish all of you a wonderful day," and left the room, smiling. With this procedure, we made it clear to participants that any of them could cheat, as David clearly did, by inflating their performance on the matrix task without fear of being caught. How honest do you think they were?

The answer to this question depended on what David was wearing—yes, really. Recall that we conducted the experiment at Carnegie Mellon University. We asked David to wear a plain gray T-shirt in what we called our "in-group-identity" condition and a University of Pittsburgh T-shirt in our "out-group-identity" condition. As you may know, the two Pittsburgh schools are rivals, and there is quite a bit of competition between them. When David showed up at sessions wearing a plain T-shirt, he fit in with the rest of the CMU participants. Participants in those sessions likely felt similar to him and believed he was one of their own. But when David showed up at sessions wearing a University of Pittsburgh T-shirt, the participants likely considered him an outsider, someone different from them.

In both of our "David" conditions, he greatly influenced the level of cheating. Compared with the shredder condition, cheating increased in the gray T-shirt condition (the in-group-identity condition) and decreased in the University of Pittsburgh T-shirt condition (the out-group-identity condition). In fact, participants reported solving, on average, about fifteen matrices in the in-group-identity condition and only eight in the out-group-identity condition. Interestingly, we also found differences between these two conditions in the percentage of participants who imitated David's behavior and reported solving all twenty matrices by the end of the allotted time period. (None of them left early, as David did.) Over 24 percent of the participants reported solving all twenty matrices in the in-group-identity condition, compared with less than 4 percent in the out-group-identity condition.

These results suggest that our social bonds have a powerful influence not only on our perceptions but also on our behavior. In our experiment, the fact that "someone like us" cheated established the norm that it was acceptable for others to cheat as well. When we feel similarly to others because we belong to the same group or because we share similar features, we are affected by their behavior. Think about how similar dynamics may explain decisions you have observed or made in the past just because people you knew were doing the same. Perhaps you have continued with a questionable investment because it was recommended by a relative. Or you bought an expensive house, larger than you needed or could afford, just because your friends bought similar houses. The psychological connectedness you felt at the time may explain what now seems to you like irrational behavior.

Feeling part of an *in group* can also affect the way we view an *out group*, especially when we are competing with out-group members. A famous social psychology experiment conducted by Muzafer Sherif (one of the founders of modern social psychology) and his colleagues in the early 1950s examined this situation.[5] The experiment was conducted with two twenty-two-member groups of twelve-year-old boys over the course of two weeks at Robbers Cave State Park in Oklahoma. The boys, who did not know one another prior to the study, were white and shared a Protestant, two-parent, middle-class background. The boys were randomly assigned to one of two groups. The groups initially did not know about the other's existence.

During their first week at the camp, the members of each group were encouraged to engage in activities that would allow them to bond, such as hiking and swimming, and to develop their own norms and culture by discussing their common goals. The two groups also chose their group names (the Eagles or the Rattlers) and created T-shirts and flags emblazoned with the group name for themselves.

During the second week of camp, the experimenter told the groups about the existence of the other group and had them engage in a series of competitive activities, such as baseball, tug-of-war, and so on. In each competition, a trophy and individual prizes (such as a medal and a pocket knife) were given to the winning group and its members. The games the two groups played during this week heightened members' competitive spirit—and their frustration every time they lost. Each group was very confident in its ability to beat the competition.

To further increase the rivalry between the two groups, the experimenters devised situations in which one group made gains at the expense of the other. For example, one group was delayed in getting to a picnic, and when the boys arrived they found the other group had eaten their food.

At this point, members of both teams started to make threatening remarks to each other and to engage in taunting and name calling. At first, this prejudice was only verbal, but as the competition wore on, the boys began to act out. The Eagles burned the Rattlers' flag; the Rattlers ransacked the Eagles' cabin, overturned beds, and stole private property. The groups became so aggressive with each other that the researchers had to physically separate them. When asked to describe members of their own group, the boys used favorable adjectives and words; they used very unfavorable terms to describe members of the out group.

These results suggest just how easily a sense of psychological connection can be created: in this case, the participants created tight social bonds despite being randomly assigned to one of the two groups. These social bonds produced prejudiced attitudes and discriminatory behavior toward the out group. Let's not forget: the participants in this field experiment were well-adjusted boys, not members of street gangs.

In these last two experiments I've described, group membership created a sense of psychological closeness to others, either by manipulating whether the confederate was an in-group member (i.e., a CMU student) or an out-group member (a student from a rival school), or by assigning participants to one of two groups in competition with each other. Often, however, people experience psychological closeness based on even subtler factors. Consider the following example. In the summer of 1993, Quincy, Illinois, was one of many midwestern towns that suffered extensive, systemic damage when overrun by rising tides along the Mississippi River. Upon hearing of the town's precarious situation, residents of Quincy, Massachusetts, mobilized, sending a lifeline of supplies. It seems even small cues, such as sharing the same name, are sufficient to psychologically bond us to others and inspire acts of altruism.

Adam Galinsky (a professor at Columbia University) and I decided to examine whether subtle similarities, such as sharing the same birthday or first name, would affect people's behavior the same way in-group membership does and generate *feelings* of similarity. To study this hypothesis, we picked a context where we thought people's behavior would be difficult to change: morality. If you really care about being a good person and being seen by others as such, the questionable behavior of those to whom you feel close will have little influence, right? The findings we just discussed cast some doubt on this possibility. So Adam and I decided to examine whether participants would be more likely to go along with another person's unethical behavior when they felt psychologically connected to him than when they did not, even if this sense of psychological connection was due to a very subtle similarity. We also wanted to learn whether a sense of psychological closeness distances people from their moral compass.

We invited seventy-two college students to participate in a study where they could earn a maximum payment of $12. A week prior to the lab session, all participants answered an online questionnaire that included a scale measuring their attitudes about cheating (such as, "Sometimes getting ahead of the curve is more important than adhering to rules" and "Cheating is appropriate behavior because no one gets hurt"). A higher score on this scale indicates a higher acceptance of cheating as morally acceptable.

At the time of the laboratory session, we randomly assigned participants to one of two conditions: "shared attributes" or "different attributes." We conducted each session with only two participants (I will tell you why in just a bit). In each session, the two participants arrived at the study location and answered a short questionnaire that contained several demographic questions. They then learned that they would engage in an anonymous problem-solving task under time pressure and that the other participant would work on the same task in the same room.

For our problem-solving task, we once again used the matrix task you are familiar with, but this time, rather than using a shredder, we changed the procedure so that we could actually determine who cheated and by how much. Unbeknownst to participants, we devised a way to match the test sheet with the math problems that participants recycled at the end of the study and the collection slip on which they reported their own performance. (As a reminder, the task involves solving math problems under time pressure: for each of twenty matrices, participants were to find the two numbers that added up to ten.) There was no apparent identifying information anywhere on the test sheet or the collection slip where participants reported their performance, so the results seemed anonymous. As before, participants received 50 cents for every matrix they reported solving correctly. Thus, participants had a financial incentive to overreport their performance to earn more money. Once the five-minute task had ended, the experimenter asked participants to write down the number of correctly solved matrices on the collection slip and drop it with the remaining money in the designated box prior to leaving the room. Participants put their test sheet in a recycling box in the same room. Afterward, since the test sheet and the collection slip could be matched, the experimenter scored the actual performance of each participant. Thus, we could compare reported to actual performance. Before leaving the lab, participants answered a short questionnaire that included the same questions about their attitudes toward cheating used in the first online survey, along with some unrelated questions.

Up until this point, our procedures sound similar to those of other studies I've discussed. Here is what we did to create a sense of connection between participants and a wrongdoer. In each session, one of the two participants was Jonathan, a confederate whom we had hired from the Department of Dramatic Art at the University of North Carolina at Chapel Hill. We gave Jonathan a script to follow in the experiment. Similar to what David did in our in-group study, Jonathan had to stand up about one minute after the problem-solving task started and state loudly: "I've solved everything. What should I do?" As in our in-group study, one minute was such a short time that it would have been clear to the other participants in the room that Jonathan was lying. Thus, thanks to this procedure, the confederate made it clear to each participant that cheating to the maximum extent was possible and would not produce negative consequences. In response to his question, the experimenter asked Jonathan to wait patiently for the other participants to finish.

Our manipulation consisted of making apparent the potential similarities or differences between Jonathan and the participants in the room with him in each session. In the shared-attributes condition, once the confederate and the participant returned their filled-out questionnaires to the experimenter, the experimenter commented, "Interesting: you two were born in the same month, [month], and are of the same school year, [school year]. Well, let's go to the main task of the study." (The experimenter mentioned the participant's birthday month in place of [month], and her school year in place of [school year].) Thus, participants in this condition believed that the confederate shared two attributes with them. As a result, we believed, they would feel similar to the confederate.

In the different-attributes conditions, the experimenter commented, "Interesting: you two were born in different months, and are of different school years. Well, let's go to the main task of the study." Thus, in this condition, the participant and the confederate shared neither of these attributes. In this case, we believed the participants would experience lower feelings of similarity with the confederate than in the shared-attributes condition.

Although very subtle, this manipulation of psychological closeness and similarity affected participants' behavior. Of the participants in the different-attributes condition (different birth month and school year), 29 percent cheated by overreporting their performance on the math task. The percentage more than doubled in the same-attributes condition (same birth month and school year): 65 percent of the participants in that condition followed the confederate's behavior and behaved dishonestly for greater payment.

To investigate this result further, we examined how participants' views of cheating changed due to a feeling of psychological closeness and their decision to overstate performance on the problem-solving task. If you remember, we assessed participants' views of cheating at two points in time: a week before the lab session and at the end of the lab session. Overstating performance on the problem-solving task increased the extent to which participants morally disengaged: people did not find cheating that problematic after lying about their performance on the problem-solving task. This finding was driven by the behavior of participants in the shared-attributes condition, who reported less moral stringency after cheating than did participants in the different-attributes condition. Our participants' opinions about cheating changed the most when they both shared attributes with a cheater and cheated themselves.

The results of this experiment suggest that when a person is psychologically connected to someone who engages in selfish or dishonest behavior, she becomes vicariously motivated to justify that person's actions and thus inclined to behave less ethically herself in subsequent situations. Psychological closeness creates distance from one's own moral compass, causing people to view unethical behavior as more morally appropriate and less wrong. Even minimal, modest connections (a shared birth month and school year) can lead people to vicariously reenact and replicate another person's traits and behaviors.

We tend to view ourselves as neutral judges who treat those we feel close to (from colleagues to family members) the same as those from whom we feel distant or dissimilar. But in fact, the actions of those we feel connected to influence us differently from the actions of those more distant from us. This special influence can lead us to cross ethical boundaries. Bernard Madoff's arrest and guilty plea for scamming investors out of billions of dollars may serve as a cautionary tale for those of us who did not know him, but could have increased the dishonest behavior of those who did know him, our research suggests. Our results are a frightening illustration of just how easily our behaviors can be swayed by the actions of those around us.

The opinions and behavior of "people like us" influence us quite powerfully, as you can see from these experiments, and it doesn't matter whether we are witnessing admirable or unethical behavior. But because we typically fail to recognize how much we are influenced by social bonds, we overlook how those bonds could be used to make improvements to people's behavior. Consider the case of environmental conservation in hotels. Motivating consumers to be more environmentally responsible (for instance, by reusing their towels during their stay) not only benefits the environment but also the hotel itself. In fact, hotels generally save about $2.50 per day for every person who reuses his towels.[6]

There are many motivational strings to pull if you wanted to encourage hotel guests to participate in environmentally friendly programs. And evidence suggests that hotel guests would appreciate such programs, since over three-quarters of them (at least in the United States) think of themselves as environmentalists. In fact, studies conducted by the largest manufacturer of hotel towel reuse signs found that approximately 75 percent of guests who have the opportunity to participate in such programs do reuse their towels at least once during their stay.[7] The industry's standard technique is to put signs in guests' bathrooms that stress the environmental benefits of such programs, such as conserving energy and natural resources.

Here's a pop quiz. Using the research findings discussed in this chapter, how can you increase the number of guests who reuse their towels? Yes, indeed: you could issue an appeal that conveys what other hotel guests did when deciding whether to reuse their towels. This is one of the possibilities that Noah Goldstein (a professor at UCLA) and his colleagues considered in a study examining how subtle changes in such signs might improve towel reuse rates.[8] Working with a national midsize, midpriced US hotel chain, the researchers created their own towel reuse cards to measure the influence of each type of appeal on the success of the hotel's conservation program.

For their first study, the researchers collected data on over one thousand instances of potential towel reuse in 190 rooms. Each room was randomly assigned to one of two messages: the standard environmental message or the treatment message, which were communicated on signs placed on the towel rack in the room's bathroom. The guests were not aware that they were participants in the study.

The sign with the standard environmental message stated:

HELP SAVE THE ENVIRONMENT.
The environment deserves our respect. You can show your respect for nature and help save the environment by reusing your towels during your stay.

The sign also included instructions on where guests were supposed to place their towels if they wanted to participate in this initiative, as well as information on the impact of participating in the initiative on the back of the sign. This sign focused guests' attention on the importance of environmental protection but did not provide any information about the behavior of other hotel guests.

By contrast, the sign used in the treatment condition had the following message:

> *JOIN YOUR FELLOW GUESTS IN HELPING TO SAVE THE ENVIRONMENT.*
> *Almost 75% of guests who are asked to participate in our new resource savings program do help by using their towels more than once. You can join your fellow guests in this program to help save the environment by reusing your towels during your stay.*

Below each of these two messages, the scholars also printed some additional information. In particular, they gave guests instructions on what to do if they were interested in participating in the program. In addition, guests could read more about the impact of participating in the program on the back of both signs. This additional information informed them:

> *DID YOU KNOW that if most of this hotel's guests participate in our resource savings program, it would save the environment 72,000 gallons of water and 39 barrels of oil, and would prevent nearly 480 gallons of detergent from being released into the environment this year alone?*

Did the new sign make a difference? When I tell managers or friends about this study, they usually believe it did not. This is because they commonly start by asking, "What would motivate me to reuse my towel during my stay?" and respond that they would be motivated by the desire to be more environmentally responsible. But their intuition is wrong. In fact, the towel reuse rate was about

44 percent in the treatment condition and only 35 percent in the industry standard condition.[9] By informing hotel guests that other guests had participated in the program, the researchers increased towel reuse rates, thus benefitting the environment and reducing costs for the hotel.

The researchers wondered if they could increase reuse rates even further. As we learned earlier in the chapter, perceived similarity strongly affects whether others' behavior affects our own. So in their next experiment, the researchers included a condition with a sign that read:

> *JOIN YOUR FELLOW GUESTS IN HELPING TO SAVE THE ENVIRONMENT.*
> *In a study conducted in Fall 2003, 75% of the guests who stayed in this room (#xxx) participated in our new resource savings program by using their towels more than once. You can join your fellow guests in this program to help save the environment by reusing your towels during your stay.*

The text "(#xxx)" was replaced with the room's unique number. Stressing the similarity between the guest and previous occupants of the same room produced an even better reuse rate than citing the behavior of hotel guests in general: 49.3 percent (as compared with 44 percent in the previously described experiment). These results are both striking and seemingly illogical. Why does the behavior of strangers affect our behavior so strongly? Because, even though they are strangers, these people share something in common with us, however trivial or happenstance: they stayed in the same room in the past. Somehow, this is enough of a commonality to make us feel similar to them and to want to mimic their behavior.

Hotels are new to the strategy of making social bonds, perceived similarity, and connections to others salient. Yet several other types of businesses have employed them with great success.

For instance, the popularity of Amazon.com's "People who bought [this book] also bought [these books]" has prompted many other websites to imitate it. The use of this type of recommender system (which is called *item-to-item collaborative filtering technique*) can be exploited in many areas. Recently, pharmaceutical companies such as London-based AstraZeneca have used the technique to enhance drug discovery. The technique recommends chemical substances that chemists might not have found on their own.[10]

As shown in the hotel field experiments, strategies that build on the power of social bonds can produce benefits to consumers, decision makers, and managers alike. But, as we saw earlier, the behavior of others can greatly influence our own behavior for the worse, whether our connections to them are strong or subtle. It is thus important to consider a fifth principle to avoid getting sidetracked:

Question your bonds.

In any context, try to examine your links and similarities to those around you and consider whether these bonds may be influencing your decisions for the worse. This will help you ensure that you are following your own plans rather than those of people around you. In doing so, you may begin to recognize the extent to which others' behavior and decisions are affecting your own.

By questioning your social bonds, you may also recognize the extent to which the behavior and decisions of others are affecting the people you evaluate (such as fellow team members, subordinates, and acquaintances). This simple recognition may affect how you allow people to join your "inner circle." As an example, HR managers might want to pay particular attention to the ways in which employees are screened for their jobs to make sure they fit into the culture of the organization.

Some companies have been successful in addressing the potential problems that social bonds among individuals can create, and have used the power of such bonds to their advantage. For instance, in 2010 Akshay Kothari and Ankit Gupta founded Pulse, a company that makes a news-reading application for mobile devices. Kothari and Gupta wanted to go beyond the typical hiring process of checking references and holding several rounds of interviews. Instead, they give prospective employees the opportunity to do their would-be job under realistic conditions. Candidates can work in Pulse headquarters for a day or two as if they are actually part of the organization. Paid for their time, candidates work on short jobs that allow them to be themselves. In this manner, Kothari and Gupta get an accurate sense of candidates' technical skills and personalities. And even more important, they can understand how these candidates interact with others in the company, and whether these social bonds seem to have the potential to lead to positive outcomes (e.g., greater motivation). After all, candidates who look great on paper may not fit in the company's culture, or they may exert the type of influence that the entrepreneurs don't want at Pulse. Through their unique selection process, Kothari and Gupta improve the odds that only social bonds that trigger productive behaviors and relationships become part of their organization.

Pulse is certainly not the only organization that is attempting to use social bonds to foster employee productivity and learning. In 2011, my colleague Brad Staats (of the University of North Carolina at Chapel Hill) and I had the opportunity to study and work with Samasource, a nonprofit start-up headquartered in San Francisco.[11] The company, founded by Leila Janah in 2008, is a leading organization in the emerging trend of *microwork*, which Samasource defines as "a new way to fight poverty by enabling capable, marginalized people to complete digital tasks in some of the world's poorest places." The company secures contracts for digital services from large companies in the Unites States and in Europe (such as Google and LinkedIn), divides the work into small chunks, and delivers it to work centers in developing communities in Africa, India, and other regions through a Web-based interface. Samasource workers perform work such as content generation, data enrichment, and transcription services.

During our conversations with Janah, Brad and I learned that the company puts a lot of thought into how to help local entrepreneurs in developing regions organize their microwork centers. For instance, shared backgrounds can have significant peer effects on workers' productivity and commitment to their jobs. Simply having workers sit next to productive others creates a sense of psychological connection that may have beneficial effects on their own learning and productivity. As in the case of Pulse, social bonds can be leveraged to improve employee work performance. This lesson can be applied more broadly throughout our work and personal lives. By paying attention to the influence others have on us, we can make sure our networks include people who bring out the best in us.

CHAPTER 6

The Power of Stickers

Salient Social Comparisons

"I got a star!" I shouted as soon as my husband picked up the phone.

"What?" Greg said, incredulous. "A star? What do you mean? What star? Where did it come from?"

"Yes, I got a star—a sticker in the shape of a red, smiley star. But I need thirty-three more . . ."

On a late October evening in 2011, I was walking home after an hour-long spinning class at a Harvard gym. Before class, I had signed up for Harvard's Group Exercise Triathlon. I received a logbook in which to record the gym classes I would take over the next seven weeks in any of the gyms on campus. To be one of the competition winners and receive a prize, I had to attend at least thirty-four gym classes over nine weeks, across three group exercise categories (strength, cardio, and aqua). Participants would receive a star after each class. This was an individual competition, not a team one, but some of my friends who regularly attend the gym also signed up for the triathlon, so going to the gym suddenly became a motivating group routine.

When I first heard about this initiative, I thought someone (maybe a colleague of mine) was conducting a field experiment to examine how social incentives influence motivation. (Maybe there was a condition where the stickers handed out were frowning stars that would be less motivating than the smiley ones I was getting?) But, after a bit of investigation, I discovered that Harvard was simply using the triathlon to promote the various gym classes taught throughout the campus.

You might be wondering why I signed up for the triathlon. My husband asked me the same question, reminding me that I am usually the one who, through my experiments, designs such initiatives to influence other people's behavior in one way or another. He was puzzled by the fact that, on multiple occasions, I stayed at the gym for a second workout so that I could get two star stickers rather than just one. All this sweat just to win a prize that, Greg thought, wasn't worth the effort: a T-shirt.

Reflecting on my own behavior, I realized that it was a nice application of the principles discussed in chapter 5: how other people's behavior influences our own, especially when we perceive these others to be similar to ourselves. Noticing that my friends in the triathlon were trying out all sorts of gym classes, I started to do the same. In the span of two weeks, I attended new classes such as Zumba, cardio kickboxing, and even Balletone. More relevant to the topic we will explore in this chapter, the star-shaped stickers had another effect on the behavior of those of us in the triathlon: they used the power of *social comparisons* to motivate us to exercise. (Like me, many of my friends were trying their best to stick to their plans of exercising regularly.)

The basic idea behind social comparison, a theory first proposed by psychologist Leon Festinger in the early 1950s, is simple: we look to others for information that will help us evaluate our own abilities, skills, and opinions.[1] We watch what others do and think and use those observations as realistic reference points for our own lives. Social comparison processes can help us evaluate ourselves more accurately and also improve our productivity.

To make this theory a bit more concrete, think about how good you are at reasoning through business problems or how skilled of a cook you are. To answer these questions, you might start thinking of other people who are similar to you, such as colleagues, friends, or family members, and compare yourself to them on these dimensions before forming a judgment of your own skills. You might think of people who are better than you on these dimensions, thus making an *upward social comparison*, or you might think of those who are worse than you—a *downward social comparison*. Festinger theorized that we are more likely to compare ourselves to people whose opinions or abilities are similar to our own, and less likely to compare ourselves to those whose views and skills are more divergent. So, you would be more likely to compare yourself to work colleagues than to Steve Jobs when assessing your ability to reason through business problems, and you would be more likely to compare yourself to friends or family members than to Mario Batali when evaluating your cooking abilities. (Unless, of course, you are a business hotshot or a rock star in the kitchen.)

As many scholars who built on Festinger's initial work have explained, we human beings make these types of comparisons constantly and on just about every dimension we deem relevant: our abilities, opinions, possessions, and relationships. Think of the last time you walked into a room filled with people, whether you knew them or not. What were some of the thoughts that passed through your mind in the early minutes of looking at and talking to them? In a brief amount of time, you probably formed an opinion of whether you were taller or shorter than certain people, happier or sadder, better or worse looking, younger or older, and so on. In other words, probably even without realizing it, you engaged in social comparisons.

Here is how the concept of social comparison applied to my own behavior regarding the gym initiative. Imagine that you are about to get a star-shaped sticker from your exercise instructor. At this point, your logbook has only three stickers. But you have seen the logbooks of your friends, and most of them have many more stars. How would you feel? I am not sure about you, but I was in this situation, and I was embarrassed by my poor performance up to that point and also motivated to work harder. (In my defense, I had signed up for the program two weeks late.) For a while, in fact, I even attended extra classes behind my friends' backs so that I could earn the stars I was missing to be on par with them.

My reaction to my friends' logbooks was consistent with research I have conducted on the influence of social comparisons on individuals' motivation and productivity. In virtually any organization, managers face the task of ensuring that their employees are motivated and devote consistent effort to their jobs. One tool for keeping employees engaged, particularly with jobs that involve repetition of tasks over time, is to provide them with performance feedback that gives them information about the effectiveness of their work behavior.

Brad Staats and I conducted a field experiment to examine how giving employees performance feedback would affect their productivity. The empirical setting for our field experiment was the processing operation for APLUS, the consumer finance subsidiary of Shinsei Bank, a midsized bank based in Japan. At the time of our study, APLUS offered credit cards, credit for large purchases, and car loans to Japanese consumers. Employees working at APLUS sat at individual desktop computers and entered data from loan applications. They completed the same set of tasks repetitively throughout the course of the day, and their individual performance was precisely tracked by the company's advanced information technology system. This seemed a perfect context for us to conduct our field experiment. Traditionally, APLUS employees did not receive performance feedback, and their pay did not vary based on their productivity. With our field experiment, we introduced variations on the type of feedback APLUS employees received on a daily basis for an entire month. In this way, we could examine the effects this feedback had on their individual productivity in a controlled manner.

We suspected that, as in the case of the star-shaped feedback I received for going to the gym, employees would respond differently to performance feedback depending on the comparisons they made between themselves and their coworkers regarding their productivity. We used feedback that promoted social comparison processes: workers learned about their performance standing relative to that of coworkers. We believed that this type of feedback captured common business practices. Although employees prefer to evaluate themselves and their standing using objective standards, such standards are rarely available in organizational settings. So, to assess how they are performing, employees compare themselves to their coworkers.

Brad and I designed various conditions for our field experiment, one of which is particularly relevant to our discussion here. The workers assigned to this condition received feedback informing them that their performance ranked in the bottom ten in their work group of twenty-four people (this was, in fact, true). How do you think they performed after receiving this feedback as compared to workers in the control condition, who received no performance feedback at all?

These workers improved their performance, on average, by approximately 14 percent the following day, as compared to coworkers in the control condition. The feedback the low-performing employees received prompted them to make upward social comparisons, just as I did upon seeing my friends' logbooks at the gym. Why? Because the knowledge that their coworkers were more productive threatened these employees' self-esteem. In general, when we receive negative feedback about our standing relative to others, we are likely to feel motivated to work harder to overcome feelings of shame and gain confidence in our ability to work effectively.

Social comparisons can be easily triggered and used to motivate people to work harder or persist longer on tasks where they can apply their abilities, knowledge, or skills. In a sense, it shouldn't be too surprising to learn that our self-evaluations are rooted in comparisons to others. The questions we most want to answer about ourselves—*Am I smart? Am I good-looking? Am I a nice and trustworthy person?*—typically can be answered only by comparing our thoughts, feelings, and behaviors with those of the people around us. In the words of psychologists Dan Gilbert, Brian Giesler, and Kathryn Morris, "We are intelligent and interesting precisely because others are so dim and dull."[2]

Social comparisons like the ones Brad and I triggered in our field experiment at APLUS powerfully influence individual behavior because they have both cognitive and emotional consequences. For instance, suppose that a professor learns that a similarly experienced professor who is teaching the same class received much higher teaching ratings than she did. The professor likely will experience a change in her beliefs ("I must not be as good a teacher as she is") and her emotions ("This makes me want to cry"). These beliefs and emotions, in turn, influence behavior ("I'll try to work harder").

Whether intentionally or not, organizations and their senior management often disclose performance rankings internally to all or some of their employees. For instance, a company might reveal performance information about the top 10 percent of their sales teams simply by giving them awards. And some organizations, such as CLEAN: The Uniform Company (of St. Louis, Missouri), disclose information about productivity to all employees. Both intuitively and based on research we've discussed, this sounds like a good idea. To improve employees' performance, you should motivate them with information about their peers' performance, right? But stories about social comparisons do not always have a happy ending.

When we compare ourselves unfavorably to someone else, we are likely to experience distress. This distress can lower our self-esteem and lead us to work harder, but it can also result in other outcomes and emotions. A story from Hollywood provides an apt illustration.

As you may know, Tom Hanks won back-to-back Best Actor Academy Awards in 1993 and 1994 for his performances in the films *Philadelphia* and *Forrest Gump*. Many critics argued that Hanks performed equally well in several of his subsequent movies, such as *Apollo 13*, *Saving Private Ryan*, and *Castaway*. But if you are an annual viewer of the Academy Awards, you probably noticed that Hanks didn't receive any Oscars for these films. In fact, Hanks didn't receive enough votes from his fellow actors to be nominated for any of these movies. Many interpreted the lack of nominations as an intentional slight that robbed Hanks of awards he deserved.[3]

This story caught the attention of researchers Katy Milkman and Maurice Schweitzer, both professors at the University of Pennsylvania. They reasoned that Tom Hanks's peers may have failed to nominate him for a third Oscar because of the envy they anticipated experiencing if he won yet another Academy Award.[4]

To test their hypothesis, Milkman and Schweitzer conducted a field experiment at a large British manufacturing company. More than three hundred employees received e-mail messages that informed them about a new employee recognition program and told them how to nominate a colleague to win an award. This was a new program that the scholars created and that the company agreed to use. The participating employees did not know it was actually a field experiment. Winners of the awards would receive both a prize (such as a plaque or a gift certificate) and recognition within the company. The award winners would be announced every quarter.

The researchers varied the e-mail messages that were sent to employees announcing the program. Half of the employees were assigned to the control condition; they received an e-mail from an HR manager that included a picture of an employee accepting an award and a description of the nomination process. The other half were assigned to the social comparison condition; these employees received the same e-mail with two additional lines of text. First, there was a caption saying "Your Coworker?" right below the image of the award recipient. Second, below the first caption was a line that read: "How would you feel if your coworker won this award?"

The researchers hypothesized that the prospect of imagining a peer receiving an award would trigger envy and that, as a result, employees who were prompted to imagine this scenario would be particularly unlikely to submit nominations. Over the next seven months, the company recorded all the award nominations submitted by the employees who participated in the experiment. In line with the researchers' predictions, employees in the control condition nominated almost three times as many coworkers as did employees in the social comparison condition.

This is not an isolated case of social comparisons triggering emotions, such as envy or threats to self-esteem, that produce consequences in interpersonal settings. Stephen Garcia, a professor at the University of Michigan, finds that when making hiring decisions, people tend to favor candidates who don't compete with their own strengths. More specifically, people who have high standing on a particular dimension (for example, a large number of publications in the case of professors) protect their own social comparisons by making recommendations that prevent others who might be competitive with them from entering the social comparison context. For example, a highly creative manager is likely to choose a job candidate who demonstrates strong attention to detail over a candidate who appears to be more creative than the manager is. It seems that people unwittingly choose to protect their personal standing rather than to improve the organization as a whole. Garcia calls this *social comparison bias*.[5]

Taken together, research on social comparisons demonstrates that when we size ourselves up relative to people who are better than we are (or as good as we are) on a particular dimension, we are likely to experience discomfort, envy, or fear. These emotions, in turn, bias our decisions.

This set of findings should cause us to pause and reflect, especially since the technology that is available to us nowadays easily triggers social comparison processes. Members of Facebook, for example, can use an application called Compare People, which (as you can tell from its name) makes the usual comparisons that pervade the social network even more explicit. Compare People shows the user random pairs of individuals from her Facebook friend list and asks her to judge them on numerous criteria (which, thankfully, are all positive), such as who is the most fun to go shopping with, who is the coolest, or who has the best profile picture. Other members of that person's network are also invited to join in the "fun" by rating one another. By comparing pairs of individuals in your network and by making a lot of comparisons, you can rank all your Facebook friends and acquaintances on given criteria— and they can rank you. The "winners" of these contests learn the results; those who lose do not. Winners, however, do not learn who rated them and how; they simply learn that they were the best in the category of interest (for example, the person best at telling jokes in Francesca's network).

These judgments are likely to influence not only the feelings and decisions of those who make them, but also the feelings and decisions of those being rated. If you used this application, for instance, you might go to work the next day uplifted by the knowledge that you dress more stylishly than all the other people in a particular Facebook friend's network. As this application illustrates, people are quite tempted to rank others and find out how others rank them. No matter what the dimension we're focused on, be it our expertise in choosing wines, our charming personality, or our attractiveness, we appreciate knowing where we stand compared to others. But even if we can appreciate this simple fact, we often fail to appreciate that these pervasive social comparison processes affect our decisions and set our plans off course.

One of the numerous dimensions on which we commonly compare ourselves to others is money. The fact that wealth-based comparisons occur frequently may not surprise you, but you might not recognize just how influential they can be.

Imagine that you just graduated from an MBA program at a top US business school and are now looking for a job. You have received the following offer from a consulting firm. The offer will expire at the end of the day, and you will have no chance to negotiate it further:

> *Job A: The offer is from Company 4 for $75,000 a year. It is widely known that this firm pays all starting MBAs from top schools $75,000 a year.*

How likely would you be to accept this offer? Now imagine that you received this offer instead:

> *Job B: The offer is from Company 9 for $85,000 a year. It is widely known that this firm is paying some other graduating students from your own program $95,000 a year.*

How likely would you be to accept this job?

Now imagine that you received both offers at virtually the same time, and both will expire at the end of the day. Which of the two jobs would you be more likely to choose, Job A or Job B?

I would bet you had a strong emotional reaction to the description of Job B. Although it pays more than Job A, Job B triggers a social comparison that may make you uneasy—the fact that the company has offered more money to others like you.

In the early 1990s, Max Bazerman and his colleagues at Northwestern University presented a group of MBA students with twelve job offers, including Job A and Job B just described, and asked them to indicate how likely they would be to accept each one.[6] Half of the students evaluated each of the twelve options sequentially, while half evaluated them in pairs (for example, the aforementioned Job A and Job B at the same time). MBA students who were presented with only one job offer at a time were more likely to accept Job A, the more emotionally appealing option. In contrast, students who were presented with these two job offers simultaneously were more likely to accept Job B. The opportunity to compare the offers allowed students to make decisions that were more consistent with their best interests. These results show that the outcomes of others serve as a reference point when we make decisions. In addition, they demonstrate that we use such information differently depending on how it is presented.

Further evidence that social comparisons based on wealth or money matter comes from a study conducted by economists David Card, Enrico Moretti, Emmanuel Saez (professors at the University of California, Berkeley) and Alexandre Mas (of Princeton University).[7] Because UC Berkeley is a public school, the salaries of all of its employees are publicly available and have been posted on the Internet since early 2008. If you were an employee at that university, would you go online to find out what your colleagues were earning? To find out, the researchers contacted a random group of UC employees in the months after the launch of the website where people could search for the salary of any state employee. Some were told about the website (the information condition); some were not (the control condition). Here is what their e-mail said in the information condition:

> *We are Professors of Economics at Princeton University and Cal Berkeley conducting a research project on pay inequality at the University of California.*
>
> *The* Sacramento Bee *newspaper has launched a website listing the salaries for all State of California employees, including UC employees. The website is located at www.sacbee.com/ statepay or can be found by searching "Sacramento Bee salary database" with Google. As part of our research project, we wanted to ask you. Did you know about the* Sacramento Bee *salary database website?*

In the control condition, instead, the e-mail introduced the study the economists were conducting and described a UC website listing the salaries of top UC administrators but not the salaries of typical UC employees. The economists wanted to know whether the employees would look up the salary information and, if they did, how they would be affected by that information.

Three to ten days after the initial e-mail introducing the study, the economists sent out another e-mail asking employees to answer a short survey with questions about their knowledge and use of the *Sacramento Bee* website, in addition to questions about job satisfaction and intentions regarding future job searches.

About 19 percent of those in the control group (who were not made aware of the website) reported having used the website sometime in the past. In the information condition, the percentage was much higher: 49 percent of these participants reported using the website after being told about its existence. The majority of the new users (four-fifths of them) reported that they used the website to look up the earnings of colleagues. How did this information affect how participants felt? As you could probably guess, access to this data triggered social comparisons. Those who learned that their colleagues earned more than they did felt underpaid and experienced negative emotions as a result. By contrast, those who discovered they were paid well relative to their colleagues felt just fine.

Wealth-based comparisons are so powerful that they can even lead people to cross ethical or legal boundaries. Lamar Pierce (a professor at Washington University in St. Louis) and I got interested in this question back when we were both visiting assistant professors at Carnegie Mellon University. Not too long after we met, Lamar and I started getting together for an afternoon coffee break a few times a week to talk about interesting patterns of behavior we observed around us. Lamar also helped me negotiate a good price for my 2002 Volkswagen Golf, the first car I had bought since moving to the United States, and I was dedicated to treating it well.

About a year after purchasing the car, I had to take it into a dealership for an emissions test. In the United States, the Environmental Protection Agency mandates that states must institute vehicle emissions programs, yet it leaves the implementation of these programs up to the states themselves. Some states directly test vehicles at state-owned facilities, but most outsource some or all of the testing to privately owned, licensed firms, which are often auto-repair shops staffed by mechanics. Emissions inspectors working at these private facilities are legally required to follow strict testing procedures, yet they typically have numerous opportunities to diverge from these policies. In fact, fraud in these settings is quite common: a 2001 covert audit in Salt Lake City, Utah, for instance, found that almost 10 percent of the facilities examined overtly tested one car in place of another.[8] Inspectors commonly have financial incentives to behave illegally during testing, since customers are more likely to return to inspection stations that have previously passed them for both future inspections and unrelated repair work.[9]

Pennsylvania, where I lived at the time, was one of the states that used private facilities for emissions tests. I remember finding a car dealership not too far from the university and bringing the car in on a rainy Friday morning. While waiting for my car to be inspected, I spent some time watching the inspectors do their jobs. I was intrigued to see that they seemed to treat their customers differently depending on the type of car they were driving.

At our next coffee break back at Carnegie Mellon, I told Lamar about my experience at the car dealership. He explained to me that mechanics earn what is commonly considered low-to-medium salaries in the United States (a little over $15 per hour, on average). Given what we now know from social comparison theory, these wages suggest that mechanics are likely to relate most closely to customers with similar or lower incomes, who are also likely to drive "standard-looking" cars. When comparing themselves to these customers, inspectors may experience empathy. By contrast, mechanics might be least likely to relate to customers who drive luxury cars. These customers may engender envy from the inspectors due to unfavorable (and salient) social comparisons.

Lamar and I wondered whether car inspectors would in fact experience such emotions and treat their customers differently as a result. Would empathy or envy due to wealth-based comparisons influence inspectors' propensity to help customers' cars pass emissions tests? We decided to explore this hypothesis.

Soon after, thanks to Lamar's persuasion skills, we obtained three years' worth of data on all vehicle inspections for gasoline-powered vehicles under eighty-five hundred pounds from the Department of Motor Vehicles of a large northern US state. In this state, emissions testing was conducted by licensed private firms. Emissions inspectors working at these private facilities were legally required to follow strict testing procedures. However, they had many opportunities to diverge from these policies. Skilled mechanics could make temporary adjustments that allowed almost any vehicle to pass the emissions tests without addressing the underlying causes of the excess pollution. Even the most polluting cars could be certified clean when inspectors used other cars during testing procedures, which occurred more often than you might think.

Lamar and I came up with an appropriate way to categorize cars as either "standard" or "luxury" depending on their make and age. For each inspector, we then measured two leniency levels by identifying their average pass rates for both luxury cars and for standard cars, and then examined differences between the two. Such differences would indicate whether inspectors were discriminating based on (perceived) customer wealth. Regardless of the type of car you drive, you may be interested in knowing what we saw in the data. We found that a striking number of inspectors appeared to be illegally helping customers who seemed less wealthy, at least as reflected in their choice of car. That is, the inspectors helped customers they likely empathized with because of favorable social comparisons.

Given the nature of our dataset, however, we weren't exactly sure how the inspectors felt when they conducted tests on cars that appeared to be either standard or luxury. So Lamar and I designed a series of laboratory studies to explore this phenomenon further: namely, to examine whether emotions helped to explain it and whether it generalized to other contexts where people compare themselves to others who appear to be better off financially.

We invited students to participate in a study on "assessing individual performance." At the beginning of each session, we randomly assigned participants to one of two roles, either "solver" or "grader." Participants in both roles were given a clear plastic lanyard to wear around their necks for the duration of the experiment. Participants were told they would receive money during the study and would need to place the money in their lanyards. Solvers were asked to take a seat on one side of a large auditorium, and graders were instructed to sit on the other side.

As the experimenter explained to participants, the study included three stages. All participants first took part in a lottery. Depending on the outcome of a visible virtual (and fair) coin toss, each participant received either $20 (wealthy condition) or $0 (poor condition). Lottery winners were asked to put the $20 in their lanyard, such that the money was visible to the other participants for the rest of the experiment. We held the lottery to make some of the participants in each role "poor" and some of them "wealthy." Through the lottery, about half of the participants in each role won $20 (these were the "wealthy" participants in our study); the rest won nothing (thus, they were "poor"). Based on the outcome of the lottery, we were able to create four types of grader/solver pairs: $20 solver/$20 grader, $20 solver/$0 grader, $0 solver/$20 grader, and $0 solver/$0 grader. Clearly, two of the types of pairings were equitable ($20 solver/$20 grader and $0 solver/$0 grader) and two of the types of pairings were inequitable ($20 solver/$0 grader and $0 solver/$20 grader).

In the other two stages of the experiment, participants were assigned different tasks based on their roles. In the second stage, all of the solvers (those who won $20 in the coin toss as well as those who earned nothing) had to individually complete an ability-based, anagram-solving task under time pressure, while graders completed a filler task. In the anagram task, solvers were asked to create words from each of four series of seven letters; the task was performed under time pressure (sixty seconds per round). Solvers were paid based on how well they performed on the task

($2 in each of four rounds in which they created more than ten words correctly from the series of letters they were given).

After the anagram task, participants entered the third stage of the study. Based on lab IDs that participants had received at the beginning of the session, each solver was randomly assigned to a grader who would grade that solver's anagram task. As the experimenter announced the pairings, solvers brought their work to their graders and then returned to their seats across the aisle to complete a filler task. Graders were given *Scrabble* dictionaries and asked to grade the solvers' work on the anagram task. After the graders finished grading, the experimenter brought the graded work back to the solvers so that they could be paid and leave the room. Graders also completed a short survey in which we recorded their emotional reactions to their partner's lottery outcome (which was clearly visible, thanks to the lanyards).

We used a procedure that gave graders the opportunity to cheat by overreporting or underreporting the solver's performance. If a grader underreported her solver's performance, then she was cheating in a way that would hurt the solver; if she overreported her solver's performance, then she was cheating to help the solver. If graders cheated, would they cheat differently depending on which condition they and their solvers were in, whether wealthy or poor? Figure 6-1 summarizes the predictions we made before conducting this experiment—both how we believed graders would feel and, consequently, how they would behave.

We conducted a series of laboratory experiments with this basic structure to test our predictions. Across studies, we varied the financial incentives for the graders and kept the solvers' participation payment the same (not including their lottery results). In some of our studies, graders received a flat fee for participating. In one study, graders were paid based on the performance of their solvers: the better the solver's performance, the more the grader earned. Thus, graders had a financial incentive to dishonestly help their solvers. Finally, in another study, we gave graders a fixed amount of money and told them to use the money to pay their solvers and to keep

FIGURE 6-1

Emotional and behavioral predictions for wealthy and poor conditions in the social comparison experiment

Grader

		Wealthy	Poor
Solver	Wealthy	Emotion: Happiness *Prediction: Honesty*	Emotion: Envy *Prediction: Hurt but not help*
	Poor	Emotion: Guilt *Prediction: Help but not hurt*	Emotion: Empathy *Prediction: Help but not hurt*

the rest for themselves. Thus, in this case, graders had a financial incentive to dishonestly hurt their solvers. By conducting these different studies, we pitted financial incentives against the emotions that might result from favorable or unfavorable social comparisons.

Imagine that you are participating in one of these experiments. At the time of the initial coin toss, you did not earn any money, but several other participants around you won $20 on the spot, including the solver with whom you were randomly paired. It is now time for you to grade the work of this solver and report his score on a performance sheet. What do you think you'd do? Would you report the solver's performance honestly, or would you lower his score? Do you think your actions would be affected by your own financial incentives?

You might think that you would be able to put your envy aside and score the person's performance honestly, but most of our participants in this experimental condition could not. When "poor" graders came up against "wealthy" solvers, they experienced envy and, as a result, deceptively lowered solvers' scores, even when doing so cost the graders real money. In fact, across our studies, 25 to 40 percent of the graders underreported their solvers' performance in the $20 solver/$0 grader condition. These results suggest that our emotional reactions to unfavorable social comparisons motivate us to level the playing field emotionally, if not financially. It seems most of us would prefer to be out a few bucks than to be plagued by uncomfortable emotions such as envy. Interestingly, and similar to what Lamar and I observed in the emissions tests dataset, the graders who hadn't earned money in the initial coin toss lied on behalf of solvers who also hadn't won any money yet—they rewarded them with cash for work they did not do. These graders appeared to experience a sense of empathy, given that both they and their solvers were "poor," and thus cheated on their solvers' behalf. Finally, we found that "wealthy" solvers graded the work of "wealthy" graders honestly. Overall, across the four conditions, the results supported our predictions.

These findings have broad implications beyond both the laboratory and car dealerships. In fact, similar patterns of behavior emerged during my nine-week gym triathlon. After one of my first few gym classes, a regular attendee who had noticed the paltry number of stars in my logbook and the dazzling constellation in my friends' books followed me to the locker room. There she told me that she, too, had joined the triathlon a few weeks late. She could help me out, she said, by giving me a few stars: she had found the same stickers at a local CVS drugstore. Like the emissions inspectors who helped customers driving standard cars, my compatriot felt a sense of empathy toward me and envy toward my friends— emotions that spurred her to break the rules of the game.

More generally, in our business and personal lives, white lies have a way of easing themselves into polite conversation, such as telling your boss you don't mind covering for a late coworker, or a friend that she should buy some pants that don't look so hot. Such subtle mistruths may seem to have little consequence, but what about when more than goodwill is at stake? As in the case of the triathlon cheater, the results of the last few studies I've discussed show that motives other than politeness may drive our deception.

One powerful factor is how the social comparisons we engage in make us feel. Unfavorable comparisons often lead to envy; favorable comparisons tend to make us feel happy for our good fortune, empathetic toward those who are less fortunate, or both.

Companies often struggle to "exploit" social comparisons in ways that motivate their employees or customers without suffering the costs that these comparisons may inflict. Consider the case of Digg, a social news website that Kevin Rose founded as an experiment in December 2004. Rose designed the website to be the prime location for people to find and source the best news and most interesting news stories. At first, Digg had a type of score sheet known as a *leaderboard*: users received points for submitting the highest number of popular stories and were then promoted to Digg's front page. These users were called "top diggers," and a prominent Web page was dedicated to them and their popular stories. The leaderboard triggered social comparisons among users: those who were not top diggers were motivated to look for interesting stories so that they could join the top diggers list. But as Digg management eventually discovered, the leaderboard triggered another behavior: gaming. Some top users were accused of trying to manipulate Digg and maintain their leadership status by pushing stories they found to the front page. This behavior was not only unexpected but also ran counter to the website's purpose. As a result, in February 2007, Digg removed the leaderboard feature from its site.[10]

So, what have we learned in this chapter? Two important points, I hope. The first is that another aspect of relationships, in addition to the type and strength of our social bonds, may derail our decisions: the comparisons we make between ourselves and others, and the types of behavior that tend to follow from those comparisons. In general, we think we are capable of judging our own behavior by comparing it to our original intentions. Yet in reality, other people often turn out to be a much more salient reference for our comparisons. Our behavior is also strongly influenced by how others appear, including how wealthy they seem to be. To overcome a sense of inequity between the resources we have and those that others have, we cheat or tell white lies. Similarly, we reject promising job candidates simply because we fear their good qualities will overshadow our own.

The second point is that we engage in social comparisons for different reasons. Sometimes we are interested in assessing our own abilities, opinions, and skills. To find out how we are doing on any of these dimensions, we compare ourselves to those who seem most similar to us. For instance, if I were to evaluate how good I am at teaching effectively, I might compare myself to colleagues with similar years of teaching experience. Other times, however, our main goal is to improve how we're doing on a given dimension. In this case, we consciously choose someone who seems much better than us as a comparison target. Any differences we note between them and us give us information about areas where we could improve. For instance, if I were to decide to become a better swimmer, I could use a friend who used to compete in swimming competitions as a comparison target. Finally, there are times when we want to feel good about ourselves or just generally feel better. In these cases, we tend to choose as comparison targets people who are doing less well than us in a particular area. So, for instance, if I wanted to feel good about my height, I would compare myself to shorter people of about my age rather than to my sister (who is about six inches taller than I am!).

These two points highlight a larger observation about how we operate as human beings: the way we define and understand ourselves is an inherently social process. As you have seen, our decisions are biased by the comparisons we strategically choose in order to alter how we see ourselves. In addition, we often do not realize that our decisions are affected by the emotions and thoughts we experience after engaging in social comparisons.

So, a sixth principle to add to our list of guidelines that can help us avoid getting sidetracked is:

Check your reference points.

This principle suggests that you need to carefully consider the motives behind your decisions. You may have developed a clear plan, such as how often to exercise or how hard to work, but when executing that plan, you may find that social comparisons are causing you to make decisions that throw you off track. Could your decisions be driven by the fact that you are feeling unhappy or, conversely, pleased because of where you stand in comparison to others?

It's important to ask yourself this question not only when making decisions that will affect your own life, but also when making decisions that affect others, as when you are hiring people or evaluating others' work. This is because your decisions may be swayed by social comparisons and the emotions associated with them, rather than being based on more objective standards. In addition, keeping your reference points in check is a useful strategy when you are making decisions that will affect the motivations and behavior of others. If you are a leader who wants to motivate your team members to perform better, if you want to motivate your partner to work out with you, or if you want to motivate your children to do their homework, you might try to leverage social comparison processes and the emotions and behaviors they trigger.

How can you use this principle effectively in your personal and professional life? An example comes from Sheldon, a teacher of game design at Rensselaer Polytechnic Institute in New York, who applied the lessons of this chapter when he introduced a new grading procedure to better motivate his students. Instead of traditional grades, students in his classes accumulate "experience points" over the course of a semester.[11] The class and its grading procedure include a number of features modeled on the computer game *World of Warcraft*, complete with "quests," "monsters," and "guilds." Throughout the semester, the students can compare their standing with that of their classmates and devise a plan to accumulate more experience points. Whenever they do well on their assignments or exams, they earn points rather than traditional grades. When Sheldon introduced this system, he found that his students worked harder and were also more enthusiastic in class. In addition, the new system triggered collaborative behavior among the students and reduced cheating.[12]

Motivating students to learn may sound quite different from motivating your spouse or your employees to do what you want them to do, yet the basic principles of social comparisons can be applied across contexts. In fact, Ross Cochrane adopted many of Sheldon's classroom techniques when he was the CEO of distribution company Express Data. Cochrane used the same principle of clearly communicating to employees how their performance would be rewarded and where they stood compared to others and their goals. Both Sheldon and Cochrane thought carefully about their systems to ensure that social comparisons would motivate participants to be more engaged and productive, without triggering the potentially damaging behaviors I have discussed in this chapter (such as sabotaging peers, cutting corners, or cheating). By instituting an open culture where performance is fairly rewarded and the guidelines for high achievement are clear, Sheldon and Cochrane ensured that participants would play by the rules.

Oh, and by the way, in case you are wondering: I did not accept any star stickers from the nice lady who wanted to give me some for free. But I did win the competition, among many other participants, and received the promised T-shirt.

PART III

Forces from the Outside

CHAPTER 7

They're Not as Dumb as You Think They Are

Irrelevant Information

On November 26, 2010, a public fight broke out between FIJI Water, a popular supplier of premium bottled water owned by a private US company, and the government of Fiji, led by its prime minister and military commander, Frank Bainimarama.[1] Since 2006, following a successful coup d'état, Bainimarama had ruled Fiji as a military dictatorship. His administration had been accused of financial mismanagement, tax evasion, bribery, and nepotism, perpetuated by a lack of proper government checks and balances. Moreover, reports alleged that the prime minister and his finance minister had stolen hundreds of thousands of dollars in public funds for their personal use and paid themselves annual salaries of about $700,000 each.

In the meantime, Fiji was experiencing serious economic difficulties. Natural disasters, including cyclones and floods, had crippled the country's already deteriorating infrastructure, reduced access to clean water supplies, and contributed to outbreaks of various diseases. From 2007 to 2010, the country faced negative

GDP growth; inflation ran into the double digits, and the poverty rate increased from 30 percent to 60 percent. In addition, the country's national debt had skyrocketed. The government compensated for its dwindling revenues by increasing taxes and reducing pension payments. Fijians had a hard time keeping up with rising food, electricity, and water prices.

To address these problems, the Fijian government decided to change its taxation system. Notably, in its 2010 annual budget, the government announced that it was increasing its tax on water extraction greater than 3.5 million liters a month from one-third of a Fijian cent to 15 cents per liter. The additional tax would add US$11.7 million annually to the government's coffers.

FIJI Water was the only water bottler on the island large enough to be affected by the new tax. On November 29, it called the tax discriminatory and shut down its bottling plant, laid off its four hundred employees, canceled its contracts, and halted its investments in development projects across Fiji. In media interviews, FIJI Water representatives declared that the country and its government were becoming increasingly unstable, making Fiji a very risky place in which to invest. Nevertheless, FIJI Water was reluctant to completely pull out of the island, where it had established its operations and earned its reputation for bottling clean, pure water. Thus, after some intense negotiations with the government, the company decided to accept the proposed tax increase.

One interesting aspect of this conflict is how it got started in the first place—with the Fijian government's decision to greatly increase FIJI Water's taxation. The government noted that FIJI Water was selling its products in the United States for high prices (around $8 a bottle in hotels) and interpreted this as a sign that the company was performing very well in the bottled water market and earning high profits. The government did not delve into FIJI Water's operations, nor did it explore the industry in which the company was operating or its competitiveness. In fact, FIJI Water was then a small player in the bottled water industry, holding only 1 percent of the global bottled water market. The company's management tried to make this fact clear to Fiji government officials, but the government nonetheless reached inflated evaluations of the company's well-being.

The way we make attributions is biased, which can have unseen effects on our decisions. This inability to adequately account for a wide range of situational factors when evaluating others helps to explain many of our most serious mistakes in life, and many derailed decisions. These errors share something in common: they involve using irrelevant information—or, alternatively, discounting relevant details—when evaluating others.

In particular, when evaluating others, we have trouble adjusting for the complexity of a situation. To use a metaphor, the most common mistake is to overlook the size of the pond when evaluating a fish. In an ideal world, for example, the coach of an athletic team should not only examine the past success of a player he is considering recruiting, but also the relative strengths and weaknesses of the player's entire team. Similarly, a manager who is evaluating salespeople should recognize that the leading salesperson in one region may simply have expertise in that region rather than a broader understanding of the sales process across all regions. Managers should carefully take such information into account when deciding which sales practices to apply throughout their organizations.

Prime Minister Bainimarama, failing to put FIJI's business in a global context, erroneously assumed that one of the most prosperous US companies based on his small island would not balk at paying whatever taxes his government demanded. And while the government in the end convinced FIJI Water to agree to the tax increase, its inaccurate evaluation of the company's standing in the global market soured the relationship between the two parties.

To investigate this phenomenon, let's start with a thought experiment. Imagine that you are the captain of your town's competitive

Quizbowl team. (In Quizbowl, teams compete against one another in a tournament to answer general knowledge questions.) Your team is preparing to enter a tournament in which you will compete against teams from other cities from across the globe. This is an important competition, and you're taking it very seriously. You have three high-performing members who have great track records at winning Quizbowl competitions, but you need one more member. You are in charge of selecting this person. To make your task a bit easier, I have narrowed down your selection to just two people with comparable background experience who have made it to the second round. The candidates were given different trivia quizzes, which were randomly assigned to them, to assess their ability and knowledge. Your task is to review the applicants' answers on their quizzes individually and decide which of the two applicants to choose for your team.

The first candidate you are evaluating received a score of 8 out of 10 on the trivia quiz he took. The average score of the people who took the same test was 8.94. How well do you think this person would perform if you chose him for your team? How likely do you think you will be to accept this candidate?

Now consider the quiz performance of your second candidate. This candidate did not do as well on the task as the first candidate did; he answered only 2 questions correctly out of 10. In this case, the average score of the people who took the same test was 1.97. How well do you think this person would perform if you were to select him for your team? How likely are you to accept him?

It seems clear that the first candidate would fit better on your team than the second one, and that you would be more likely to accept the former rather than the latter as your new team member. In a few pages, I will explain why I believe you reached this decision—and, if you did, why it may have been a mistake.

The problem I presented you with—assessing the informative value of the scores the two candidates received on their trivia quizzes—illustrates a more general question: how should we infer a person's attributes (such as intelligence and leadership potential) from her behavior while properly accounting for the influence of the given context?

This general problem underlies many selection decisions. For instance, would you have more confidence in your company's new CEO if she had previously led a successful company in a highly profitable industry or if she had led a firm that was barely surviving in an industry in which most firms had been decimated? Would you rather promote a salesperson who has performed very well in a region with high levels of demand or someone who has been less successful in a region with low demand? And would you evaluate a graduate student as more ambitious and hardworking if she had a 3.6 grade point average (GPA) from a school where the average GPA is 3.4 or if she had a 3.3 from an institution where the average GPA is 2.8?

These very different decisions share a fundamental challenge: they require you to evaluate a person's ability by making attributions about him or her. This challenge may seem simple. After all, you already know that individual behavior depends on a person's disposition as well as the influence of the situation in which she finds herself. And yet, as human beings, we seem to have difficulty applying this simple principle when making decisions like the Quizbowl problem you just completed.

As you may have already guessed, such decisions are complicated by the fact that we do not have access to people's inner selves. We cannot directly observe their true character, beliefs, intentions, desires, or motives. Yet all of these elements are critical to our understanding and evaluation of others. Since we cannot directly observe these intangible factors, we must undertake the tricky business of inferring them from what we can in fact observe: people's words and behavior. Not surprisingly, then, judging intangible factors by observing tangible ones leads to mistakes.

In particular, one mistake we systematically make is known as the *correspondence bias*. When making attributions as we evaluate others, we tend to ascribe too little influence to the situation and too much to their dispositions. In simpler terms, we tend to believe that people's behavior reflects their unique dispositions and skills, when many times it actually reflects aspects of the situation in which they find themselves. Imagine, for example, that you are shopping for a sweater to give to a friend for her birthday. When you ask a sales clerk for help, she shows you a few different sweaters, but she doesn't say much about them. In fact, she is not even smiling or making eye contact with you. What kind of impression do you think you'd have of the clerk? You might judge her as rude (as I probably would). But it is also possible she just had an unpleasant encounter with a verbally abusive customer. Thus, her attitude during her brief encounter with you may not be a good descriptor of the type of person she is. If you fail to consider this possibility, you are showing the correspondence bias in your judgments.

A laboratory experiment conducted in the late 1970s by psychologist Lee Ross and his colleagues provides a nice demonstration of this common bias.[2] In one of their studies, the researchers asked participants to take part in a "quiz show." Some were randomly assigned to the role of quizmasters, and some were assigned to the role of quiz taker. The quizmasters were in charge of formulating questions within an area of their expertise that the quiz takers would then be asked to answer. In addition, a third group of participants was assigned to the role of observer: these participants were asked to observe a quiz taker's behavior as he or she attempted to answer the quizmaster's questions. The researchers were examining the following questions: would the average observer recognize that his or her quiz taker's performance was not a clear signal of this person's intelligence or knowledge? Would the observer fail to recognize that the quizmaster probably asked difficult questions on subjects the quiz taker might not be familiar with and that others also would have trouble answering?

Imagine that you are participating in this experiment in the role of quiz taker. Your quizmaster turns out to be an expert in 1960s and 1970s pop/rock music. Here are some of the questions he asks:[3]

1. At what age did Janis Ian learn "the truth"?

2. Where might the Hollies lead you to expect to find a "long cool woman"?

3. Who sang backup vocals on Lou Reed's "Satellite of Love"?

4. According to Pete Townshend, where does "nothing ever go as planned"?

5. What did Smokey Robinson say would be easy to trace (if you look closer)?

6. From what state does the writer of "Mary Queen of Arkansas" hail?

Feel free to take a few minutes to review these questions. How many were you able to answer with confidence? (The answers are at the bottom of the page.*)

I personally did not perform very well on this task, and I am guessing you weren't too happy with your performance either (unless you happen to be an expert on this topic). If you performed poorly, to what do you attribute your poor performance? I would blame the quizmaster for asking questions that were too difficult and specific to his area of expertise rather than blame myself for not knowing the answers.

In the original experiment, the observers weren't able to recognize the influence of the situation. In fact, when asked to rate the knowledge of the quiz takers and of the quizmasters, the observers failed to appreciate the role of the situation—they failed to realize that the quizmasters drew on specialized expertise to formulate their questions and that quiz takers likely were not familiar with this narrow subject matter. As a result, the observers rated the people in the role of quizmasters as generally more knowledgeable—more intelligent—than those in the role of quiz takers,

---

*(1) At 17; (2) In a black dress; (3) David Bowie; (4) By the sea and sand; (5) The tracks of my tears; and (6) New Jersey.

though quiz takers clearly were disadvantaged by the situation. When evaluating others, observers didn't recognize that, because of the experiment's random assignment, they could have been in a quiz taker's shoes and performed just as poorly.

In this experiment, quizmasters were unlikely to be more knowledgeable overall than quiz takers (given random assignment to roles). But this information would have been of little help to observers, who had to decide whether a specific quizmaster was more or less intelligent than a particular quiz taker. To accurately judge the power of the situation, observers needed to know what proportion of questions *all* of the quiz takers, on average, failed to answer correctly. Armed with this information, observers would have been able to identify whether a particular quiz taker performed above or below average. This would allow them to account for the situational differences between the quizmaster and the quiz taker. Would they?

To answer that question, we can go back to the problem you faced earlier: choosing the final member of your Quizbowl team. In addition to showing you the performance of each candidate on the quiz, I also gave you all the information you needed to adjust your attributions of the candidates' abilities based on the influence of the situation. If you remember, I highlighted the fact that the candidates had taken different tests, and I gave you information about the average performance on each type of test. I conducted similar thought experiments in the laboratory a few years ago in collaboration with Don Moore and two PhD students at Carnegie Mellon University, Sam Swift and Zachariah Sharek.

For one of the experiments, we recruited seventy-one undergraduates from Carnegie Mellon University and asked them to imagine that they had to select members for a Quizbowl trivia team, exactly like you did. They reviewed the prior performances of ten applicants on a US geography quiz. Five of these applicants had taken an easy test that included questions such as, "The Bronx is part of what US city?" The other five had taken a difficult test that included questions such as, "How many US states border Canada?" For each of the ten candidates, participants saw actual completed and corrected quizzes from participants who had taken part in a pilot study. In addition to learning each candidate's score on the test, participants learned the average score and standard deviation among all ten test takers on that quiz. By looking at the questions on the quiz, they could easily tell whether the quiz the applicants had taken was the easy or the difficult one.

We asked participants to examine the ten contestants and to identify the five they thought would be most likely to perform well on a third quiz of medium difficulty. This quiz, which participants saw before making their evaluations, was the same for all ten applicants. In addition, participants had to rate the extent to which each candidate was knowledgeable about US geography. Participants earned $2 for each contestant they picked whose score was in the top half of the performers on the third quiz. Thus, if they correctly picked the five top scorers, they would receive $10, and if they incorrectly picked the five worst performers, they would not earn any additional money. Our hypothesis was that participants would select test takers who had high scores as a result of taking the easy quiz more often than those who had less impressive scores as a result of taking the more difficult test.

In addition to varying the type of test the participants took, we manipulated whether those making the selection decisions had personal experience with the task. Half of the participants (in the experience condition) were asked to take both the easy and the difficult test prior to evaluating candidates and to provide as many correct answers as possible. The other half of participants (those in the no-experience condition) did not take the tests prior to evaluating candidates. We introduced this manipulation because we were interested in understanding whether experience would reduce the correspondence bias we hypothesized we would observe. We theorized that experience with a task would help make situational pressures salient through their effects on participants' own behavior.

Not surprisingly, people are far more sensitive to situational effects on their own behavior than on the behavior of others.

The information we gave participants about the task did not help to improve their selection decisions. Participants who had seen a contestant's easy quiz rated that contestant as almost twice as knowledgeable as the same contestant rated by participants who had seen his or her difficult quiz. Interestingly, experience taking the test made no difference: it did not reduce the impact of test difficulty on participants' judgments. Participants were also more likely to pick contestants whose easy quiz scores they had seen when predicting which contestants would score better on the third quiz. In sum, participants weighted contestants' actual test scores much more heavily than the difficulty of the quiz. In fact, moving from an average score on the difficult quiz (1.11 out of 10) to an average score on the easy quiz (8.78 out of 10) increased a contestant's probability of being selected from 27 percent to 70 percent.

These results demonstrate that people tend to use obvious information about the impact of a situation—in this case, the difficulty of the task—insufficiently, if at all, to discount obvious information about an individual's performance. This common mistake leads to biased selection decisions in a variety of contexts, including promotions in organizations and admissions to college or graduate school. In our own research, using data from admission decisions of top-tier US schools, we have found evidence of grade inflation, such that students with high grades from institutions with lenient grading benefit from this leniency. On a more anecdotal level, sports fans may have noticed cases in which a coach or manager enjoys great success with one team for a season or two and is praised to the skies. Then he gets poached at great expense by a second team, where he performs very poorly. The team stuck paying his contract probably failed to consider the complex context in which the manager operated and the fact that his success may have been due to factors other than his managerial skills.

We commonly see ourselves as accurate and rational evaluators of others and their actions. But, as the studies on the correspondence bias show, the way information is presented to us greatly influences our evaluations of others and our decisions. In addition to the correspondence bias, there are two other common evaluation mistakes I want to tell you about. The first has to do with how we use information about a person's actions, even when such information is irrelevant.

If you are a fan of the hit TV comedy *Seinfeld*, you may remember an episode in which Jerry's friend George leaves his car parked at work on purpose. George wants his boss, New York Yankees owner George Steinbrenner, to believe that he is putting in long hours. George hopes that his apparent productivity will impress his boss and net him a raise. Researchers would call George's behavior an attempt to invoke the *input bias*—the tendency to use signs of effort (in this case, the presence of George's car in the parking lot) to judge outcomes (how hard George works) when this information may be irrelevant and uninformative. Because of the input bias, we tend to automatically associate a high degree of effort or expense with a high-quality outcome.

Beyond TV shows, people often purposefully manipulate input measures such as effort (and even the perception of input measures) to influence their assessments of outcomes. This desire to manage impressions can even influence the way companies are structured. For example, the National Bicycle Industrial Company manufactures and delivers custom-ordered bicycles three weeks after receiving an order, even though it takes the firm less than three hours to manufacture and assemble a bicycle.[4] The company could invest resources in speedy delivery without too much trouble, but it believes that consumers may not appropriately value faster delivery. Slow delivery time, the reasoning goes, may give customers the sense that their customized product, which purportedly took a long time to build, has greater value than a bike that seems to have been rushed off the assembly line.

Karen Chinander (a professor at Florida Atlantic University) and Maurice Schweitzer tested this very possibility in a cleverly designed laboratory experiment. They began with a pilot study in which they had a participant prepare and deliver a seven-and-a-half-minute presentation about electronic ink; the researchers recorded the presentation for use in their main study. For the main study, sixty-three college students were asked to view the presentation and then answer a few questions about its quality. After viewing the presentation but before formally assessing its quality, participants received information about the amount of time the person had spent preparing his presentation. Half of the participants were told that the preparation time was long: eight hours and thirty-four minutes (high-input condition). The other half were told that the preparation time was short: thirty-seven minutes (low-input condition). After receiving this information, participants in both conditions rated the quality of the presentation along various dimensions, such as the quality of the information and its organization. Participants also indicated whether the information about preparation time influenced their assessment of the quality of the presentation and if they believed that the amount of preparation time should influence their ratings.

The results were in line with the predicted outcome of George's strategy in the *Seinfeld* episode: participants rated the presentation to be of greater quality when preparation time was long rather than short. Even those participants who believed that preparation time *should* not influence their ratings (65 percent of them) and those who believed preparation time *did* not influence their ratings (67 percent of them) showed the same pattern of results.

The input bias also skews our evaluations outside the domain of judging others' effort and decision quality. In follow-up experiments, Chinander and Schweitzer had participants taste chocolate and tea that they were told had been produced by either expensive or inexpensive machinery. Individuals preferred the chocolate and tea that they thought was produced using expensive methods—though the same products were used throughout the experiment.

These results illustrating the input bias may not seem surprising to you. It's only common sense, you might reason, that the more effort we devote to a task (the "input"), the more likely we will be to reach a given performance goal (the "outcome"). Similarly, R&D expenditures are often used as a measure of the innovativeness of a firm (another outcome). Yet in many situations, effort does not reflect the quality of the outcome. For instance, the fact that I spent an endless number of hours working on this book may tell you little about its quality. Similarly, learning that your car was at the shop for a long time to get an oil change probably tells you little about the quality of the service you received on it.

It is often difficult to know how loosely or tightly correlated information about someone's effort is with that person's intended results. Even if we understand this observation intuitively, as most of the participants in Chinander and Schweitzer's experiments did, our judgments continue to be swayed by impressive inputs. Moreover, as both the *Seinfeld* storyline and the results of these experiments suggest, we frequently make decisions based on biased or manipulated information about effort. As Schweitzer once noted when talking about his research, "There's this billboard for Lexus that says something like, '35,000 people took vacations in the south of France last year; none of them was a Lexus engineer.' I don't really care that they went on vacation. Is it a good car? That's what I care about. People can misperceive what these inputs are measuring."[5]

So far, I have discussed how our judgments of others and subsequent decisions that may affect them are influenced by the correspondence bias and by the input bias. We have seen that we tend to attribute people's behavior to their personality rather than the situations in which they find themselves, and that we attribute people's outcomes too much to the effort they seem to have expended. There is a third common mistake that we tend to make when processing information about others' actions as we try to evaluate them: when judging the quality or nature of someone's initial decision, we overweight information regarding his or her outcomes, a tendency known as the *outcome bias*. (In a sense, this mistake is the input bias in reverse.)

To see a simple demonstration of this error, consider the following hypothetical scenario of a surgeon deciding whether or not to recommend a risky operation:

> *A fifty-five-year-old man had a heart condition. He had to stop working because of chest pain. He enjoyed his work and did not want to stop. His pain also interfered with other things, such as travel and recreation. A type of bypass operation would relieve his pain and increase his life expectancy from sixty-five to seventy. However, 8 percent of the people who have this operation die from the operation itself.*

The decision of whether or not to recommend the surgery is obviously a difficult one for the doctor. What do you think he should do? You may be undecided, but keep reading.

> *His physician decided to go ahead and recommend the operation, and the patient went through with the surgery. The operation was a success.*

Based on this information, how would you evaluate the quality of the surgeon's decision? Was the decision to recommend an operation the right one? Moreover, how competent do you think the surgeon is?

Now consider a different version of the same scenario. The surgeon is faced with the same decision. This time, however, you learn that the surgeon went ahead with the operation, but the patient died. In this case, how would you evaluate the quality of the surgeon's decision to recommend the operation? And how would you evaluate the surgeon's competence?

Jonathan Baron and John Hershey, both of the University of Pennsylvania, presented a group of college students with this scenario, along with a few similar ones.[6] The researchers were interested in testing whether the information about the outcome of people's decisions would influence participants' ratings of the decision quality. Their results indicated that it did: when the patient survived, participants supported the surgeon's decision; when the patient died, participants condemned the surgeon for proceeding with the operation. Of course, objectively speaking, participants' judgments should have been based on the soundness of the surgeon's decision-making process rather than on his results. The results were similar for the other scenarios the two researchers used, suggesting that the outcome bias is robust across contexts.

One of the contexts I examined in my own research is how we evaluate others' ethical behavior. Don Moore, Max Bazerman, and I became interested in this context because it presents a unique problem for organizations. Consider the case of US auditing firms. For decades, auditing firms worked for their clients not only as auditors, but also as consultants, providing financial and other types of advice. Conducting such nonaudit services compromised the independence of accounting firms' audits. The core problem is that an auditing firm that wants to score lucrative consulting contracts has a motivation to keep its client happy; thus, it is predisposed to be less likely to notice problems in the client's books in the course of an audit. This conflict of interest is recognized by outside observers, but it was largely ignored by auditing firms, clients, government officials, and society at large. The public expressed little concern, even in the face of evidence of auditor nonindependence—until a series of disasters occurred. The collapse of Enron and its auditor Arthur Andersen, and that of many other corporations in the early 2000s, resulted at least in part from a failure to notice or to report unethical and illegal behavior. These dramatic failures of American corporations helped spur the passage of the Sarbanes-Oxley Act of 2002, which placed tighter controls on auditors' engagements in an attempt to bolster auditor independence. Yet, it is somewhat ironic that change occurred only after a series of crises that could not be ignored.

It may be a natural human failing that, in many realms, we resist change until disaster strikes. Unions were created only after companies repeatedly mistreated their employees to extreme degrees. Similarly, tightened regulation of children's products emerged only after parents organized following immense personal tragedies. Why do we question poor decisions only when we see that they have led to a negative outcome? Lisa Shu (of Northwestern University), Max Bazerman, and I designed a series of experiments to address this question. We hypothesized that people would judge the unethical behavior of others more harshly when it led to a negative outcome (namely, when it harmed other people) than when the same behavior led to a positive outcome.

In one of our experiments, which we described to our participants as a study of monetary allocation decisions, we randomly assigned 223 individuals (mostly students) to one of six roles. Depending on their role, we asked them to allocate money to themselves or to other participants playing a different role. The roles were: Player A, Player B, and one of four types of Player C.

Participants in the role of Player A had to choose payments for themselves and another participant (Player B) by choosing between the following two options: "(1) You receive $5, and Player B receives $5, or (2) You receive $6, and the experimenter will toss a fair coin. If heads, then Player B will receive $5. If tails, then Player B will receive nothing." Participants in the role of Player B were truthfully told that their payment would depend upon the choice of Player A. Player A's decisions did, in fact, determine Player B's payoff in the study.

We introduced our two manipulations of interest for participants in the role of Player C, who received $5 for their participation. First, we manipulated whether Player B had a real name (i.e., a gender-neutral name, Chris) or not (i.e., Player B), as we wanted to see if people would behave differently toward a person who was somewhat personalized rather than anonymous. Player Cs received the following instructions for the game:

> *In this study, you will observe the actions of two randomly chosen participants in the same study—Player A and [Player B/Chris]. Player A will be asked to consider the following two options: option (1) A receives $5, and [Player B/Chris] receives $5; option (2) A receives $6, and the experimenter will toss a fair coin. If it comes up heads, then [Player B/Chris] will receive $5. If tails, then [Player B/Chris] will receive nothing.*

Player Cs then waited for Player A to make her or his decision. This waiting time was actually fictitious, as the choice of Player A that Player Cs saw on their computer screen was always the same: Player A chose the option in which Player A receives $6 (that is, option 2).

Second, we manipulated outcome information by changing the information that participants in the role of Player C received about the coin toss. In the negative-outcome information condition, participants were told that the result of the coin toss was tails. In the positive-outcome information condition, participants instead were told that the result of the coin toss was heads.

In all conditions, after receiving this information, participants in the role of Player C were given the option of forfeiting money to punish Player A. Player C faced the following choices:

a. Pay $0.00, and thus reduce Player A's payoff by $0.00

b. Pay $0.05, and thus reduce Player A's payoff by $0.25

c. Pay $0.10, and thus reduce Player A's payoff by $0.50

d. Pay $0.15, and thus reduce Player A's payoff by $0.75

e. Pay $0.20, and thus reduce Player A's payoff by $1.00

f. Pay $0.25, and thus reduce Player A's payoff by $1.25

Participants in the role of Player C were told, truthfully, that any money they paid to reduce Player A's payoff would be deducted from their $5 participation fee at the end of the study. (Note that although we were interested only in the decisions of Player C, we included Player A and Player B so that the game would be perceived as realistic. Participants in the role of Player C saw the participants in the other roles when they were all waiting outside the laboratory for the experiment to start.)

Imagine that you are participating in this experiment. You have been randomly assigned to the role of Player C. You learn that Player A decided to act unfairly by choosing option 2, which ensures him or her $6 and a different payment for Player B that depends on a coin toss. The experimenter tosses the coin: it is heads, so Player B will receive $5. What would you do?

Now, consider a different scenario: the experimenter tosses the coin, but the outcome is tails rather than heads. Player B will receive nothing. What would you do in this case? Would you behave any differently from in the previous scenario?

Most of our study participants in the role of Player C were affected by the outcome information related to the coin toss. To punish Player A, participants were willing to reduce their own payoff by a higher amount in the negative-outcome than in the positive-outcome condition. In addition, the level of punishment was higher when the victim of wrongdoing was identified ("Chris") than when he or she was not ("Player B"). Overall, participants were over three times more likely to punish others when their unfair behavior toward a third party produced negative rather than positive consequences and when the third party being harmed was identified rather than unidentified. These findings are particularly interesting given that punishing others meant not only reducing the perpetrator's payoff, but also one's own payoff.

It appears, then, that the same behaviors produce more ethical condemnation when they happen to produce bad rather than good outcomes, even if the outcomes are determined by chance. Consequently, if a colleague massages the data when touting the superiority of your company's products to a customer, your evaluation of your colleague's behavior is likely to differ based on the outcome. If the customer decides to buy the product, you may see little wrong in your colleague's actions. But if the customer doubts your colleague's analysis and decides not to make a purchase, you may be more likely to recognize that your colleague's pitch was not ethically sound.

The three common decision mistakes I have discussed so far demonstrate various ways in which our judgments of others and their actions are swayed by subtle changes in how information is presented to us. This illogical use of information not only influences our evaluations of others but also our evaluations of our own actions.

Imagine that you are working at your desk. You have been sitting in front of your computer for quite some time today, and as you are thinking about whether to take a short break, you notice the pile of papers next to your computer—a stack of work that you have completed. As you glance at the pile, you think to yourself that you have been very productive today. Is the size of the pile on your desk a valid indicator of your productivity?

In the early 1990s, psychologist Robert Josephs (of the University of Texas at Austin) and his colleagues designed a series of studies to address this question.[7] They had participants complete a task in which they had to put a slash mark through every letter c that they saw in paragraphs of text. Participants were stopped after completing five paragraphs and told to put their completed work in an "outbox." In one condition, pages were attached to journals (journal condition). In the other condition, the pages were not attached to journals (page condition). On average, participants in the journal condition rated their productivity as higher than did participants in the page condition. These results indicate that an irrelevant quantity factor (in this case, the height of a pile in an outbox) can influence judgments of our own productivity. Thus, irrelevant outcome information influences not only our judgments of others' actions but also our own. These results serve as a good reminder to myself not to judge my productivity by the number of pages I have written, but rather by the extent to which readers respond to the book!

We may all desire and attempt to see others as they truly are and to judge our actions for what they really are. And yet, too often, it is the charlatan who wins our praise and the altruist who receives our scorn. We may interpret others' low-quality decisions (or our own) as effective ones when in fact they are not. The correspondence bias, the input bias, and the outcome bias point to the same human flaw: the tendency to rely on irrelevant, but seemingly important, information when making judgments. Because of this general human tendency, juries commonly misjudge defendants, voters misjudge candidates, lovers misjudge each other, and, as a result, the innocent are executed, the incompetent are elected, and the ignoble are embraced.

How can we overcome the common mistakes I've described? Here is a seventh principle to avoid getting sidetracked:

Consider the source.

This principle highlights the value of carefully considering the information surrounding important decisions, including evaluations of your own actions and those of others. When making inferences about others, for instance, it is important to pause to consider whether your judgment is warranted based on all the information available to you. The "gut feeling" you have about a person's competence or trustworthiness may simply be an outcome of the biases I discussed. And remember that others are affected by these common errors too. So, avoid being observed in situations that could cause people to make negative inferences about your general character. For example, if you want your staff or colleagues to think that you are a hard worker, put in "face time" at the office rather than working from home or at coffee shops.

Considering the source likely will lead you to reexamine the data you rely on to form your decisions and follow through on your plans. I once worked with a chain of retail stores in the United States that attempted to motivate employees by providing clearer performance guidelines and specific sales targets, which were associated with monthly bonuses. The results of this change were quite striking: productivity increased soon after its introduction, and most employees began reaching their sales targets. Managers started using this information in their performance evaluations as a sign of a committed, hardworking workforce. But a few months later, company management decided to look at the data a bit more closely. They observed that employees were netting increased sales in the last week of each month. Moreover, some stores were experiencing an increase in returned merchandise during the week following the payment of bonuses. Motivated by the change in the guidelines, employees had been buying merchandise toward the end of the month in order to reach their sales targets, but returned it right after receiving their bonuses. Managers were evaluating their employees based on incomplete information about their behavior and performance.

This example speaks to the importance of considering information critically and questioning whether you are evaluating the *right* information. For organizations, the "consider the source" principle may work best when accompanied by structural interventions in the way others' actions are evaluated, particularly in the case of hiring and promotion decisions. In many organizations, incentives are not aligned with desired behaviors. For instance, law firms reward people for the number of hours they bill, thus providing employees an incentive to work slowly. IBM used to reward employees based on the number of lines of code they produced, despite the fact that programmers are generally more efficient when producing fewer lines of code. In your organization, you might reduce the effect of the three biases discussed in this chapter by requiring managers to assess the means employees have used to achieve given objectives, the inputs that led to their outcomes, and the situational influences on their performance. In fact, companies such as Novartis have already adopted such structural changes to their performance evaluations. For many years, the company has conducted performance reviews that focus not only on the "what" (whether performance goals are met) but also on the "how." Feedback from several sources allows company management to evaluate employees' performance based on more thorough information about input, means, and ends.

Considering the source may help you identify more effective performance measures by reducing the influence of irrelevant information on the judgments and decisions you make as you execute your plans. This principle may prove valuable not only in terms of evaluating coworkers but also in your parenting decisions and your judgments of those close to you. By considering the source, you can become more confident that, when following through on your plans, you are using relevant information to weigh others' actions as well as your own.

CHAPTER 8

Traveling to Europe on Pudding

Subtle Changes in Framing

In the spring of 1999, David Phillips, a civil engineer working at the University of California at Davis, was shopping at a local supermarket in California.[1] As he was pushing his shopping cart down the frozen-foods aisle, David noticed an interesting promotion on a Healthy Choice frozen entrée: he could earn five hundred air miles for every ten bar codes from Healthy Choice products that he mailed to the company by December 31. The promotion included an even more attractive "early bird special": any Healthy Choice bar codes sent to the company earlier in the same year (by May 31) could be used to double the mileage. That is, every ten labels guaranteed customers participating in the promotion one thousand miles.

For quite some time, David had been thinking about taking his family to Europe on vacation. Such a trip would be expensive, though, and he couldn't afford it. This promotion seemed like the right opportunity to make his dream come true. He quickly did the math. Each frozen entrée cost about $2. A plane ticket to Europe would require fifty thousand miles per family member. If he bought enough entrées to accumulate the number of miles needed to take his entire family to Europe, would it be worth the expense? As it turns out, thanks to this promotion, the cost David would have to sustain to make his plan work could be significantly lower. In fact, David soon discovered that Healthy Choice also offered cans of soup for 90 cents each that were subject to the same promotion. David filled up his shopping cart with as many cans of soup as he could find and checked out. He then drove directly to a grocery outlet—a warehouse-style discount store—in search of more Healthy Choice products. Bingo! At the discount store, he found individual servings of Healthy Choice chocolate pudding for only 25 cents each. David noticed that each cup of pudding had its own bar code. In less than an hour, he had bought every cup of pudding available in the store. He then spoke with the store manager and asked for the addresses of all the chain's outlets in the area. With the help of his mother-in-law, David spent the next weekend driving his van from store to store, from Davis to Fresno, looking for more cups of chocolate pudding to buy. By the end of the weekend, he had visited all of the chain's ten stores and cleaned them out. David also asked the manager of the local store he had originally visited to order sixty more cases of chocolate pudding on his behalf.

In the end, this effort led to quite an impressive outcome: 12,150 individual servings of chocolate pudding. Now David needed only to get the bar codes off the packaging and send them off to Healthy Choice. He and his wife got to work, but since the May 31 promotion deadline was fast approaching, David had to come up with a creative solution for tearing off all the bar codes in time. After reflecting on the problem, he came up with a solution. He negotiated with two local food banks and the Salvation Army and struck an interesting deal: the food banks and the Salvation Army would help him and his wife finish removing the labels off the packets in exchange for the food donation. (In addition to the miles he would earn, this win-win negotiation also assured David a tax write-off of $815.)

In the end, David's careful math and clever plan paid off: he was able to convert $3,150 worth of chocolate pudding into 1.25 million miles, plus the tax write-off. David figured he had enough miles for thirty-one round-trip coach tickets to Europe, or twenty-one round-trip tickets to Australia, or fifty tickets anywhere in the Unites States. He estimated that the total value of those miles would be around $50,000. Clearly, David's close attention to the fine print on Healthy Choice's bargain paid off. He had turned a one-time promotion into a multiyear vacation and travel plan.

In David's eyes, the promotion was not only an opportunity to earn a few air miles but also an opportunity for him to realize his dream of traveling to Europe with his family. By framing the promotion the way he did, David was able to focus on what he could gain by purchasing a large number of Healthy Choice products, and he was also able to successfully execute his plan. In addition, through his framing of the promotion, David was able to get the full support of his family (even that of his mother-in-law!): everyone felt motivated to help. Looking beyond the uncertainty of executing the plan by the deadline and the short-term costs it involved, David reached his goal.

The way we frame information when we present it to others can substantially influence their decision making and judgment about that information. In fact, framing is such an important aspect of the way we communicate information to others that researchers have been exploring its effects for over thirty years, starting with the pioneering work of psychologists Daniel Kahneman and Amos Tversky on the framing of risky choices. This research has found that equivalent descriptions of a decision-making problem (or of attributes of a product) can lead to systematically different decisions depending on the way the problems are framed.[2]

For instance, people tend to evaluate the same products more favorably when they are described using positive proportions ("75 percent lean beef") than when they are described using negative proportions ("25 percent fat").[3] Think about the famous glass of water: is it half full or half empty? The frame you use to describe the glass is likely to trigger different reactions from your audience. In this chapter, I will focus on the effects of framing on motivation by discussing how framing can sway our decisions regarding how much effort to exert in completing a given task, from a reward program to one's own job. Across these domains, as we will learn, even subtle changes in framing can cause us to veer from our predetermined path.

Framing can be used across a variety of contexts to influence people's motivation to act or to exert effort. One context where framing can take many flavors and produce surprising differences in behavior is loyalty programs and promotions. Companies across industries regularly offer these to their customers. For instance, consider "customer loyalty" promotions that offer customers a free service or product after they have purchased a predetermined amount of the company's products (e.g., a coffee shop gives you a free coffee once you have made ten purchases there). Suppose you are responsible for designing such a promotion. How would you frame it to consumers? You could give interested consumers a stamp card with space for ten stamps and tell them they'll get their eleventh purchase free. Can you think of another way to frame the same promotion—one that might increase business?

In 2004, Joseph Nunes, a professor at the University of Southern California, and Xavier Drèze, a professor at UCLA, conducted a field experiment to examine this question: they wanted to explore how differences in the way promotions are framed influence the effectiveness of the promotion.[4] Nunes and Drèze contacted a local car wash business in a busy metropolitan area and convinced its management to let them run the business's loyalty program for a month. After some negotiation, the management agreed. As a result, for a month, the researchers stood at the car wash's pay station every Saturday, handing out loyalty cards to paying customers. Nunes and Drèze used two different types of cards depending on the week. The customers who visited the pay station on the first and fourth weeks received a standard "buy eight car washes, and get your ninth one free" stamp card. Customers who visited during the second and third weeks of the month received a similar stamp card. This one required them to buy not eight, but ten car washes before they received one for free. This card also came with a "special promotion": customers were told they were being gifted with two free stamps. The car wash's two promotions were the same in absolute terms: both required exactly eight stamps before customers could redeem a free car wash. The only difference between the two offers was the way they were framed.

How likely do you think you would be to return to the car wash to begin accumulating stamps if you received the first promotion card? Do you think you would feel or behave any differently if you instead received the second promotion card?

Let's turn to the results of Nunes and Drèze's study. Over the next nine months, the two researchers collected each card that was redeemed for a free car wash and recorded the dates of each of the eight visits. They found that 19 percent of the standard "buy eight and get one free" customers completed the program. In contrast, a whopping 34 percent of the customers who'd been given the two free stamps completed it—almost double the percentage of those who got the first card. What's more, not only were the customers who had been given two free stamps more likely to return and complete the program, but they also took shorter breaks between visits, averaging almost three days less between visits as compared with the standard card holders.

As I have noted, the two promotions were the same in absolute terms but differed in the way they were framed. The first card framed the promotion as a new program that the customer could choose to begin or not begin. By contrast, the second card framed the promotion as a program the customer had already started and made some progress on.

Why did the framing of the promotion make such a difference in customers' decisions? Over the years, scholars from various disciplines have found that goals motivate individuals, especially when those goals are specific and difficult.[5] Such goals make us work harder and perform better than ambiguous goals (such as "do your best") or no goals at all. Nunes and Drèze exploited this consequence of goals by encouraging customers to return to the same car wash multiple times. Their results also identified another notable human quirk: the tendency for people to expend greater effort toward achieving goals that they have already started than those they have yet to undertake. Thus, people will be more committed to completing a task framed as one they have undertaken rather than one they have not yet begun. The two "free" stamps gave customers a semicompleted goal, one they had already started even if someone else initiated it. As a result, they were more likely to persist at the task until they achieved their goal and earned their reward. That meant that customers in the special-promotion condition who had planned to have their cars washed once per month may have veered off course and visited the car wash much more frequently.

Nunes and Drèze coined this pattern of results the *endowed progress effect. Endowed progress* means that people who receive an artificial advancement toward a goal (such as a free trip or extra stamps on a promotion card) pursue it with greater persistence than they otherwise would. By framing the promotion in a way that included artificial advancement, the car wash company appeared to give customers a head start toward a goal even though the same effort was required to achieve it. The subtle difference in framing produced a large difference in behavior.

So, what's the broader point here? It's that we often fail to recognize that the way information is framed can have a strong effect on our and others' decisions. That can be a problem if framing causes us to abandon our carefully thought-out goals and plans.

Providing a head start is not the only way through which framing a task or promotion differently influences people's behavior. My colleague Scott Wiltermuth and I conducted a series of experiments where we changed something even more subtle about the rewards participants received for completing the experiment: the presence of seemingly irrelevant categories.

The motivation for this project came from a simple observation: many of the choices we are faced with every day are presented to us in the form of categories. Consumers, in particular, often face abundant product categories, as in the case of credit-card reward programs that present a multitude of product options for those looking to cash in their points. As another example, I recently had dinner at a restaurant where the menu included quite a few categories: appetizers, first courses, second courses, cheese selections, palate cleansers, fruit assortments, and desserts. I felt excited to be choosing from such a wide range of categories and spent quite some time carefully selecting dishes from each of them. But after spending over three hours eating, I started wondering whether I would have been less motivated (or tempted) to eat so much if the menu had only a couple of categories, as is often true of restaurant menus that include only appetizers and entrées. As another example, imagine that you are browsing the magazine rack at an airport, trying to choose one or more magazines to read during your flight. You are likely to find dozens of publications grouped under category headings such as Sports, Business, Cooking, Fashion, Current Events, and so on. Do you think that the fact that there are so many categories of magazines to choose from would affect your decision? More broadly, does the presence of numerous categories influence consumers' motivation and likelihood to purchase products?

Inspired by the common use of categories in our daily lives, Scott and I wanted to test whether splitting rewards into arbitrary categories would lead people to apply more effort toward a given reward than when no categories were present. We chose effort as our main variable of interest since scholars across disciplines have long sought to understand how to foster individual motivation. Much of this research has examined mechanisms that either increase or make salient the monetary or nonmonetary benefits that people can obtain by applying effort. For instance, prior work has found that people become more motivated when the benefits that their jobs can produce for others is highlighted (as in the case of call centers raising money for student scholarships), when their work is otherwise imbued with significance, and when they come to see the performance of a task as central to their own identity.[6] Scott and I wondered if there are also factors that should *not* rationally affect the amount of effort people apply toward attaining incentives—but have an effect anyway. Seemingly irrelevant categories struck us as a potentially interesting factor to test.

To study this possibility, on a sunny spring day in 2010, Scott and I invited sixty-three college students at the University of Southern California to participate in an experiment for pay. We told participants that they would be transcribing a number of passages of typewritten text to help us prepare for a future experiment in which we would examine how handwriting can affect the perceptions people form of others. Participants could spend as much or as little time as they liked transcribing these passages. After receiving these initial instructions, participants examined their potential rewards for completing the task. The rewards had been placed in two plastic storage containers (without any labels on them) and consisted of a mix of stationery and food items (such as boxes of hot cocoa, packages of pens, calculators, notebooks, etc.). Each item in the containers was unique, but they were all of equal value, as we had purchased them from a local dollar store.

We manipulated the way we framed rewards to participants so that they would perceive the rewards as belonging to two distinct categories or only one. In the categorization condition, we told participants that there were two categories of rewards that they could potentially choose from by spending time transcribing: category 1 was in one container and category 2 in the other. (While we did not label the containers, we referred to them using categories in this condition.) If the participants spent ten minutes transcribing the passages of text, they could choose to take one item from either container. If they spent twenty minutes transcribing the passages, they could choose to take one item from each container—from each of the two categories. In the no-categorization condition, we informed them that if they spent ten minutes transcribing the passages of text, they would be able to choose and take home one item from either container (from the entire set of rewards available to them), but if they spent twenty minutes transcribing the passages of text, they would be allowed to take home a second item from either container. Thus, in the no-categorization condition, participants had more choices regarding the rewards they could take, as they could choose two rewards from the same container if they liked.

Participants in both conditions visually inspected the rewards and then began transcribing the passages of text. After they decided to stop transcribing, they selected their reward(s). Finally, they completed a short questionnaire asking them to indicate how motivated they were to earn the first reward, how motivated they were to earn the second reward, and how much they enjoyed the task.

Participants had access to a greater variety of rewards in the no-categorization condition. Yet the fictitious categories Scott and I created influenced participants' motivation in the opposite direction: in the categorization condition, they were over three times as likely to transcribe for the full twenty minutes (34.4 percent) than were participants in the no-categorization condition (9.7 percent). Participants also reported being more motivated to obtain the second reward than were participants in the no-categorization condition, and they reported enjoying the task more. Thus, even though the categories of rewards Scott and I had created were completely arbitrary, participants spent more time working on the transcribing task and reported enjoying it more when the potential rewards were divided into categories. By framing rewards such that they belonged to categories, Scott and I thought we may have triggered a sense in participants that they would be missing out if they did not get a reward from the second category.

It seems this fear of missing out drives many of the decisions we make in our professional and personal lives. We are willing to stand in long lines so that we can be among the first to see a highly rated movie or to buy the latest iPhone, and we sign up for all sorts of store e-mail lists so that we won't miss the latest deals.

As another example, take one of the products offered by SCVNGR, a start-up based in Cambridge, Massachusetts, that was founded in 2008. The company creates mobile applications for iPhone and Android phones. In the late summer of 2010, SCVNGR introduced a new software platform that allows local businesses to build their own reward programs. The program launched with fifty-plus stores in the Boston area. One of the businesses that agreed to partner with SCVNGR is an ice cream shop that I visit on a regular basis: Toscanini's. At Toscanini's, you can log in on SCVNGR and suggest the ingredients you'd include to create a new flavor; by doing so, you earn a free scoop of ice cream (one of the current flavors). Other businesses in town offer similar reward programs. The purpose of the app is to reward consumers for frequenting the same businesses. And if you asked consumers why they use this app, you'd discover that many do so because they are afraid of "missing out" by not taking advantage of fun opportunities and rewards. Like this app, most forms of social software on the market nowadays both foster and cure our fear of missing out. If you didn't know about a cool party, you'd be home contentedly rereading your favorite book or watching a good movie. But since you do, you hungrily watch for each new Facebook update or tweet as the date approaches.

In the experiment Scott and I conducted to examine the effects of framing rewards such that they belonged to meaningless categories, we seemed to have triggered the same sorts of feelings: participants apparently did not want to miss out on choosing from the contents of the second container. But at this point, we were just speculating. We had not yet tested whether fear of missing out explained why dividing rewards into meaningless categories increased motivation. So, once again, we returned to the laboratory.

To test this hypothesis, we examined whether the effects of framing rewards into categories differed across conditions that varied in their degree of eliciting fear of missing out. For instance, if people can choose only two rewards out of more than two categories as compensation for their performance, we reasoned, they will be less motivated to work hard than when there are only two categories and they can choose a reward from each. In the latter case, increased effort would more effectively reduce people's fear of missing out, since by working hard they could obtain a reward from each of the available categories of rewards.

We recruited 123 individuals to participate in an experiment in which they would be forming words out of a series of scrambled letters. Participants would receive different rewards based on their performance on the task. Before they started working on the unscrambling task, participants examined the rewards from which they could choose if their performance placed them in the top 30 percent of test takers. Participants would earn a second reward if they finished in the top 10 percent of test takers.

The way rewards were framed varied across four conditions. In the no-categorization condition, participants could choose one reward if they performed in the top 30 percent of test takers, and two rewards if their performance placed them in the top 10 percent of test takers. Participants in the two-of-two-categories condition could choose a reward from either of two categories of rewards if their performance placed them in the top 30 percent of test takers, and they could choose a second reward from the other category if their performance placed them in the top 10 percent of test takers. Participants in the one-of-two-categories condition could choose a reward from either of two categories of rewards if their performance placed them in the top 30 percent, and they could choose a second reward from the same category if their performance placed them in the top 10 percent of test takers. Finally, those in the two-of-four-categories condition could choose a reward from one of four categories of rewards if their performance placed them in the top 30 percent of test takers, and they could choose a second reward from a second category if their performance placed them in the top 10 percent of test takers.

Imagine you are participating in this experiment. Here is your first set of letters to scramble to form meaningful words: I S T E B O M.

You have one minute to write down, on a separate sheet of paper, as many English words as you can form out of these letters. This is your first round; then you will have five more rounds to complete with different sets of letters. In which of the four conditions do you think you'd feel the most motivated to work hard on this task?

Scott and I included these four conditions on the theory that framing rewards as belonging to different categories improves motivation most dramatically when participants' performance can allow them to attain rewards from each category. We therefore expected participants' performance to be higher in the two-of-two-categories condition than in the other three conditions.

As we predicted, participants' performance was higher in the two-of-two-categories condition (over twenty-six words formed on average across the six rounds) than it was in the no-category condition (almost nineteen words), the one-of-two-categories condition (sixteen words), and the two-of-four-categories condition (about eighteen words). Participants' performance in the latter three categories did not differ (statistically) from performance in any other category. These results tell us that dividing rewards into categories increased the degree to which participants anticipated they would miss out if they did not attain multiple rewards from different categories. When participants had the opportunity to obtain rewards from each of the available categories (even if meaningless), their motivation increased. However, when there was no possibility of receiving rewards from each of the available categories, their motivation did not increase.

In our experiments, Scott and I focused on people's motivation to achieve given rewards. It is common for people to make plans about how much effort they'll devote to their jobs or how hard they want to work. But, as the results of our experiments suggest, simple changes in the framing of potential rewards for effort can affect motivation and cause people to fall short of their goals. Framing information by using categories also influences people's motivation in other contexts. Let's return to a question I asked you earlier in this chapter: imagine that you are shopping for magazines at the airport; you are carefully browsing the many categories available to you, including Fashion, Current Events, Music, Sports, and Cooking. Do you think the presence of these categories will influence your purchase decisions? If so, why? This is an interesting question, as companies and store managers must decide the best way to categorize magazines and other products. Cassie Mogilner (a professor at the University of Pennsylvania) investigated this question together with two colleagues from Columbia University, Tamar Rudnick and Sheena Iyengar.[7]

In one of their experiments, the researchers examined whether framing menu options by presenting them in categories affected consumption choices. For their experiment, they had a female research assistant approach individuals randomly at a food court on the campus of Stanford University. Participants were told they would earn $5 for their choices and answers in a thirty-minute study as well as a free cup of coffee. In the end, 138 people agreed to participate. They were presented with one of four different coffee menus, which varied in their design. Each menu included fifty different coffee flavors drawn from those offered by actual coffee shops. Across conditions, the researchers varied whether the coffee flavors were divided into categories and, if so, how informative the categories were. They included four conditions: uncategorized menu, menu with informative categories (attribute-based categories), menu with somewhat informative categories (coffee-shop-based categories), and menu with completely uninformative categories (alphabet-based categories). (The researchers confirmed that the categories were perceived as more or less informative in a pilot study on a different group of participants.)

Across conditions, the research assistant approached people at the food court and gave them some time to look at the menu. She took each person's order and left for a few minutes to get the coffee. When she returned, she handed the participant the cup of coffee, which was labeled to reflect the person's order. She asked the participant to taste the coffee and then to fill out a short survey, which was designed to measure the participant's satisfaction with the coffee and the degree of variety he or she perceived in the menu consulted. (Unbeknownst to participants, all participants were served the same coffee flavor.) Do you think participants' satisfaction and perceptions of variety were related to the presentation of the menus? Which menu or menus do you think generated the highest sense of satisfaction and variety?

I've left out one important detail about the study. Before giving participants their menus, the researchers divided them into two groups depending on their familiarity with coffee (the decision context). Some participants were regular coffee drinkers and thus had established preferences regarding coffee. Others were less familiar with types of coffee and had not yet identified their preferences. I'll focus on this second group of people in describing the results, since they are the ones whose choices were most likely to be swayed by a menu's presentation of offerings. No matter what information the category labels provided, framing options by presenting them in categories led to greater satisfaction than did no categorization; participants were less satisfied with their coffee in the no-categories condition than they were in the three conditions where the menus included categories. Menus with categories produced about the same level of consumer satisfaction, suggesting that how informative the categories were did not affect participants' satisfaction with their chosen coffee. In addition, participants perceived greater variety in menu offerings when the menu included categories, irrespective of the content of the category labels. Together, these results indicate that framing assortment options using categories, even arbitrary ones, leads to both greater perceptions of variety and greater satisfaction with the chosen options for people whose preferences for a particular choice domain (in this case, coffee) are not yet well defined. In related research, Mogilner and her colleagues also found that the number of categories used to partition the display of magazines in a supermarket chain positively influenced customers' perceptions of variety and their satisfaction, while the actual number of magazines did not.

Returning to the context of choosing magazines from a rack, Mogilner and her colleagues asked a group of experts—namely, fifteen magazine company executives—a simple question: whether they believed that the number of categories of magazines in a display would have a stronger or weaker effect on customers' satisfaction with magazines they purchased than the number of different magazines offered. Of these experts, 87 percent predicted that the number of different magazines would have a greater impact on consumers' satisfaction than the number of categories. Yet the research that Mogilner and her colleagues conducted suggests just the opposite. In their research, subtle changes in framing lead to consequences that may not seem particularly costly or harmful: in the end, participants may have just enjoyed a cup of coffee or magazine of one variety rather than another. But think of a situation where the offerings differ quite substantially in price, such as a display of computers in a showroom. Or imagine a menu where offerings vary greatly in terms of calories. In such cases, the presence of categories could lead consumers to buy a more expensive computer than they had planned or to go off their diet.

The experiments I have described so far in this chapter point to the same conclusion: the framing of potential rewards, incentives, and choices affects our motivation to achieve those rewards, though we usually are unaware of such framing effects. Even when we have clear plans for how often to wash our car or how many hours we want to spend at work, we are likely to veer off course because of a boost or a reduction in motivation due to the framing of potential rewards. This basic tendency influences our behavior across a variety of contexts, from the motivation to receive free products or services through promotions and loyalty programs, to the motivation to work hard on a task to reap certain rewards, to the decision to purchase various products or services. There is another interesting consequence that the framing of tasks can produce: it can change our commitment to the task at hand and the extent to which we identify with it.

To explain what I mean by this, let's travel to a beautiful region of Italy, Tuscany, which is well known for many reasons, including its peaceful valleys, picturesque seascapes, and delicious traditional cuisine. And for over eight hundred years now, the Tuscan town of Siena has been known for the horse race it hosts twice each summer, called the *palio*. In the palio, two Siena neighbors compete while a crowd of over a hundred thousand people watches the race. This seventy-five-second event may sound trivial to you, but it is taken quite seriously by the locals. Each side has its club, costumes, hymn, museum, and elected president. As one journalist recounted, "The winners are worshipped. The losers embarrass their clan."[8] Because the entire event is framed as a competition, people who live in one part of the town see the other side as the enemy: the framing of the palio heightens each side's identity. The competitors engage in behaviors that many Italians outside Siena consider barbaric—the horses often die during races due to falls or collisions—but locals still associate the competition with strong feelings of pride or shame depending on whether they win or lose the race. To ensure that even newcomers to Siena will experience these strong feelings and sense of communal identity at the time of the palio, they are put through an orientation process upon moving to town where they learn the history of the competition, information about the various factions that are competing, and the rituals associated with the event.

This type of orientation process is not too different from what all of us go through when we join a new organization or special group, such as the Harley Owners Group in the United States. As many of the riders who belong to this group would tell you, riding a Harley is a way of life. To acknowledge this fact, many members have the company logo tattooed on their skin when they join the club. Similarly, when I worked in the R&D group of the Walt Disney Company in the summer of 2010, I learned that new employees are taught a great deal about the life of its founder as well as the culture and traditions of Disney in their initial training (called "Traditions 101"). Through such orientation processes, organizations transform newcomers into knowledgeable members who are committed to the company's mission.

In fact, the orientation processes people go through when joining a new group often share this focus: they are framed as an opportunity for newcomers to learn about the organization and the benefits of joining. Although different people have different motives for joining a particular organization, they commonly share a desire to fit in and be productive. This seems like a simple plan. But can the framing of the orientation process alter one's plan of becoming a committed and productive worker? And does the framing that organizations commonly use increase new members' commitment to their new roles, or would some other type of framing be more effective in reaching this goal? Intuitively, we might assume that it does, but this is a question that—at least in my mind—had to be tested.

I joined forces with Dan Cable (of the London Business School) and Brad Staats to test how the framing of information about a new job during orientation processes influences newcomers' behavior. To carry out a convincing study of this idea, Dan, Brad, and I conducted a field experiment at Wipro, a large business-process-outsourcing organization based in India. This company provides telephone and chat support for its customers around the globe; Wipro's employees answer customer queries about the services (such as buying an airline ticket) or products (for example, how to configure a printer) offered by the company's clients. Like other companies in this industry, at the time of the field experiment, Wipro was experiencing high turnover of its call-center employees, with many employees burning out and quitting only a few months after completing their training. Like many service industry jobs, Wipro's positions can be stressful. Not only must employees try to help solve problems for frustrated customers, but also Indian call-center employees are often expected to "de-Indianize" many aspects of their behavior—for example, by adopting a Western accent, attitude, and pseudonym. Employees at Wipro traditionally complete all of their training—orientation, voice and language training, six weeks of process training, and six weeks of on-the-job training—in groups of fifteen to twenty-five. During process training, employees learn about their customers and learn the steps necessary to complete their work. Next, the employees move to "the floor," where they undergo on-the-job training, which consists of taking calls under supervision and engaging in additional classroom training to address issues identified on calls. As their last step in the process of joining the organization, employees transition to line operations, where they take calls independently full-time.

Dan, Brad, and I introduced a simple manipulation during the orientation process and randomly assigned incoming groups of new employees to different experimental conditions. In particular, we were interested in comparing how employees would react if onboarding processes were framed as an opportunity for the organization to add value to their lives versus if these processes were framed as an opportunity for newcomers to add value to the organization. In our "individual" condition, a senior leader from Wipro began a one-hour orientation session by discussing how working at Wipro would give each employee the opportunity to express himself or herself and generate individual opportunities for growth. After this presentation, employees worked individually on a series of exercises that encouraged them to reflect on their unique skills and characteristics and to consider how they could express these qualities in their new job. By contrast, in the "organizational" condition, the senior leader from Wipro began the one-hour session by discussing the company's values and explaining why it was an outstanding organization. Next, employees engaged in a series of exercises in which they had the opportunity to reflect on the organization's unique features and strengths, and the qualities that made them proud to be a part of it.

In both conditions, at the end of this one-hour session, the employees received two fleece sweatshirts and a badge. They were asked to wear the sweatshirts and badges as much as possible during training. The sweatshirts and the badge had the employees' names on them in the individual condition, and the company name on them in the organizational condition.

A total of 96 and 101 employees were part of the individual and organizational treatments, respectively. The control group, comprising 408 employees, went through a regular orientation process, in which the company focused on the organization's strengths and what the job entailed, a process similar to the one we used in our organizational condition. To examine the effect of our manipulation on turnover, we started data collection in November 2010 and determined whether employees were still working at Wipro about seven months later.

Employees in the organizational and control conditions were more likely to leave the organization than were employees in the individual condition. In fact, being in the organizational or the control condition increased the odds of turnover by 250 percent and 157 percent, respectively. (Why no difference, at least from a statistical standpoint, in employee turnover between the organizational and control conditions? Probably because employees in the control condition engaged in an orientation process that also emphasized the organization's strengths.) We found similar results in the case of productivity as measured by employees' performance on measures of customer satisfaction.

These results suggest that orientation and training tactics that encourage self-expression of personal identities and signature strengths produce beneficial effects for employees *and* the organization. Here, once again, framing produced powerful consequences. These findings confirmed our hypotheses. More importantly, they encouraged Wipro's management to think carefully about how best to frame employees' work in a way that keeps them motivated and lengthens their tenure and to change the way they frame their orientation processes for new employees. Managers' initial intuition had been that stressing what the organization had to offer employees would be more effective than emphasizing employees' strengths. Dan, Brad, and I demonstrated just the opposite, thus showing that our intuitions are not always correct.

The results also highlight another important point: newcomers' plans to fit in and be productive at work were affected by the way the onboarding process was framed.

In this field experiment, framing a new job as a way for the newcomers to express their personalities and strengths—their identity—produced benefits in terms of performance and retention. This identity-based framing has been shown to be effective in other contexts as well. For instance, Christopher Bryan (a psychologist at Stanford University) and a group of colleagues examined the role of identity-based framing in the context of voter turnout.[9] In one of their experiments, conducted in early November 2008, just before the presidential election, the researchers recruited 133 participants (all native English speakers) who were registered to vote in California and had not already voted in the election. This experiment required participants to complete a short, ten-question survey. Participants were randomly assigned to one of two conditions: the noun condition or the verb condition. In the noun condition, all survey questions referred to voting using a self-relevant noun (for example, "How clear are your thoughts about being a voter in tomorrow's election?" with *voter* being the self-relevant noun). In the verb condition, the survey included the same questions, but this time the wording referred to voting using a verb (for example, "How clear are your thoughts about voting in tomorrow's election?").

As you can see from the wording of the sample questions from the survey, the manipulation was very subtle. Imagine that you took part in this experiment. Would you feel differently when answering the two versions of the questions? Do you think your likelihood to vote would be affected by such an unobtrusive manipulation?

By wording survey questions using nouns (versus verbs), Bryan and his colleagues increased the likelihood that individuals would see attributes as representative of who they are. So, they predicted that using a noun rather than a verb to refer to voting in an upcoming election would generate a greater interest in and likelihood of voting. To test their prediction, the researchers analyzed the official records from the State of California after the election, which indicated whether or not each of the study participants voted. The results were quite clear: almost 96 percent of the participants in the noun condition voted, while in the verb condition a significantly lower percentage—not quite 82 percent—of the participants voted. Thus, framing voting as a reflection of the type of person one is rather than as a behavior increased voter turnout by 14 percent. A subtle change in the framing of the survey questions produced quite a significant difference. People often choose to vote to be consistent with their desire to be good citizens. But, as voter turnout numbers suggest, the decision to vote often gets derailed. This research identifies a possible factor that may help people avoid derailed decisions in this context: changing the framing of what the action of voting signals.

In the research I conducted with Dan Cable and Brad Staats, framing the decision to join an organization as a way of expressing one's own personality and strengths appeared to have a similar effect of heightening newcomers' identity and authenticity. Although our field experiment could not confirm this connection, we assessed it in a laboratory experiment. We invited 115 participants to the laboratory and told them that they would have the opportunity to join our research team for about three hours on two consecutive days. As the instructions clarified, they would be working on a data-entry task from a recent experiment we had conducted, as well as on the idea-generation and problem-solving tasks we commonly face in our research team.

We employed a manipulation similar to the one used in the field study we conducted. In the individual condition, the experimenter first spent a few minutes discussing how working in the research lab she was leading would give each participant the opportunity to express himself or herself and generate individual opportunities. Next, participants were asked to think about and write down their unique skills and strengths and how they could use them in the tasks they would be completing. Finally, they received a piece of paper, colored pens, and markers that allowed them to write their own names creatively—to create a personalized logo—so that they could be recognized as a member of the research team. They were asked to use their self-created nametag during the lab session by placing it next to the computer they'd be using.

In the organizational condition, the experimenter spent a few minutes discussing the research lab's values and why the team was an outstanding group. Second, the participants were asked to think about and write down what they knew about the group and what made them feel proud to be part of it, even if for a short period of time. At the end of this procedure, the participants were given the same materials and asked to creatively write the name of the research lab name on the piece of paper. As in the other condition, they were asked to place the logo they created next to their computers throughout the session.

In both conditions, participants then spent the next hour working on tasks the research team commonly engages in, such as data entry and problem-solving tasks. Before the end of the session, they were asked to fill out a short survey. They were then paid for the day and told that they could come back the next day to work on similar tasks for another hour and a half. Dan, Brad, and I were interested in testing whether our manipulation produced differences in the extent to which participants felt committed to the research team and in the likelihood they would return. As in our field experiment in India, a simple difference in the focus and wording of the orientation process made quite a difference: participants reported being more engaged and satisfied with their jobs in the individual condition than in the organizational condition, and they were also more likely to come back a day later to do more work as part of our research team. Almost 68 percent of the participants in the individual condition came back, as compared to 50 percent in the organizational condition. The type of framing that most organizations use derailed newcomers' decisions to fit in and be productive workers.

In this chapter, I discussed how our decisions are often influenced and potentially sidetracked by the framing of tasks, rewards, and choices, even beyond our own awareness. Here is the eighth principle for avoiding getting sidetracked:

Investigate and question the frame.

This principle highlights the importance of asking questions about the way tasks, rewards, and choices are structured and thinking carefully about different ways in which you could frame the same information. By becoming more attentive to frames, you can avoid being unduly influenced by them and increase your odds of sticking to your initial plans and goals.

One way to implement this principle is to think *counterfactually* about the decision at hand. Thinking counterfactually means imagining different choices you could make or could have made when faced with a decision. For example, think about a past decision you've made, such as a big purchase or investment. To engage in counterfactual thinking, consider different courses of action you might have taken (rather than buying the car you chose, you could have selected a less expensive model, for instance). By reflecting on the alternatives to a given decision, you will come to better understand the factors that led you down that particular path in the first place (such as focusing on a car's brand name rather than its mileage per gallon).

You may recognize that, had the problem been framed differently, you likely would have made a different decision. Consider, for instance, the plot of the 1998 movie *Sliding Doors*. The movie alternates between two story lines. One follows what happens to Helen (played by Gwyneth Paltrow) after she narrowly makes it through a pair of sliding doors onto a train; the other follows what happens when she misses the train. By viewing both stories, the viewer can more clearly examine the forces that influence Helen's decisions at different points in time. Similarly, you can use counterfactual thinking as you reason through choices you are facing. Since engaging in counterfactual thinking involves considering alternatives to a given outcome, it expands our focus from just one frame of reference to many other frames. This type of reflection encourages you to take note of different frames and reach a more balanced view of a decision you made or are about to make. By thinking counterfactually, you can increase your understanding of how frames influence your choices.

A beautiful example of the effects of framing comes from Teddy Roosevelt's 1912 presidential campaign.[10] Right before the brochures with Roosevelt's photograph were about to be distributed, the campaign manager realized something important: three million campaign brochures had been printed using a photograph of Roosevelt without the permission of the photo's copyright owner. Imagine being in the campaign manager's shoes. What would you do? Would you reprint all of the brochures without a picture? Would you contact the photographer and plead your case?

Choosing the second option, the campaign manager prepared a telegram to send to the photographer. Rather than telling him about the error, however, he framed the message to make it more appealing to the photographer. The telegraph stated, "We are planning to distribute millions of pamphlets with Roosevelt's picture on the cover. It will be great publicity for the studio whose photograph we use. How much will you pay us to use yours? Respond immediately." The excited photographer quickly replied with an offer to pay $250. Thanks to the campaign manager's careful analysis and framing of the issue, he was able to transform a worrisome error into a profitable opportunity.

In the end, the campaign manager was able to stick to his plan of running a successful campaign free of costly errors by understanding the general principle of investigating the frame. Similarly, you can use this principle to understand how to best frame a task, message, or job in a way that improves your own decisions and those of others. Reflecting on this principle may also help you recognize a force that has derailed some of your decisions in the past.

CHAPTER 9

Cheaters in Sunglasses

Ambience and Opportunity

In the summer of 2008, I moved from Pittsburgh to Chapel Hill to start my new position as a faculty member at the business school at the University of North Carolina. Although I was sad to leave Carnegie Mellon and my colleagues there, I was excited to meet new ones and to move into our new home. A few months earlier, my husband and I had bought a lovely house surrounded by quiet, leafy streets just a few blocks away from the center of town.

Within a few days of moving in, Greg and I received a letter from Chapel Hill's City Hall welcoming us and informing us that new street lighting would be added in the neighborhood in the following weeks since that part of town had recently experienced a surge in crime. In addition to raising my fears (and not making me feel any safer), the letter also piqued my curiosity, since it highlighted an intriguing assumption: that lighting would reduce crime.

In a sense, this assumption was consistent with what Ralph Waldo Emerson once wrote: "As gaslight is the best nocturnal police, so the universe protects itself by pitiless publicity."[1] According to conventional wisdom, darkness conceals identity and also decreases inhibitions; as a result, it may be linked to crime. The idea that darkness promotes unethical behavior dates back to the myth of the "Ring of Gyges," which was recounted by Plato in *The Republic* (360 BC). In the myth, a shepherd in Lydia named Gyges finds a ring that makes him invisible. He travels to the king's court, seduces the queen, conspires with her to kill the king, and takes control of Lydia. Thus, invisibility corrupted the wearer of the ring. The story leads Plato to ask the following question: is there anyone alive who could resist taking advantage of the invisibility ring's powers, or is it only others' monitoring that prevents us from committing immoral acts?

From this perspective, by providing anonymity, darkness may facilitate dishonest behavior. When transgressors believe others will not be able to identify them, are they more likely to behave dishonestly? Scholarly work conducted in the 1960s and 1970s found that criminal assaults most frequently occur during hours of darkness and that improving street lighting in urban areas is commonly followed by reductions in crime of between 33 percent and 70 percent—impressive gains.[2] Although interesting, the scientist in me notes that this evidence is inconclusive, as the relationship between darkness and crime suggested by this data could be explained by other factors. I wondered whether there is a direct relationship between darkness and crime rates. Even more interestingly, does darkness increase dishonesty?

Soon after Greg and I received our letter from City Hall, Chen-Bo Zhong (a professor at the University of Toronto), Vanessa Bohns (a professor at the University of Waterloo), and I designed a series of experiments to test whether darkness—or even dim lighting— would increase dishonesty.

Chen-Bo, Vanessa, and I tested this possibility by conducting an experiment where we manipulated darkness by varying the level of lighting in rooms. Upon arriving at our laboratory, our eighty-four student participants were randomly assigned to one of two rooms (with about half in each room): one of them was well lit (our control condition); the other one was similar in size but was dimly lit (specifically, lit by four fluorescent lights rather than by twelve). Participants in the dim room could see the materials and one another, but the room was more dimly lit than the average room at a university. Participants completed the add-to-ten problem-solving task that I described in the introduction and chapter 5: they had five minutes to solve twenty problems (which involved finding two three-digit numbers that add up to ten in a matrix of twelve numbers), and were paid 50 cents for each problem they solved correctly. After the five minutes was up, participants in both conditions were asked to self-report their performance on the problem-solving task. They were able to lie by overstating their performance and thus walk away with undeserved money. As in other experiments concerning dishonesty that I've described in earlier chapters, we tracked whether participants cheated and, if so, by how much. If you were a participant in this experiment, do you think you would cheat by overstating your performance?

Maybe you would stay true to your moral compass. But, as it turns out, many of our participants did not: in fact, on average, about half of them cheated across conditions. More interestingly, the level of darkness in the room dramatically influenced participants' likelihood to lie by overreporting their performance: almost 61 percent of the participants in the dim room cheated, while "only" about 24 percent of participants in the well-lit room cheated. In other words, eight additional fluorescent lights reduced dishonesty by about 37 percent. This is quite a large difference, especially considering that the task Chen-Bo, Vanessa, and I used in the experiment was completely anonymous: the only difference between the two rooms was the level of darkness.

These results were consistent with our initial predictions, but we wanted to take them a step further. We reasoned that, beyond simply producing conditions of actual anonymity, darkness may create a sense of what we refer to as *illusory anonymity*. This type of anonymity is likely to loosen inhibitions surrounding dishonest behaviors such as lying and cheating. People in a room with slightly dimmed lighting, we reasoned, may feel anonymous not because the relative darkness has reduced others' ability to see or identify them (which it hasn't), but because they are anchored in their own experience of darkness. When people experience impaired vision as a result of darkness, they might unconsciously generalize that experience and expect that others will conversely find it difficult to perceive or see them, even when these others are sitting in a different location (such as another room). Just as small children close their eyes and believe that others can't see them, the experience of darkness, we theorized, would trigger the belief that we are warded from others' attention and inspections. Since people often have a myopic focus, this reasoning seemed to hold. If it's true, then manipulating darkness in other, more subtle ways than reducing ambient lighting likely would have the same effects on ethical behavior that we observed in our first experiment.

For our next experiment, we invited eighty-three students from the University of North Carolina at Chapel Hill to participate in an experiment for which they would receive a $5 show-up fee and a potential bonus payment of $6. Half of the participants were asked to wear a pair of sunglasses, and the other half were asked to wear glasses with clear lenses. They were then assigned to work with someone they were told was another participant (but was actually the experimenter) in a different room. They would be working with this person by communicating through computers. Participants knew that they would not interact face to face with their partner, nor would they later learn their partner's identity.

Clearly, when you are wearing a pair of sunglasses, no one else's sight is affected, especially when you are not looking at each other. Nonetheless, we expected that the relative darkness caused by wearing sunglasses would trigger a sense of illusory anonymity and influence participants' dishonest behavior. We measured dishonesty by examining how selfish people were in allocating a sum of money between themselves and their partner.

Each person had $6 to divide between him- or herself and the recipient. The recipient had no choice but to accept the offer, and participants were told they could leave with the money they kept for themselves. Although we told participants that they had been randomly assigned to a role (either initiator or recipient), they all played the initiator against the experimenter. After participants made their choice, they answered a few questions measuring the extent to which they felt anonymous during the experiment.

Participants could offer any amount between $0 and $6. On average, they offered $2.35, a bit less than a 50/50 split. Their offers differed based on whether they wore sunglasses: those who wore sunglasses gave less than $2, on average, while those who wore clear glasses offered an average of almost $3. Participants in the sunglasses condition gave significantly less than an equal division; those in the clear-glasses condition gave significantly more. As we predicted, wearing sunglasses also affected participants' psychological state: they felt more anonymous during the study than did those wearing clear glasses. Although darkness had no bearing on actual anonymity, it still increased morally questionable behaviors.

What about our moral compass? It gives us good guidance, but forces from the world around us also easily influence it, even if we fail to realize it. Our daily lives provide many examples of "minor" ethical failures, such as people standing in the express line with too many grocery items, cutting in line at the movie theater, lying about why they are late for an appointment, taking home office supplies from work, or inflating business expense reports. We can add even more troubling behaviors to this list, such as those that have caused many organizations to go bankrupt in recent years.

Motivated by the surge of business scandals in the news over the last ten years, several scholars have focused on trying to understand when and why people cross ethical boundaries. The empirical evidence seems to point to the conclusion that we lie and cheat much more often than we care to admit. At the same time, we strive to maintain a positive image of ourselves, and moral values are a central component of our self-image. We like to think of ourselves as honest and deserving; we strongly believe in our own morality. So, how can we explain this apparent conflict between our desire to be good and behavior that suggests otherwise?

Here, another situational force—darkness—powerfully influenced people's decisions and moved them away from their moral compass. This chapter focuses on morality, arguably an area where it should be quite difficult to affect people's behavior. In fact, however, although we care about being good and moral, situational forces can change the direction set by our moral compass, even if only temporarily.

This is shown very powerfully in a modern take on an ancient story from the Bible. In the early 1960s, John Darley (of Princeton University) and Daniel Batson (of the University of Kansas), two scholars who have made important contributions to the field of social psychology, decided to test the parable of the Good Samaritan in the modern world.[3] As you may know, the parable concerns a Jewish man who is traveling to Jericho. After being attacked by bandits, the man lies half dead at the side of the road. The first two people who pass him are a priest and a temple assistant; they offer no help. Then a Samaritan (a member of a group that was known for hating Jews) approaches and stops to offer his assistance. The moral of the story is clear enough (we should set aside our prejudices and show compassion for others, independent of our specific religious beliefs), but Darley and Batson wondered whether the actions of the priest and the temple assistant could be interpreted differently. They suggested that because both the priest and the temple assistant were prominent public figures, they could have been hurrying to a meeting. The Samaritan, by contrast, probably did not have important people counting on him to be at a particular place at a particular time.

Is it possible that the priest and the temple assistant were in such a rush that they didn't notice the person in need? There was no way to tell, really, but to reenact the story. Darley and Batson did just that, recruiting sixty-seven students from the Princeton Theological Seminary for a study that they were told concerned religious education and vocations. The students had to answer a personality questionnaire and then give a brief talk in a nearby room. Half of the students were asked to talk about the types of jobs suitable for seminary graduates. The other half were asked to talk about the parable of the Good Samaritan. They were all given a few minutes to gain familiarity with the materials they would be talking about and prepare for their speech.

Next, the experimenter informed the students that they would be giving the talk in a different building that had more spacious rooms. The experimenter gave the students a campus map and told them how to reach the room where their talk would be recorded (referred to as "Professor Steiner's laboratory"). They were also given some additional instructions. Within each group (the group assigned to talk about the Good Samaritan parable or the group assigned to talk about job prospects), there were three versions of the instructions. In the "high-hurry" version, the experimenter looked at his watch and said, "Oh, you're late. They were expecting you a few minutes ago. We'd better get moving. The assistant should be waiting for you, so you'd better hurry. It shouldn't take but just a minute . . . " In the "medium-hurry" version, they were told, "The assistant is ready for you, so please go right over." Finally, in the "low-hurry" version, the students were told, "It'll be a few minutes before they're ready for you, but you might as well head on over. If you have to wait over there, it shouldn't be long." Thus, some students left the office thinking they needed to go to the next location quickly, others less so, while some were more relaxed. With these manipulations, the scholars could test the effect of both the talk's type of content and the effect of being in a rush on participants' helping behaviors.

On their way to the lab, the students passed through an alley and were confronted with the opportunity to help a person in need. A man (a confederate) was lying in the doorway, doubled over, coughing, with his eyes closed. Would participants stop to help the apparently highly distressed man? Would they be good Samaritans?

On average, less than half of the seminary students actually offered help—in fact, a few even *stepped over* the apparently injured man! Even more interesting, the degree of hurry the students were in significantly affected their behavior. In the low-hurry condition, 63 percent of the students offered help. In the medium-hurry condition, 45 percent helped. And in the high-hurry condition, only 10 percent helped. The type of talk students were about to give also affected their behavior. Only 29 percent of those who had been asked to talk about careers for seminarians offered help; 53 percent of those asked to talk about the parable of the Good Samaritan stopped to help.

These findings demonstrate that subtle aspects of a situation can have large effects on the way people behave. And remember: all participants were seminarians, and thus quite religious. In fact, the students were assessed for their degree of religiosity in the personality questionnaire they completed. Guess what? When Darley and Batson compared the effect of this personality trait with the effect of the situation (how much of a hurry the students were in or whether they were thinking about a relevant parable), the effect of religiosity was almost insignificant. Situational influences trumped a notable personality factor. Even seminary students (presumably very good people) were perfectly happy to ignore the sight of an apparently sick man slumped in a doorway when they were rushing to get to their classrooms.

It can be sobering to come to grips with the degree to which human beings can rationalize their immoral behavior. Think of all the Nazi soldiers who followed orders to exterminate 6 million Jews in World War II or, more recently, the American soldiers following orders to torture and humiliate detainees at the Abu Ghraib prison in Iraq. Psychologists attempted to explain such behaviors in a series of well-known experiments carried out in the 1960s. In one famous study by Stanley Milgram, participants were instructed to deliver a shock every time a student (who in reality was a confederate) gave an incorrect answer on a quiz.[4] *All* of Milgram's participants—who were well-adjusted, well-intentioned people—delivered electric shocks to victims who seemingly were in great pain, complaining of heart problems, or even apparently unconscious. Over 60 percent of participants delivered the maximum shock. All of us, these results suggest, are capable of acting in ways that depart significantly from our moral compass under various situational pressures.

Moving on from darkness, time pressure, and pressure from an authority figure, let's consider another situational force that might influence how we behave when it comes to ethical decision making: the presence of abundant resources.

A few years ago, a colleague of mine told me an interesting story. He used to be on the faculty of a well-known university. Like most academics, he sometimes used his office phone to make calls related to his consulting work (which fell outside of his job at the university), and he sometimes used the school's FedEx service to ship letters and packages to friends and family members. He also sometimes took paper from the office's copy center home for his personal use. In all likelihood, such behaviors violated the university's implicit norms or official policies. In fact, recognizing this possibility, about every six months, this professor would estimate how much of the university's money he had spent for personal use and wrote a check to his university for this amount. Impressive, right?

The professor eventually moved to a different university. Although his new position was once again with a very well-respected school, something was visibly different: his new school clearly had more resources, as was evident in the free coffee and snacks offered in the hallways, the well-stocked supply cabinets, and a number of other perks that had not come with the professor's previous job. At his new school, my colleague's work life continued on a similar track. Sometimes he found himself making client calls from his office or using the school's prepaid mailing system for personal letters and packages. But his behavior changed on one dimension: he no longer wrote a check to his employer to cover his personal expenses. After all, this new school appeared to have so many resources that it seemed it would not be affected by minor losses.

At the time my colleague told me this story, I was working on a research project that looked at this exact phenomenon: how a perceived abundance of resources can sway our moral compass and influence our behavior. Lamar Pierce and I were interested in examining a particular type of abundance: cold, hard cash. Inspired by the legendary story of Robin Hood, we wanted to examine whether the presence of monetary wealth influenced people's likelihood to behave dishonestly. In our first few studies, we decided to manipulate resource abundance by varying the amount of cash present in the room where the experiment took place while holding the opportunity for unethical gain constant.

In one experiment, we invited fifty-three individuals to take part in an experiment that we told them concerned the relationship between perception and creativity. We conducted the experiment in two adjacent rooms. In the hall outside the rooms, we randomly assigned participants to one of the rooms and thus to one of two conditions: the "wealthy" condition or the "poor" condition. When the participants entered their assigned classroom, they could clearly see that there was some cash piled on a table in the center of the room. In both conditions, as participants passed by the table, the experimenter handed them each a stack of twenty-four one-dollar bills. Participants were told they would use this money to pay themselves at the end of the study based on their performance. In the wealthy condition, the experimenter distributed the money from a large pile of cash—about $7,000 in real one-dollar bills. In the poor condition, only the amount of cash needed to pay the participants was on the table. After receiving their cash, participants took seats at individual desks that were positioned such that they could not see one another's answers, but they could see the table where the pile of cash was (in the wealthy condition) or had been (in the poor condition).

Next, the experimenter told the participants that they would play multiple rounds of a word game. Each game involved using a set of seven letters to create words, which participants were instructed to list in a workbook they had received. They were told that at the end of the study, they would anonymously record the number of valid words they had created in each round on the answer sheet found on their desk. Participants were also directed to put the workbook in a sealed box at the front of the room and turn in their answer sheet to the experimenter at the end of the study. The participants were told that none of their identifying information would be on the workbook or the answer sheet. In addition, they were told that they would earn $3 for each round in which they met the goal of creating twelve words. (We had conducted a pilot to determine that this was a difficult goal to reach in the allotted time.)

After an initial practice round, participants completed eight rounds of this task. In each round, they received seven letters and had two minutes to create words that followed a set of rules (each word needed to be two or more letters long, etc.). Lamar and I had developed a system to track whether participants cheated by overstating their performance on the task: the last round contained a unique set of letters for each participant that we used to match participants' workbooks with their answer sheets. After working on the anagram task, participants had time to check their work, fill out their answer sheets, and then pay themselves. Participants were instructed to keep the money they had earned and to return the unearned money and their answer sheet before leaving the room.

Imagine being a participant in the wealthy condition. Just a few minutes earlier, you passed by a big pile of money, and now, as you work on the problems, it's staring you straight in the face. When it's time to check your work, you find that you reached the goal in two out of the eight rounds. In three other rounds, you were close to the goal: you created ten correct words rather than twelve. What would you do? Do you think you'd report reaching the goal in four or five rounds rather than just two?

You are probably having a hard time imagining what you'd do in this situation. So, let me tell you what happened in the actual experiment. The pile of cash made a big difference: about 85 percent of participants overstated their productivity in at least one round in the wealthy condition, and "only" about 39 percent did in the poor condition. The abundance of cash in the wealthy condition produced more than twice as many cheaters as the poor condition.

After we had conducted initial experiments and pilot studies at Carnegie Mellon University, Lamar and I wanted to replicate the findings in other contexts and using other populations. So, after talking it over, we decided to conduct a study at Harvard (since I had worked there before and knew my way around), and I made preparations to run the study myself. If you remember, our experiment involved quite a bit of money. After thinking about this issue for a while, we decided that it would be more proper for me to travel with the money rather than putting it into my account and taking it out in Boston. (Lamar and I are still discussing this issue: I remember this being his idea, but he remembers it was a joint decision!) As a result, I ended up traveling from Pittsburgh to Boston with a carry-on suitcase containing seven thousand one-dollar bills, somewhat apprehensive that Transportation Security Administration officials would question me about the money at airport security. As it turned out, the TSA didn't interrogate me, but my boyfriend (now my husband) did. He was living in Boston then, and he questioned me for quite some time when, helping me unpack, he opened the carry-on and found only cash. He seemed to be wondering what I was up to—and what sort of woman he was dating.

But, all's well that ends well. Greg bought my (true!) story, and Lamar and I successfully replicated our findings at Harvard and at other universities.

When given the opportunity, we often cross ethical boundaries but still maintain a positive self-image. This may occur in part because, as human beings, we examine our behavior and then come up with self-serving stories to explain why we acted in a certain way. Imagine, for instance, that you tripped in front of your colleagues, giving them all a good laugh. Tripping might affect your view of yourself in one of three ways: you might update your self-view negatively ("I am clumsy"), fail to update your self-view ("The floor must have been slippery, because I don't usually trip"), or, in the most interesting scenario, update your self-view positively ("My friends thought that was really funny!"). These three options are available to all of us when interpreting our own behavior. The positive-update option is particularly intriguing, since it is suggestive of a specific type of storytelling following poor or embarrassing behavior: self-deception.

Self-deception occurs when we update our self-view not in spite of our poor behavior but *because* of it. As Demosthenes (384–322 BC), the prominent Greek statesman and orator of ancient Athens, once wrote, "Nothing is easier than self-deceit. For what each man wishes, that he also believes to be true." Take the context of sports. Over the last decade, sports fans have endured a steady diet of news about high-profile athletes who have been rumored or proven to have used steroids. In one recent case, Major League Baseball pitcher Andy Pettitte was accused of using human growth hormones, a substance banned by the league. Pettitte publicly admitted that he had used the drugs but said he had not done so "to try to get an edge on anyone," nor "to try to get stronger, faster, or to throw harder." Rather, he claimed he took the drugs to try to recover more quickly from an injury and get off the disabled list so that he "would not let [his] team down." Reflecting on his behavior, Pettitte decided to interpret it in a manner that would reflect positively on him, both in his own mind and in the public eye. In this way, he transformed his cheating into the helpful actions of a player who cared deeply about his teammates.

Here is another concrete example of how self-deception works. Please prepare to take the ten-item trivia quiz in figure 9-1. As you will see, the questions are of medium difficulty. While taking the quiz, imagine that you will be paid $1 for each correct answer. In just a few minutes, you could make up to $10. Pretty good, right?

Figure 9-1

Trivia quiz for the self-deception experiment

Trivia Quiz

1.   What African river is the longest river in the world?

2.   What is the capital of and largest city in Japan?

3.   The "Ring of Fire" is located around what ocean?

4.   In what US state is Atlantic City located?

5.   What is the highest mountain range in the world?

6.   What is South America's highest peak?

7.   In what US state is the ski-resort town of Aspen?

8.   What is the capital of Australia?

9.   Sweden, Denmark, Poland, and Finland all border what sea?

10.   Bechuanaland was the colonial name of what country?

Answers

1. Nile; 2. Tokyo; 3. Pacific; 4. New Jersey; 5. Himalayas;
6. Aconcagua; 7. Colorado; 8. Canberra; 9. Baltic; 10. Botswana

---

Now, after taking the quiz, how many questions do you think you solved correctly?

As you may have noticed, to speed up the grading process, I included the answers at the bottom of the page, as a newspaper might for a quiz or puzzle. Did you find yourself peeking at the answers? If you did, do you think you would take your peeks into consideration when reporting your performance on the trivia quiz?

You may have been able to keep your eyes focused on the questions. But, as it turns out, most people feel tempted to "just have a quick look" at the answers at the bottom of the page. When I was in grade school, I certainly experienced this temptation when a teacher would give us the answers to our math homework. The teacher provided the answers to encourage us to keep working if the answer we found didn't match the provided solution. But I sometimes used the answers simply to improve my score.

I used quizzes similar to the one you just took when testing for self-deception in a series of experiments in collaboration with Zoë Chance (of Yale University), Mike Norton, and Dan Ariely. We wanted to examine situations in which self-deception is fueled by cheating.

We recruited 131 students from the University of North Carolina at Chapel Hill to participate in the experiment for pay. Participants took a ten-question general knowledge test of medium difficulty with questions similar to those you just answered (for example, "How many US states border Mexico?" and "In which US state is Mount Rushmore located?"). Participants were paid based on their performance on the test ($1 per correct answer). For half of the participants, the answer key for the test was included at the bottom of the page (answers condition); the other half did not receive the answers (control condition). After completing and scoring this test, participants were asked to look over a second general knowledge quiz and predict their scores. This time, none of the participants could see the answers. Then they were asked to complete the second test. Once again, they received $1 for each correct answer on the second test.

Having completed one of these tests with access to the answers, you probably realize how difficult it is not to look at them. So, we expected score inflation for those who could see the answers on the first test. Indeed, this is exactly what we found: participants in the answers condition solved more problems correctly on the first test (about nine correct answers on average) than did those in the control group (about six correct answers). More interestingly, participants in the answers condition predicted that they would give eight correct answers on the second test, whereas those in the control condition predicted that they would give only six correct answers. Participants' actual performance on the second test—around five correct answers—did not differ between the two groups, indicating that those who had the answers on the first test deceived themselves into believing they were more knowledgeable than their results on the second test proved them to be.

These results demonstrate that having access to the answers both enhanced performance on the first test and triggered self-deception, namely by causing people to hold positive beliefs about themselves ("I am a good test taker") despite negative information to the contrary ("I saw the answers"). The results also show how easy it is to trigger self-deception, with potential costly consequences in the future. If cheating on a test causes you to think you are smarter than you are, for example, you may not spend enough time studying for future tests.

While problematic as an individual tendency, self-deception is even more worrisome and potentially more costly when situational forces exacerbate it. Zoë, Mike, Dan, and I decided to examine one particular force: social feedback. We investigated whether such feedback would exacerbate self-deception on a group of 136 students from the University of North Carolina. Our process was similar to the experiment I just described, but we included a second manipulation in addition to giving the answers to half of the participants. After completing the first test, but before predicting their performance scores on the second, participants in both conditions (answers and control) were randomly assigned to either receive or not receive a certificate of recognition on which their name and score were written. The experimenter told each participant who was given a certificate that everyone who scored above average on the test was receiving one. In addition, in this experiment, the second test was longer: it included one hundred questions rather than just ten.

As in our previous experiment, participants in the answers condition reported higher scores on the first test than did those in the control condition (about nine correct answers on average versus only four), and they also predicted higher scores on the subsequent longer one-hundred-question test that lacked answers (about seventy-three versus about fifty-one). Receiving a certificate also increased performance predictions. Most importantly, as shown in table 9-1, the certificate's enhancement of self-deception was restricted to the answers condition and had no effect on the control group.

Those who were given the answers were even more likely to inflate their beliefs about their subsequent performance when commended for their performance.

Overall, the results of these experiments suggest that when people cheat on a task, they take the good performance that results as a sign that they are knowledgeable, thus deceiving themselves, and mispredict their performance on a future task. Receiving social feedback makes the problem of self-deception even worse.

If you step back from the details of these studies on self-deception and think about the general lesson they highlight more broadly, you might identify times in your own life when you were not perfectly honest about how outside factors influenced your behavior. For instance, you may have interpreted an outstanding performance review as a sign of your leadership skills without recognizing that people on your team may have made your job easier. Or, after a successful party, you might reflect on how great you are at entertaining, overlooking how crucial your partner's contributions were.

In addition to fostering self-deception, the common tendency to positively reinterpret information about our own behavior can manifest itself as the desire to appear good to others without

TABLE 9-1

Impact of social feedback in the self-deception experiment

	Answers condition	Control condition
Certificate	81.2	52.7
No certificate	64.7	48.5

suffering the costs of actually being good. Take the case of Eliot Spitzer, the governor of New York from 2007 to 2008. Prior to being exposed as "Client #9" in a prostitution ring, the prominent, highly regarded politician actively shaped the public agenda and zealously pursued organized crime, white-collar corruption, and even prostitution. It seems that Spitzer viewed his own illegal behavior as less egregious than that of others. Similarly, former senator John Edwards had an affair and fathered a child with his videographer even as he made his supposedly ideal marriage and family life a centerpiece of his presidential campaign.

These may seem like extreme illustrations of our ability to deceive ourselves about our own morality. However, convincing empirical evidence suggests otherwise: as human beings, we often engage in moral hypocrisy—that is, we desire to appear moral without bearing the real cost of being moral.[5] Philosophers noted this tendency centuries ago. Immanuel Kant once wrote about how self-love rather than ethical principles may explain people's behavior: "We like to flatter ourselves by falsely taking credit for a more noble motive . . . A cool observer, one that does not mistake the wish for the good, however lively, for its reality, may sometimes doubt whether true virtue is actually found anywhere in the world . . . (sec 2., para. 2).[6]

Psychologist Daniel Batson and his colleagues used a series of cleverly designed experiments to test whether people engage in moral hypocrisy. In one of the experiments, each participant was asked to assign him/herself to one of two tasks, knowing that another participant (in actuality, a fictitious person) would be asked to complete the other task.[7] The positive task involved the opportunity to win a small cash prize ($30 in a raffle without having to exert any effort!); the neutral task involved engaging in a "rather dull and boring" task with no chance of winning a prize. When facing this allocation decision, each participant was told that most people consider a coin flip to be the fairest way to assign tasks. This information was intended to make the moral standard of fairness salient. Each participant decided whether or not to flip the coin, then flipped the coin (if he or she chose to do so), and reported the outcome of the coin flip. Notably, the participant was the only person who saw the outcome of the coin flip. Finally, participants rated the morality of the procedure they used to assign the tasks.

What do you think you would do in this situation? Would you flip the coin? What if you flipped the coin and ended up being assigned to the boring task?

The majority of participants in the experiment chose to flip the coin. Among those who did, 90 percent of them assigned themselves to the positive task. This percentage is interesting for two reasons. First, it is much higher than 50 percent, which is approximately the average percentage we would expect from the coin tosses of a group of people. Second, 90 percent of participants who did *not* flip the coin assigned themselves to the positive task. Thus, it is likely that some of the people who flipped a coin and got an undesired outcome (assignment to the boring task) cheated by reporting that they got the outcome they desired.

There's another interesting finding: when evaluating the morality of their actions, participants who flipped the coin judged the morality of their assignment decision much higher than did those who decided not to flip the coin (respectively, 7.11 versus 3.56 out of 9 on average). So, after (likely) cheating on the coin flip, participants indicated that their allocation procedure was morally acceptable. In other words, they behaved in ways consistent with moral hypocrisy.

Often, in both our professional and personal lives, the line between what is right and wrong blurs, especially when we are going after short-term rewards, such as a promotion or a financial benefit. This research on moral hypocrisy tells us that our judgments of our own behaviors also can be blurry, such that we fail to recognize the immorality of our own actions. Is moral hypocrisy an innate tendency? Are we born this way?

To answer these questions, my colleagues Marco Piovesan (of the University of Copenhagen), Natalia Montinari (of the Max

Planck Institute in Germany), Mike Norton, and I conducted a large-scale experiment with children. We traveled to Italy and recruited almost six hundred children from ten schools in Northern Italy, between the ages of six and eleven.

We employed a simple paradigm to test our ideas that mirrored the one that Batson and his colleagues used to assess moral hypocrisy in adults. We asked each child to assign two prizes, one to him/herself and a second to another child (they did not know who the child would be): a "good" prize (a colored highlighter pencil) or a "bad" prize (a normal pencil). Children could use two methods for assigning the prize: they could choose a prize immediately, or they could flip a coin in private to make their decision. Children who chose to flip the coin were asked to flip the coin only once behind a screen that ensured their privacy and then write down the outcome on a sheet of paper, which they were to give to the experimenter.

What percentage of children do you think decided to flip the coin, and do you think the percentage varied by age? Finally, do you think that children behaved differently from the adults in Batson's experiments?

We found that as age increased, the percentage of children choosing to flip the coin increased as well, from about 37 percent for ages six to seven, to over 47 percent for ages eight to nine, to almost 67 percent for ages ten to eleven. But does this preference reflect a real desire to be fair or simply a desire to *appear* fair, as we predicted? To test this prediction, we needed to show two things: first, we needed to show that children had a strong preference for the good prize, which might induce a desire to cheat on the coin flip; second, we needed to show that children cheated when reporting the outcome of the coin flip in order to win the good prize.

To address the first point, we looked at the results of children who immediately chose a prize rather than flipping the coin. The good prize was the overwhelming favorite, chosen by almost 90 percent of children independent of their age. Thus, across ages, children likely had a motivation to misreport the results of the fair coin flip to obtain the good prize. As for the second point, we examined the behavior of children who chose to flip the coin. About 62 percent of them reported winning the good prize, a percentage greater than 50 percent—the percentage of good prizes that a fair coin, on average, would have caused them to actually win. The percentage of those who reported winning the good prize did not differ across age groups.

Self-interest remains constant across the ages we tested, but children as young as six are aware of the effectiveness of hiding their self-interested decisions under a veil of fairness. So, between childhood and adulthood, the desire to *appear* fair increases—and, consequently, so does unethical behavior—but the desire to actually *be* fair does not. Just as the research on self-deception has shown, we need only the right opportunity (here, the decision to choose outright or flip a coin) to come up with reasons to reinterpret our behavior—and we learn this skill at a very young age.

In this chapter, I examined how subtle situational forces can influence our decisions. While previous chapters examined a range of personal and business decisions, here I focused specifically on decisions that may lead us to cross ethical boundaries, even beyond our own awareness.

It sometimes seems as if a day doesn't go by without a revelation of bad behavior by a politician, movie star, professional athlete, high-ranking executive, or politician—not to mention all the "ordinary" people who get caught doing outrageous things. As I have discussed in this chapter, when we're faced with evidence suggesting that we may have behaved dishonestly, we become excellent storytellers, coming up with excuses for our behavior and sweeping our dishonesty under the rug.[8] Consider the earlier example of Andy Pettitte, who justified his behavior by focusing on the benefits it produced for his team. External factors also help us to feel we haven't done wrong when we actually have.[9] As we learned earlier in this chapter, darkness lends a psychological sense of anonymity that increases unethical behavior, and the presence of wealth offers us an excuse to rationalize unethical behavior that we might otherwise resist.

The experiments I described point to a ninth principle for avoiding getting sidetracked:

Make your standards shine.

This principle suggests that the best way to maintain our high ethical standards is to keep them salient in our minds and to stick with them, especially in situations that we may perceive as tempting. In fact, a simple reminder at the right time may help make our standards salient. To see what I mean, think about the times you have reported figures that are supposed to be truthful, as when you are filling out tax forms or business expenses. In these cases, we usually sign the form after completing it. But what if you were asked to sign before filling out the form?

My colleagues Lisa Shu, Nina Mazar (of the University of Toronto), Dan Ariely, Max Bazerman, and I examined this question in a field experiment with an insurance company located in the southeastern United States. In the study, we manipulated the automobile policy review form that was sent out to customers at the end of the year. The form asked customers to record the current, exact odometer mileage of all cars that were currently insured under their policy, in addition to other information. Note that policy holders had a financial incentive to report lower mileages: the fewer miles they drove, the lower their insurance premium. Thus, they might have faced a dilemma between truthfully indicating the current odometer mileage and dishonestly indicating a lower mileage, as there was no indication that a lie could be caught.

We randomly assigned customers to receive a form that asked them to sign the following pledge of honesty: "I promise that the information I am providing is true." In one version of the form, they were asked to sign after having completed the form. In the other version, they were asked to sign at the top of the form—before filling it out. Otherwise, the forms were identical. We received completed forms from 13,488 policies for a total of 20,741 cars, and we compared odometer readings between the two conditions. As we expected, the calculated usage (based on reported odometer readings) was significantly higher among customers who signed at the top of the form (26,098 miles on average) than among those who signed at the bottom of the form (about 23,671 miles on average)—an annual difference of 2,428 miles per car, on average. A very simple change in the location of a signature led to a 10.25 percent increase in the calculated miles driven over the current practice of asking for a signature at the end. Such change served as a powerful reminder of people's ethical standards and greatly influenced the extent to which they misreported information to advance their self-interest.

Another way to make our standards shine is to discuss them more often. Increasingly, organizations are doing this by design. For instance, Kathleen Edmond, the Chief Ethics Officer at Best Buy, created a website where company employees can read about the company's policy regarding ethically questionable behaviors and learn tips on how to best defend themselves from crossing ethical boundaries. The website highlights the extent to which the organization cares about morality and honesty, and Best Buy reports that it has positively influenced employee behavior.

We may not need to sign the top of every important document or read up on the details of corporate policy to follow our moral compass. But, as should be clear from the evidence I presented in this chapter, our moral compass often fails us under the influence of subtle situational forces. Finding ways to make our standards shine should help us to stay on track.

Sticking to the Plan

According to Herodotus, the ancient Greek historian, more than twenty-five hundred years ago, during a period of famine, the king of Lydia came up with a plan to help ease his people's suffering. He began by inventing a game using dice made out of sheep's knuckles. (The dice were the first game pieces ever designed, at least according to Herodotus.)

When introducing the game to his kingdom, the king also presented his plan: each of his subjects would play games one day and eat the following day, and continue to alternate between playing games and eating, day after day, until the famine ended. The king's plan was based on a simple prediction: that the citizens would get so involved playing the games that they would forget they were hungry. According to Herodotus, the king's plan was successful: most of his citizens survived eighteen years of famine by dicing every other day.

But the famine persisted. So the king developed another plan: he divided the kingdom in half and asked the two sides to play one final game of dice against each other. The winners would leave Lydia in search of a new place to live, and the losers would remain to survive on the resources that were available. With any luck, those who left Lydia would take their civilization to hospitable new territory where they could thrive.

Once again, the king's plan was successful, and the Lydians survived. Recently, scientists argued that Herodotus's story may even have the virtue of being true: they found evidence showing that the Etruscans, who led to the Roman Empire, shared DNA with the ancient Lydians. In addition, geologists found evidence of a global cooling that lasted for nearly twenty years that could have explained the famine.

But, true or not, the point of the story is that by developing a clear plan that accounted for the forces affecting his citizens' preferences and decisions, the king of Lydia met his goal of saving his kingdom. The story reminds us that when developing our plans, we need to carefully consider the forces that are likely to impede our decisions or the decisions of those we are trying to influence.

To take advantage of the principles I described in this book to avoid getting sidetracked, you need to acknowledge and recognize the limitations in the way the human mind functions. You need to acknowledge that forces from within ourselves, forces from our relationships with others, and forces from the outside have powerful and predictable effects on our decisions. Consider that most of us have no trouble acknowledging that we do not know how our kidneys or other body parts work, and we are open to learning more about them, especially when we are sick. Too often, however, we assume that we know exactly what's going on in our minds when we face and make decisions, despite the fact that many of our past decisions have led to disappointing outcomes.

I hope the evidence that I've presented throughout the book has convinced you that there are real forces that can get us sidetracked. Forces from within ourselves, forces from our relationships with others, and forces from the outside all come together to sabotage our well-thought-out plans. Although we are motivated to behave in ways that are consistent with our self-image as competent, effective, and honest people, even when we are fully committed to following our best intentions, we often reach outcomes that bear little resemblance to our initial goals. Our decisions veer off course and lead to poor outcomes.

Throughout this book, we've looked at a variety of decisions, from how much effort and integrity to devote to a task, to how to weigh others' opinions in an important decision. Evidence from both real-world stories and research has documented the many ways in which our decisions are easily and predictably side-tracked. These examples have shown why we so often fall short of our intended goals. If the chapters you've read were not convincing enough, numerous recent events—from the failures of prominent banks across the globe to political scandals to man-made ecological disasters—point to the conclusion that, like computer software, the human mind also has bugs that make it difficult for us to stick to our plans.

Although important, acknowledgment and recognition of our "mind bugs" is not enough to help us avoid getting sidetracked. Equipped with the principles discussed in this book, we also need to revisit our plans and think about developing new ones. While this may seem an obvious point, we often lack a clear plan of action, and the forces we've discussed sabotage us as a result. As with the king of Lydia, having a plan gives us the opportunity to clarify our intentions and think through what could make it difficult for us to accomplish our goals.

Let me give you an example from a familiar context: voting. David Nickerson (of the University of Notre Dame) and Todd Rogers (of the Kennedy School of Government at Harvard University) conducted a large field experiment during the 2008 presidential election to examine whether they could increase voter turnout by prompting people to come up with a concrete plan for getting to the polls.[1] The researchers recruited Pennsylvania residents who were eligible to vote in the 2008 presidential primary (and who conformed to other criteria, such as having voted in zero or one primary election since 2000). Participants received a phone call from a professional telemarketing firm that was delivering "get out the vote" calls between Saturday and Monday before the Tuesday Election Day.

The script that callers used varied across conditions. In one of the conditions, the caller read the standard set of statements and questions used in such calls. In another condition—the one of interest here—the script helped the person being called develop a plan for voting. Participants in this condition were asked at what time they would vote, where they would be traveling from, and what they would be doing beforehand. Thus, the script encouraged people to develop a plan (if they did not already have one) for voting. The result? Facilitating the formation of a voting plan increased turnout by over 4 percent among those contacted. Considering how difficult it is to create a meaningful behavioral change in this domain—not to mention the closeness of many recent election races—this increase is quite impressive.

One of the main lessons I try to impress upon the students in my decision-making and negotiation classes is the importance of developing a plan. Too often, we find ourselves underprepared at the bargaining table. We rush into negotiations without taking the time to clarify our objectives, interests, and positions; the range of emotions we could experience during talks; and the information we have about the other side.

Having a clear plan also makes it easier for us to check our progress. In the same way we may count calories when we are on a diet, we can track our progress by outlining a detailed plan. For instance, when engaging in a team project at work, you and your coworkers might agree in advance that you will spend time together reflecting on your performance throughout the process. Doing so can help you determine whether you are on track and make any needed adjustments. Similarly, before attending an important meeting at work, spend some time thinking about the questions you plan to raise and the information you want to gather so that you can keep your goals in sight as others cover their own agendas.

As you develop and start implementing your plans, keep in mind the nine principles from the previous chapters:

1. *Raise your awareness.* Because our views of how capable and competent we are as individuals are often overly positive, we rely too much on our own information and ignore the valuable opinions that others have to offer. By raising your awareness, you can keep your self-views in check and recognize when they may be taking you off track.

2. *Take your emotional temperature.* Even when triggered by situations or events unrelated to the decision at hand, emotions can derail us. They can lead to inaccurate analyses of the information at hand, thus moving us away from our plan of producing correct analyses. By taking your emotional temperature, you can examine what your emotions are telling you and whether they are clouding your decisions.

3. *Zoom out.* We often focus too narrowly on the decision at hand and our own views about it. As a result, we fail to see the bigger picture, including other people's roles. By zooming out, you can include more relevant information in your decision-making process so that you can avoid derailment.

4. *Take the other party's point of view.* There is always another side to a story: the other person's viewpoint. Failing to recognize the potential for a different perspective can prevent us from sticking to the plan. By taking the other side's point of view, you can analyze the decision you face from another person's perspective.

5. *Question your bonds.* As social beings, we easily form connections with others based on subtle factors, such as sharing the same birthday. These connections may expand our networks, but they can also derail our decisions. By questioning your bonds, you can carefully reflect on your ties and similarities to those around you and consider whether these bonds are affecting your choices for the worse.

6. *Check your reference points.* The people around us provide natural reference points to help us understand where we stand across a variety of dimensions, from attractiveness to performance. How we measure up in these comparisons matters and can easily result in derailment. By checking your reference points, you can uncover the real motives behind your decisions and readjust accordingly.

7. *Consider the source.* We look at the effort others put into their decisions to evaluate the quality of those decisions. When evaluating the quality of decisions, we examine their outcomes. Finally, we also discount how situational factors led to a given outcome. These biases lead us to judge others inaccurately. By questioning your sources, you can carefully examine the information surrounding your decisions.

8. *Investigate and question the frame.* We can view the same glass as half empty or half full. Similarly, we can frame our offers and messages to others in different ways. Simple changes in framing can have significant effects on our motivation to act. By investigating the frame, you can ask questions about the way tasks, rewards, and choices are structured and learn how to avoid decisions being derailed.

9. *Make your standards shine.* Our plans commonly reflect our desire to be moral individuals and to listen to our moral compass. Yet, from the amount of lighting in a room to the amount of resources at our disposal, subtle forces can send us off course. By making your standards shine, you can remind yourself of the importance of keeping your standards salient and become more likely to stick with them.

By identifying and acknowledging the forces that sidetrack decisions and applying these principles, you can learn to successfully stick to the plan. You can also use these principles to build systems to help you and others behave according to your goals.

A recent example of how this might work comes from a novel experiment conducted by the car company Volkswagen. In 2009, as part of a public service project, the company developed a plan aimed at encouraging commuters to access the subway system in Stockholm, Sweden, via a flight of stairs rather than via the escalator right next to the stairs. The main purpose of the project was to encourage people to be more active. The plan implicitly was designed to harness the eighth principle to avoid getting sidetracked: investigate and question the frame. The car company applied this principle by shifting the common view of using the staircase from being effortful to being fun. Overnight, a team transformed the stairs leading out of the Odenplan subway station in Stockholm into a functioning piano keyboard, such that every step was a different key and made a different sound. As people applied pressure on each step, a musical note played. More and more commuters chose to use the new stairway, enjoying the sounds they made as they went up or down the scale. In fact, 66 percent more people than usual chose the musical stairs over the escalator.[2]

Following this successful project, Volkswagen created a website called "the fun theory" and invited people across the globe to submit engaging ideas that would produce a positive change in people's behavior in any context.[3] As an example, one person submitted a plan to encourage safe driving that involved capturing on camera not only those who violate the speed limit, but those who drive within it. This group of law abiders would be entered into a lottery and have the opportunity to win cash prizes, which would come from the fines collected from drivers caught speeding. This fun solution to a significant problem reflects my fourth principle: take the other party's point of view. By asking drivers who follow rules how they feel about speed violations, Volkswagen identified a potential plan for action.

These final few examples demonstrate that you can use the nine principles in this book not only to plan more carefully going forward, but also to design systems for yourself and others that can account for the various forces that tend to sidetrack our decisions.

In the research and examples described in the book, getting sidetracked has a negative connotation, as it leads to outcomes that are not only inconsistent with initial plans but that are also poor or inferior to them. Typically, we are unhappy with the outcome of a sidetracked decision and experience regret that we didn't follow through on our plans. But it is also possible for the same forces to sway our decisions for the better, thus leading to outcomes we do not regret.

When I was eighteen, I had a very clear goal in mind: I wanted to become an architect, a career that in Italy requires a degree in engineering. I thought about my future in architecture quite a bit and, in my free time, drew plans for the houses and office spaces I might one day build. I had just finished high school and was spending the summer studying for a general test that prospective students need to take to be admitted to engineering programs in most Italian colleges.

One day in early September, it was raining heavily as I drove my father's small Fiat from Tione, the small town in Northern Italy where I grew up, to the University of Trento to take the exam. As I approached the beautiful city of Trento and the rest of the university, I saw the engineering department, where I was due to take my test, looming on the top of a hill. The building had been beautifully designed, but looked somewhat intimidating to me that day. I remember thinking that the questions on the test are usually quite difficult but that I had prepared for them for quite some time.

I was rushing to the exam room when a student handed me a colorful brochure advertising the university's program in economics and management. The student, who introduced himself as Stefano, told me he was in his second year of the program. He seemed genuinely enthusiastic about what he was learning. He spoke very highly of his management and economics professors and stressed how impressive the department's facilities were. He described his classes as quite entertaining and depicted his peers as smart people with broad interests.

This brief encounter with Stefano had a deep, unexpected impact on my plans. A week later, I was enrolled in the same program as him: economics and management. Just like that, my future career as an architect was over.

We expect our goals and desires to work like a compass that guides our choices, but as I've described throughout this book, the decisions we need to make to reach our goals are often sidetracked by subtle, unanticipated factors. Perhaps even more important, we are often unaware of *why* we made a decision that sabotaged an important plan. I could say that the gloomy weather in Trento soured my mood as I was driving to take the qualifying exam and turned me away from a career in architecture. Or I could credit Stefano for his wonderful ability to persuade prospective students. No matter what the real reason was, I was unaware of it at the time, and it led to an outcome that was quite different from my well-defined initial plan.

I have no regrets about abandoning architecture, and I look at my derailed plan as one that ultimately produced a good outcome. But more typically in life, this is not the case. As you have seen in this book, getting sidetracked can led to unethical behavior, poor analyses of existing information, inaccurate decisions, biased evaluation of others, and low motivation. By reflecting on the forces that derail your decisions and the nine principles to avoid getting sidetracked, you can be more confident that you will be able to stay on track going forward.

As the French author and philosopher Albert Camus once said, "Man is the only creature that refuses to be what he really is." By acknowledging our limitations and recognizing the forces that sidetrack our decisions, we can start debugging our choices, and we can design systems to help us and others follow through on our plans or come up with better ones. That might be the best way for us to get closer to being "infinite in faculties" and "noble in reason," as Shakespeare once wrote.

So, what's next? I did my part; the rest is up to you. But I do have one more piece of advice for you. As my dear colleague and friend Max often tells me, "Make good decisions."

NOTES

Introduction

1. These realizations make us question our fundamental ability to make effective decisions that are consistent with our initial plans. In fact, for decades now, behavioral decision researchers have been studying the systematic mistakes we make under certain circumstances. In 1978, Herbert Simon won a Nobel Prize in Economic Sciences for arguing that our mental faculties are limited rather than infinite. Simon argued that, as human beings, we are "boundedly rational," since our ability to perceive, remember, and process information is restricted. In 2002, Daniel Kahneman won the same Nobel Prize for his work in collaboration with Amos Tversky, which suggested that people reason in ways that produce systematic errors over time. Their research showed that the way we collect information, integrate it, and draw inferences about the world is predictably biased. Since then, empirical evidence on the many ways in which our capacities are systematically "bounded" has been mounting, and brilliant books have been written on this topic. If you are interested in learning more, you can read one or more of the following books: Dan Ariely, *Predictably Irrational: The Hidden Forces That Shape Our Decisions* (New York: Harper Perennial, 2008); Max H. Bazerman and Don A. Moore, *Judgment in Managerial Decision Making*, 7th ed. (Hoboken, NJ: John Wiley & Sons, Inc., 2008); Daniel Kahneman, *Thinking, Fast and Slow* (New York: Farrar, Straus, and Girox, 2011).

2. Joe Marks told me this story over lunch when I was working at Disney R&D as a research consultant in California during the summer of 2010. Marks told me that the story made him realize the importance of understanding human behavior in order to be successful in business.

3. We chose to focus on women not because of the particular behavior we were about to examine (cheating); we had plenty of evidence from other studies that men and women do not differ when it comes to morality—they cheat about the same amount. But we do know that women typically care more about fashion than men, and they certainly care more about feminine-looking sunglasses. So, given that we had chosen to work with a women's brand, we focused our efforts on women.

4. Since the effect of wearing counterfeits was robust across different tasks in the previous study, we decided to focus only on the matrix task in this second study, and we added a questionnaire that would help us understand what participants experienced while wearing authentic or seemingly fake sunglasses.

Chapter 1

1. These arguments are discussed in detail in the following book: James Surowiecki, *The Wisdom of Crowds: Why the Many Are Smarter Than the Few and How Collective Wisdom Shapes Business, Economies, Societies and Nations* (New York: Doubleday; Anchor, 2004).

2. These results were shown quite compellingly in this paper: Ganna Pogrebna, "Naïve Advice When Half a Million Is at Stake," *Economics Letters* 98 (2008): 148–154. For additional research using data from *Affari Tuoi*, interested readers can check out this paper: Pavlo Blavatskyy and Ganna Pogrebna, "Risk Aversion When Gains Are Likely and Unlikely: Evidence from a Natural Experiment with Large Stakes," *Theory and Decision* 64 (2008): 395–420.

3. The full story is available at http://www.nytimes.com/2008/08/05/business/05freddie.html.

4. As reported by Edmund L. Andrews, "Fed Shrugged as Subprime Crisis Spread," *New York Times*, December 18, 2007, http://www.nytimes.com/2007/12/18/business/18subprime.html.

5. For more information about this example, see Edgar H. Schein, *DEC Is Dead, Long Live DEC: The Lasting Legacy of Digital Equipment Corporation*, 1st ed. (San Francisco: Berrett-Koehler, 2003).

6. See http://www.nytimes.com/2006/08/02/business/worldbusiness/02walmart.html.

7. The concept of better-than-average beliefs refers to a cognitive bias that causes people to overestimate their positive qualities and abilities and to underestimate their negative qualities, relative to others. For more information, consult the following papers: Vera Hoorens, "Self-Enhancement and Superiority Biases in Social Comparison," *European Review of Social Psychology* 4 (2003): 113–139; David Dunning, Judith A. Meyerowitz, and Amy D. Holzberg, "Ambiguity and Self-Evaluation: The Role of Idiosyncratic Trait Definitions in Self-Serving Assessments of Ability," *Journal of Personality and Social Psychology* 57 (1989): 1082–1090. The first empirical investigations of these better-than-average effects were conducted by: Mark D. Alicke, "Global Self-Evaluation as Determined by the Desirability and Controllability of Trait Adjectives," *Journal of Personality and Social Psychology* 49 (1985): 1621–1630; Jean-Paul Codol, "On the So-Called 'Superiority Conformity of the Self' Behavior: Twenty Experimental Investigations," *European Journal of Social Psychology* 5 (1975): 457–501; Shelley E. Taylor and Jonathon D. Brown, "Illusion and Well-Being: A Social Psychological Perspective on Mental Health," *Psychological Bulletin* 103 (1988): 193–210.

8. It is important to note that in order to demonstrate better-than-average effects, most scholars point to the fact that it is impossible for the majority of participants to report that they are above average on a certain desirable dimension (e.g., intelligence). However, it is in fact logically possible for nearly all of the participants in the given group of interest to be above the mean if the distribution of intelligence is highly skewed. An example is that the mean number of human legs is slightly lower than two, because of the small minority that has one or no legs. Yet, many of the experiments on better-than-average effects compare study participants to the median of their peer group, since by definition it is impossible for a majority to exceed the median.

9. This test is adapted from J. Edward Russo and Paul J. H. Schoemaker, *Decision Traps: Ten Barriers to Brilliant Decision Making and How to Overcome Them* (New York: Simon & Schuster, 1989), 39.

10. This is a validated and popular way to induce a sense of high or low power, and it was first used by Adam Galinsky, Deborah H. Gruenfeld, and Joe C. Magee, "From Power to Action," *Journal of Personality and Social Psychology* 85 (2003): 453–466.

11. Edmund L. Andrews, "Greenspan Concedes Error on Regulation," *New York Times,* October 23, 2008.

12. Interview with Steve Henn on National Public Radio's *Marketplace,* May 13, 2011.

Chapter 2

1. You can read more about the story here: http://www.usatoday.com/money/industries/technology/2007-06-18-yahoo-ceo-switch_N.htm.

2. If you want to watch the clip and get a better sense of the emotions it triggers, you can find it here: http://www.youtube.com/watch?v=sKMjpN2iCmc.

3. Early research on emotions primarily studied positive and negative moods rather than specific emotions such as sadness, anger, or happiness. In the 1990s, however, researchers found that *valence* alone—that is, a positive or negative mood—doesn't fully explain the relationship between affective states and unrelated judgments. Emotions can be characterized not only by the primary appraisal of valence, but also by a number of secondary appraisals, including perceptions of certainty (how certain am I about the situation?), required attention and effort (how much attention must I devote to this situation?), and control over the outcome (to what extent am I, another person, or outside factors responsible for this situation?). These secondary appraisals are important in helping us understand emotions and their influence on individuals' judgments and decisions.

4. This relationship was identified in the late 1970s. See Michael R. Cunningham, "Weather, Mood, and Helping Behavior: Quasi-Experiments with the Sunshine Samaritan," *Journal of Personality and Social Psychology* 37 (1979): 1947–1956. For a more recent paper on the same issues, see Matthew C. Keller, Barbara L. Fredrickson, Oscar Ybarra, Stéphane Côté, Kareem Johnson, Joe Mikels, Anne Conway, and Tor Wager, "A Warm Heart and a Clear Head: The Contingent Effects of Weather on Mood and Cognition," *Psychological Science* 16 (2005): 724–731.

5. Here are some interesting papers in the finance literature that examine the relationship between weather (and the emotions it triggers) and stock trades: David Hirshleifer and Tyler Shumway, "Good Day Sunshine: Stock Returns and the Weather," *Journal of Finance* 58 (2001): 1009–1032; Edward M. Saunders Jr., "Stock Prices and Wall Street Weather," *The American Economic Review* 83 (1993): 1337–1345; and Mark A. Trombley, "Stock Price and Wall Street Weather: Additional Evidence," *Quarterly Journal of Business and Economics* 36 (1997): 11–21. In addition, this study shows that prospective college students are more likely to enroll in a school if they visit campus on a cloudy day: Uri Simonsohn, "Weather to Go to College," *The Economic Journal* 120 (2010): 270–280. For more

information about the relationship between weather and consumer behavior, check out the following paper: Andrew G. Parsons, "The Association Between Daily Weather and Daily Shopping Patterns," *Australasian Marketing Journal* 9 (2001): 78–84.

6. The statement was part of a speech Brinegar gave in the 2011 Duke Marketing Club's CEO Speaker Series (see http://dukechronicle.com/article/ceo-stresses-emotion-advertising).

7. Additional information about the interviews we conducted in this case can be found at Francesca Gino and Gary P. Pisano, "Ducati Corse: The Making of a Grand Prix Motorcycle," Harvard Business School Case 605-090 (2005).

8. More details regarding the study can be found here: Alice M. Isen, "Positive Affect and Decision Making," in *The Handbook of Emotions*, eds. Michael Lewis and Jeannette M. Haviland (New York: Guilford Press, 1993).

Chapter 3

1. See Donald Sull, "Look Out for the Tunnel Vision Trap," *Financial Times*, August 3, 2004, http://www.ft.com/cms/s/2/e0bcb1ac-e576-11d8-bfd2-00000e2511c8.html.

2. Feel free to try this selective attention test yourself by watching the video: http://www.youtube.com/watch?v=vJG698U2Mvo.

3. This and other experiments on attention and tricks our minds play on us are beautifully described in a book by the scholars who designed the "gorilla" study: Christopher Chabris and Daniel Simons, *The Invisible Gorilla and Other Ways Our Intuitions Deceive Us* (New York: Crown Publishers, 2010).

4. Additional information about the case can be found here: Francesca Gino, Vincent Dessain, Karol Misztal, and Michael Khayyat, "Poles Apart on PZU (A)," Harvard Business School Case N9-912-013 (2011); Gino et al., "Poles Apart on PZU (B)," Harvard Business School Case N9-912-014 (2011); Gino et al., "Poles Apart on PZU (C)," Harvard Business School Case N9-912-015 (2011).

5. This study is described in Daniel J. Simons and Daniel T. Levin, "Failure to Detect Changes to People During a Real-World Interaction," *Psychonomic Bulletin and Review* 5 (1998): 644–649. The same researchers also have demonstrated that people regularly fail to notice editing errors in commercial movies, despite the intense scrutiny given to movies during the post-production process; see Daniel T. Levin and Daniel J. Simons, "Failure to Detect Changes to Attended Objects in Motion Pictures," *Psychonomic Bulletin and Review* 4 (1997): 501–506. You can read more about change blindness in another paper by these authors: Daniel J. Simons and Daniel T. Levin, "Change Blindness," *Trends in Cognitive Science* 1 (1997): 261–267.

6. Additional information about the case can be found here: Francesca Gino and Gary P. Pisano, "Teradyne Corporation: The Jaguar Project," Harvard Business School Case 606-042 (2005).

7. If you are interested in reading the details of the original study, you can find it here: Elizabeth Newton, "Overconfidence in the Communication of Intent: Heard and Unheard Melodies" (unpublished doctoral dissertation, Stanford University, 1990).

8. These comments are described on page 114 of Lee Ross and Andrew Ward, "Naive Realism in Everyday Life: Implications for Social Conflict and Misunderstanding," in *Social Cognition: The Ontario Symposium*, eds. Edward S. Reed, Elliot Turiel, and Terrance Brown (Hillsdale, NJ: Erlbaum, 1996), 305–321.

9. In case you want to read more, you can find them here: Jack Handey, *Deep Thoughts* (New York: Penguin, 1992).

Chapter 4

1. This manipulation was first used by Glen Hass; see R. Glen Hass, "Perspective Taking and Self-Awareness: Drawing an *E* on Your Forehead," *Journal of Personality and Social Psychology* 46 (1984): 788–798.

2. See http://www.vip.it/tim-silurato-fabrizio-bona-colpa-degli-spot-di-belen/.

3. See http://www.ft.com/intl/cms/s/1/099ae96a-b4f0-11d9-8df4-00000e2511c8.html#axzz1XOH0hWnX.

4. For more information about this case, you can read the original case studies: Kathleen L. McGinn, Paula J. Laschober, and Dina Pradel, "Endesa Chile: Raising the Ralco Dam (A)," Harvard Business School Case 906-014 (2006); and Kathleen L. McGinn, Paula J. Laschober, and Dina Pradel, "Endesa Chile: Raising the Ralco Dam (B)," Harvard Business School Case 906-015 (2006).

5. The experiment is described in detail in this paper: Boaz Keysar, Shuhong Lin, and Dale J. Barr, "Limits on Theory of Mind Use in Adults," *Cognition* 89 (2003): 25–41.

6. The study is described in detail here: Michael Ross and Fiore Sicoly, "Egocentric Biases in Availability and Attribution," *Journal of Personality and Social Psychology* 37 (1979): 322–336.

7. The phrase "curse of knowledge" was first used in this article: Colin Camerer, George Loewenstein, and Martin Weber, "The Curse of Knowledge in Economic Settings: An Experimental Analysis," *Journal of Political Economy* 97 (1989): 1232–1254. Other papers discuss this common tendency in both children and adults. If you interested in learning more, you can read the following papers: Susan A. J. Birch, "When Knowledge Is a Curse: Children's and Adults' Reasoning About Mental States," *Current Directions in Psychological Science* 14 (2005): 25–29; Baruch Fischoff and Ruth Beyth, "'I Knew It Would Happen': Remembered Probabilities of Once-Future Things," *Organizational Behavior and Human Performance* 13 (1975): 1–16.

8. This study is described here: George Loewenstein, Don Moore, and Roberto Weber, "Paying $1 to Lose $2: Misperceptions of the Value of Information in Predicting the Performance of Others," *Experimental Economics* 9 (2006): 281–295.

9. This study is described in detail here: Kenneth Savitsky, Leaf Van Boven, Nicholas Epley, and Wayne M. Wight, "The Unpacking Effect in Allocations of Responsibility for Group Tasks," *Journal of Experimental Social Psychology* 41 (2005): 447–457.

10. See http://gadgetwise.blogs.nytimes.com/tag/glowcap/.

Chapter 5

1. Cited on page 129 in Albert H. Hastorf and Hadley Cantril, "They Saw a Game: A Case Study," *The Journal of Abnormal and Social Psychology* 49 (1954): 129–134.

2. Cited on page 129 in Hastorf and Cantril, "They Saw a Game."

3. See Matthew Rand, "Lessons from the Trenches: How to Mix Business and Friendship," Forbes.com, August 16, 2006, http://www.forbes.com/2006/08/16/google-yahoo-entrepreneurs-cx_mr_0816friends.html.

4. See Matthew Rand, "Lessons."

5. Muzafer Sherif, O. J. Harvey, B. Jack White, William R. Hood, and Carolyn W. Sherif, *Intergroup Conflict and Cooperation: The Robbers Cave Experiment* (Norman: University of Oklahoma Book Exchange, 1954/1961).

6. These estimates are mentioned in Noah J. Goldstein, Robert B. Cialdini, and Vladas Griskevicius, "A Room with a Viewpoint: Using Social Norms to Motivate Environmental Conservation in Hotels," *Journal of Consumer Research* 35 (2008): 472–482.

7. These estimates are mentioned in Goldstein, Cialdini, and Griskevicius, "A Room with a Viewpoint."

8. The study is described in Goldstein, Cialdini, and Griskevicius, "A Room with a Viewpoint." A similar set of studies was conducted to examine how to reduce energy conservation by highlighting the behavior of other people; see P. Wesley Schultz, Jessica M. Nolan, Robert B. Cialdini, Noah J. Goldstein, and Vladas Griskevicius, "The Constructive, Destructive, and Reconstructive Power of Social Norms," *Psychological Science* 18 (2007): 429–434.

9. At this point, you may be wondering why the new sign informed participants that 75 percent of the guests reused their towels when only about 44 percent of the guests who participated in the study actually did reuse their towels. Two main reasons explain this discrepancy. As the authors note in the original paper, "First, in keeping with the data reported by the towel hanger suppliers, the signs in our study informed the guests that the majority of individuals recycled at least one towel sometime during their stay. Because we only examined towel reuse data for participants' first eligible day, the compliance rate we observed is likely an underestimation of the number of individuals who recycle their towels at least once during their stay. Second, we used the most conservative standards for counting compliance; that is, we did not count as a reuse effort a towel that was hung on a door hook or doorknob—a very common practice for towel recyclers who misunderstand or do not thoroughly read the instructions—as we wanted to eliminate the likelihood of guests complying unintentionally with the request. Thus, the overall percentage of towel reuse was artificially suppressed" (Goldstein, Cialdini, and Griskevicius, "A Room with a Viewpoint," 475).

10. See Jonas Boström, Niklas Falk, and Christian Tyrchan, "Exploiting Personalized Information for Reagent Selection in Drug Design," *Drug Discovery Today* 16 (2011), 181–187.

11. If you are interested in learning more about this company, you can read: Francesca Gino and Bradley R. Staats, "Samasource: Give Work, Not Aid," Harvard Business School Case N9-912-011 (2011).

Chapter 6

1. Leon Festinger, "A Theory of Social Comparison Processes," *Human Relations* 7 (1954): 117–40.

2. See Daniel T. Gilbert, R. Brian Giesler, and Kathryn A. Morris, "When Comparisons Arise," *Journal of Personality and Social Psychology* 69 (1995): 227–236.

3. Elizabeth Weitzman, "Movies and Actors Who Were Robbed of Oscar Gold," *New York Daily News*, February 21, 2008, http://www.nydailynews.com/entertainment/movies/2008/02/22/2008-02-22_movies_and_actors_who_were_robbed_of_osc.html.

4. See Katherine L. Milkman and Maurice E. Schweitzer, "Will the Best Man Win? Social Comparisons, Envy, and the Tension Between Cooperation and Competition" (working paper, Wharton School, University of Pennsylvania, 2011).

5. To learn more about this bias, you can read Stephen M. Garcia, Hyunjin Song, and Abraham Tesser, "Tainted Recommendations: The Social Comparison Bias," *Organizational Behavior and Human Decision Processes* 113 (2010): 97–101.

6. The study is described in detail here: Max H. Bazerman, Holly A. Schroth, Pri Pradhan Shah, Kristina A. Diekmann, and Ann E. Tenbrunsel, "The Inconsistent Role of Social Comparison and Procedural Justice in Reactions to Hypothetical Job Descriptions: Implications for Job Acceptance Decisions," *Organizational Behavior and Human Decision Processes* 60 (1994): 326–352.

7. The study is described here: David Card, Alexandre Mas, Enrico Moretti, and Emmanuel Saez, "Inequality at Work: The Effect of Peer Salaries on Job Satisfaction," *American Economic Review* (forthcoming).

8. See Virginia Groark, "An Overhaul for Emissions Testing," *New York Times*, June 9, 2002, http://www.nytimes.com/2002/06/09/nyregion/an-overhaul-for-emissions-testing.html?pagewanted=all&src=pm; and Thomas N. Hubbard, "An Empirical Examination of Moral Hazard in the Vehicle Inspection Market," *RAND Journal of Economics* 29 (1998): 406–426.

9. See Thomas N. Hubbard, "How Do Consumers Motivate Experts? Reputational Incentives in an Auto Repair Market," *Journal of Law and Economics* 45 (2002): 437–468.

10. The announcement was made by the company's founder on February 1, 2007; see http://about.digg.com/blog/couple-updates%E2%80%A6.

11. From http://gamingtheclassroom.wordpress.com/syllabus/.

12. When I asked him about his innovative system, Sheldon told me: "Since all of my classes are focused on a guild project at the end, one of the checks I institute is the anonymous peer review. Anyone not carrying his or her weight becomes clear very quickly. I was worried though that guild members might agree to just vote the highest possible XP for everyone. Yet that has never happened. Everyone in a guild is responsible to help the others, or they are either demoted or kicked out. Since the students couldn't in this case kick anyone from the guild, they individually used the procedure to make certain everyone got the XP they had earned. There are also opportunities for one guild member to do well, and the entire guild gets credit. The bottom line is they are playing the game, and enjoying it."

Chapter 7

1. Additional information about the case can be found here: Francesca Gino, Michael W. Toffel, and Stephanie Van Sice, "FIJI Versus Fiji: Negotiating Over Water," Harvard Business School Case N9-912-030 (2012).

2. This experiment is described in detail here: Lee D. Ross, Teresa M. Amabile, and Julia L. Steinmetz, "Social Roles, Social Control, and Biases in Social-Perception Processes," *Journal of Personality and Social Psychology* 35 (1977): 485–494. If you are interested in learning more about how individuals engage in attribution processes, you can read the following papers: Edward E. Jones and Victor A. Harris, "The Attribution of Attitudes," *Journal of Experimental Social Psychology* 3 (1967): 1–24; and Richard E. Nisbett and Eugene Borgida, "Attribution and the Psychology of Prediction," *Journal of Personality and Social Psychology* 32 (1975): 932–943.

3. These examples were used in Gordon B. Moskowitz, *Social Cognition: Understanding Self and Others* (New York: The Guilford Press, 2005).

4. This example was originally discussed in Susan Moffat, "Japan's New Personalized Production," *Fortune*, October 22, 1990, 132–135. It was also mentioned in Karen R. Chinander and Maurice E. Schweitzer, "The Input Bias: The Misuse of Input Information in Judgments of Outcomes," *Organizational Behavior and Human Decision Processes* 91 (2003): 243–253.

5. See Stephanie Overby, "Bias Beware: More Time Does Not Equal Better Quality," *CIO*, March 1, 2004, http://www.cio.com/article/32143/Bias_Beware_More_Time_Does_Not_Equal_Better_Quality_.

6. This study is described in detail here: Jonathan Baron and John C. Hershey, "Outcome Bias in Decision Evaluation," *Journal of Personality and Social Psychology*, 54 (1988): 569–579.

7. This experiment and other interesting ones are described here: Robert A. Josephs, R. Brian Giesler, and David H. Silvera, "Judgment by Quantity," *Journal of Experimental Psychology: General* 123 (1984): 21–32.

Chapter 8

1. Kathleen Holder, "Engineer Finds Sweet Travel Deal in Cups of Pudding," UC Davis, News and Information, Dateline, February 4, 2000, http://dateline.ucdavis.edu/020400/DL_pudding.html. See also Claudia Puig, "The Proof of 'Punch-Drunk Love' Is in the Pudding," *USA Today*, October 7, 2002, http://www.usatoday.com/life/movies/news/2002-10-07-pudding_x.htm.

2. More precisely, *framing* refers to a cognitive bias indicating that presenting the same option in different formats can alter people's decisions. This tendency was initially demonstrated in this paper: Amos Tversky and Daniel Kahneman, "The Framing of Decisions and the Psychology of Choice," *Science* 211 (1981): 453–458.

3. The example of the framing of the amount of fat in beef comes from a study described in this paper: Irwin P. Levin and Gary J. Gaeth, "How Consumers Are Affected by the Framing of Attribute Information Before and After Consuming the Product," *Journal of Consumer Research* 15 (1988): 374–378. If you are interested in learning about the various forms of framing, you can read the following paper: Irwin P. Levin, Sandra L. Schneider, and Gary J. Gaeth, "All

Frames Are Not Created Equal: A Typology and Critical Analysis of Framing Effects," *Organizational Behavior and Human Decision Processes* 76 (1998): 149–188.

4. This interesting study is described here: Joseph C. Nunes and Xavier Drèze, "The Endowed Progress Effect: How Artificial Advancement Increases Effort," *Journal of Consumer Research* 32 (2006): 504–512. See also Joseph C. Nunes and Xavier Drèze, "Your Loyalty Program Is Betraying You," *Harvard Business Review* (April 2006): 124–131.

5. A large stream of research has consistently and robustly demonstrated that specific, challenging goals lead to greater performance as compared to vague, easy goals (e.g., "do your best"). For a recent review, see Edwin A. Locke and Gary P. Latham, "New Directions in Goal-Setting Theory," *Current Directions in Psychological Science* 15 (2006): 265–268.

6. If you are curious about this research, you can read: Adam M. Grant, "The Significance of Task Significance: Job Performance Effects, Relational Mechanisms, and Boundary Conditions," *Journal of Applied Psychology* 93 (2008): 108–124.

7. If you are interested in reading the research discussing this study, you can find it here: Cassie Mogilner, Tamar Rudnick, and Sheena S. Iyengar, "The Mere Categorization Effect: How the Presence of Categories Increases Choosers' Perceptions of Assortment Variety and Outcome Satisfaction," *Journal of Consumer Research* 35 (2008): 202–215.

8. Delphine Saubaber, "Sienne: La cavalcade infernale [Siena: The horse race from hell]," *L'Express*, September 8, 2007, 42–45, http://www.lexpress.fr/ styles/voyage/la-cavalcade-infernale_475955.html.

9. The study is described in detail here: Christopher J. Bryan, Gregory M. Walton, Todd Rogers, and Carol S. Dweck, "Motivating Voter Turnout by Invoking the Self," *Proceedings of the National Academy of Sciences* 108 (2011): 12653–12657.

10. This example was mentioned in Deepak Malhotra and Max H. Bazerman, *Negotiation Genius: How to Overcome Obstacles and Achieve Brilliant Results at the Bargaining Table and Beyond* (Boston: Harvard Business School, 2008). It was originally described in David A. Lax and James K. Sebenius, *3-D Negotiation: Powerful Tools to Change the Game in Your Most Important Deals* (Boston: Harvard Business School, 2006).

Chapter 9

1. Ralph Waldo Emerson, "Worship," in *The Conduct of Life*, ed. Edward W. Emerson (Boston: Houghton Mifflin Company, 1904), 224.

2. If you are interested in learning more about early studies on the relationship between lighting and crime, you can read the following: J. E. Hartley, *Lighting Reinforces Crime Fight* (Pittsfield, MA: Buttenheim, 1974); and E. B. Karnes, "Well-Planned Lighting Is City Progress," *American City Magazine* 75 (1960): 104–105.

3. John M. Darley and C. Daniel Batson, "'From Jerusalem to Jericho': A Study of Situational and Dispositional Variables in Helping Behavior," *Journal of Personality and Social Psychology* 27 (1963): 100–108.

4. Stanley Milgram, *Obedience to Authority: An Experimental View* (New York: Harper Collins, 1974).

5. If you are interested in learning more about moral hypocrisy, you can read the work of Daniel Batson and his colleagues. Here are a few papers: C. Daniel Batson, Diane Kobrynowicz, Jessica L. Dinnerstein, Hannah C. Kampf, and Angela D. Wilson, "In a Very Different Voice: Unmasking Moral Hypocrisy," *Journal of Personality and Social Psychology* 72 (1997): 1335–1348; C. Daniel Batson, Elizabeth R. Thompson, and Hubert Chen, "Moral Hypocrisy: Addressing Some Alternatives," *Journal of Personality and Social Psychology* 83 (2002): 303–339; C. Daniel Batson, Elizabeth R. Thompson, Greg Seuferling, Heather Whitney, and Jon A. Strongman, "Moral Hypocrisy: Appearing Moral to Oneself Without Being So," *Journal of Personality and Social Psychology* 77 (1999): 525–537.

6. Immanuel Kant, *Fundamental Principles of the Metaphysic of Morals*, trans. Thomas Kingsmill Abbott (Rockville, MD: ARC Manor, 2008).

7. The experiment described here is Study 2 from Batson et al., "In a Very Different Voice."

8. In fact, the more creative we are, or the more we are asked to think creatively about a problem, the more we are at risk of crossing ethical boundaries, at least in situations where cheating is tempting. You can read more about these relationships here: Francesca Gino and Dan Ariely, "The Dark Side of Creativity: Original Thinkers Can Be More Dishonest," *Journal of Personality and Social Psychology* 102 (2012): 445–459.

9. In the discussion, I have focused on cases in which cheating is deliberate (i.e., people realize that they are crossing ethical boundaries), but people may fail to realize that situational forces are influencing their decisions. There is also research on cases in which people do not even realize that they are behaving dishonestly. If you are curious about such research, you can read the following recent book on this topic: Max H. Bazerman and Ann E. Tenbrunsel, *Blind Spots: Why We Fail to Do What's Right and What to Do About It* (Princeton, NJ: Princeton University Press, 2011).

Conclusion

1. You can read the original study here: David W. Nickerson and Todd Rogers, "Do You Have a Voting Plan? Implementation Intentions, Voter Turnout, and Organic Plan Making," *Psychological Science* 21 (2010): 194–199.

2. If you are curious to see the video of this project, you can find it here: http://www.youtube.com/watch?v=2lXh2n0aPyw&feature=player_embedded.

3. If you want to learn more or see more interesting videos, here is the website: http://thefuntheory.com/.

BIBLIOGRAPHY

Introduction

Based on:

Gino, Francesca, Michael I. Norton, and Dan Ariely. "The Counterfeit Self: The Deceptive Costs of Faking It." *Psychological Science* 21 (2010): 712–720.

Chapter 1

Based on:

Gino, Francesca. "Do We Listen to Advice Just Because We Paid for It? The Impact of Advice Cost on Its Use." *Organizational Behavior and Human Decision Processes* 107 (2008): 234–245.

Gino, Francesca, and Don A. Moore. "Effects of Task Difficulty on Use of Advice." *Journal of Behavioral Decision Making* 20 (2007): 21–35.

Tost, Leigh Plunkett, Francesca Gino, and Richard P. Larrick. "Power, Competitiveness, and Advice Taking: Why the Powerful Don't Listen." *Organizational Behavior and Human Decision Processes* 117 (2012): 53–65.

Related readings:

Arkes, Hal R., and Catherine Blumer. "The Psychology of Sunk Cost." *Organizational Behavior and Human Decision Processes* 35 (1985): 124–140.

Moore, Don A., and Tai Gyu Kim. "Myopic Social Prediction and the Solo Comparison Effect." *Journal of Personality and Social Psychology* 85 (2003): 1121–1135.

Yaniv, Ilan, and Eli Kleinberger. "Advice Taking in Decision Making: Egocentric Discounting and Reputation Formation." *Organizational Behavior and Human Decision Processes* 83 (2000): 260–281.

Chapter 2

Based on:

Gino, Francesca, Alison Wood Brooks, and Maurice E. Schweitzer. "Anxiety, Advice, and the Ability to Discern: Feeling Anxious Motivates Individuals to Seek and Use Advice." *Journal of Personality and Social Psychology* 102 (2012): 497–512.

Gino, Francesca, and Maurice E. Schweitzer. "Blinded by Anger or Feeling the Love: How Emotions Influence Advice Taking." *Journal of Applied Psychology* 93 (2008): 1165–1173.

Gino, Francesca, and Maurice E. Schweitzer. "Seeing and Believing: How Expressed Emotions Influence Trust and Advice Taking." Working paper, 2011.

Grant, Adam M., and Francesca Gino. "A Little Thanks Goes a Long Way: Explaining Why Gratitude Expressions Motivate Prosocial Behavior." *Journal of Personality and Social Psychology* 98 (2010): 946–955.

Related readings:

Mattes, Kyle, Michael Spezio, Hackjin Kim, Alexander Todorov, Ralph Adolphs, and R. Michael Alvarez. "Predicting Election Outcomes from Positive and Negative Trait Assessments of Candidate Images." *Political Psychology* 31 (2010): 41–58.

Schwarz, Norbert, and Gerald L. Clore. "Mood, Misattribution, and Judgments of Well-Being: Informative and Directive Functions of Affective States." *Journal of Personality and Social Psychology* 45 (1983): 513–523.

Wiltermuth, Scott S., and Larissa Z. Tiedens. "Incidental Anger and the Desire to Evaluate." *Organizational Behavior and Human Decision Processes* 116 (2011): 55–65.

Chapter 3

Based on:

Gino, Francesca, and Max H. Bazerman. "When Misconduct Goes Unnoticed: The Acceptability of Gradual Erosion in Others' Unethical Behavior." *Journal of Experimental Social Psychology* 45 (2009): 708–719.

Gino, Francesca, and Don A. Moore. "Why Negotiators Should Reveal Their Deadlines: Disclosing Weaknesses Can Make You Stronger." *Negotiation and Conflict Management Research* 1 (2008a): 77–96.

Gino, Francesca, and Don A. Moore. "Using Final Deadlines Strategically in Negotiation." *Negotiation and Conflict Management Research* 1 (2008b): 371–389.

Related readings:

Kruger, Justin, Nicholas Epley, Jason Parker, and Zhi-Wen Ng. "Egocentrism Over E-Mail: Can We Communicate as Well as We Think?" *Journal of Personality and Social Psychology* 89 (2005): 925–936.

Chapter 4

Based on:

Brooks, Alison Wood, Francesca Gino, and Maurice E. Schweitzer. "Smart People Ask for (My) Advice: The Surprising Benefits of Advice Seeking." Working paper.

Cavanaugh, Lisa A., Francesca Gino, and Gavan J. Fitzsimons. "'Mirror . . . Mirror on the Wall, Who's the Greenest Giver of Them

All?': Understanding When and Why Men and Women Gift Ethically Made Products." Paper presented at the Association for Consumer Research Annual Conference, Pittsburgh, PA, October 22–25, 2009.

Cavanaugh, Lisa A., Francesca Gino, and Gavan J. Fitzsimons. "When Going Good Is Bad for You: Effects of Socially Responsible Gifts on Recipients' Appreciation." Working paper, 2011.

Gino, Francesca, and Francis J. Flynn. "Give Them What They Want: The Benefits of Explicitness in Gift Exchange. *Journal of Experimental Social Psychology* 47 (2011): 915–922.

Related readings:

Gilovich, Thomas, Kenneth Savitsky, and Victoria Husted Medvec. "The Illusion of Transparency: Biased Assessments of Others' Ability to Read Our Emotional States." *Journal of Personality and Social Psychology* 75 (1998): 332–346.

Hass, R. Glen. "Perspective Taking and Self-Awareness: Drawing an *E* on Your Forehead." *Journal of Personality and Social Psychology* 46 (1984): 788–798.

Chapter 5

Based on:

Gino, Francesca, Shahar Ayal, and Dan Ariely. "Contagion and Differentiation in Unethical Behavior: The Effect of One Bad Apple on the Barrel." *Psychological Science* 20 (2009): 393–398.

Gino, Francesca, and Adam D. Galinsky. "Vicarious Dishonesty: When Psychological Closeness Creates Distance from One's Moral Compass." *Organizational Behavior and Human Decision Processes* 119 (2012): 15–26.

Gino, Francesca, Jun Gu, and Chen-Bo Zhong. "Contagion or Restitution? When Bad Apples Can Motivate Ethical Behavior." *Journal of Experimental Social Psychology* 45 (2009): 1299–1302.

Related readings:

Cialdini, Robert B., and Noah J. Goldstein. "Social Influence: Compliance and Conformity." *Annual Review of Psychology* 55 (2004): 591–621.

Griskevicius, Vladas, Robert B. Cialdini, and Noah J. Goldstein. "Peer Influence: An Underestimated and Underemployed Lever for Change." *Sloan Management Review* 49 (2008): 84–88.

Chapter 6

Based on:

Gino, Francesca, and Lamar Pierce. "Dishonesty in the Name of Equity." *Psychological Science* 20 (2009): 1153–1160.

Gino, Francesca, and Lamar Pierce. "Robin Hood Under the Hood: Wealth-Based Discrimination in Illicit Customer Help." *Organization Science* 21 (2010): 1176–1194.

Gino, Francesca, and Lamar Pierce. "Lying to Level the Playing Field: Why People May Dishonestly Help or Hurt Others to Create Equity." In "Regulating Ethical Failures: Insights from Psychology," special issue, *Journal of Business Ethics* 95 (2010): 89–103.

Gino, Francesca, and Bradley R. Staats, "Driven by Social Comparisons: How Feedback About Coworkers' Effort Influences Individual Productivity." Working paper, 2011.

Related readings:

Garcia, Stephen M., Hyunjin Song, and Abraham Tesser. "Tainted Recommendations: The Social Comparison Bias." *Organizational Behavior and Human Decision Processes* 113 (2010): 97–101.

Larkin, Ian, Lamar Pierce, and Francesca Gino. "The Psychological Costs of Pay-for-Performance: Implications for the Strategic Compensation of Employees." *Strategic Management Journal* 33 (2012): 1194–1214.

Chapter 7

Based on:

Gino, Francesca, and Max H. Bazerman. "When Misconduct Goes Unnoticed: The Acceptability of Gradual Erosion in Others' Unethical Behavior." *Journal of Experimental Social Psychology* 45 (2009): 708–719.

Gino, Francesca, Don A. Moore, and Max H. Bazerman. "See No Evil: When We Overlook Other People's Unethical Behavior." In *Social Decision Making: Social Dilemmas, Social Values, and Ethical Judgments*, edited by Roderick M. Kramer, Ann E. Tenbrunsel, and Max H. Bazerman, 241–263. New York: Psychology Press, 2009.

Gino, Francesca, Don A. Moore, and Max H. Bazerman. "No Harm, No Foul: The Outcome Bias in Ethical Judgments." Working paper, 2012.

Gino, Francesca, Lisa L. Shu, and Max H. Bazerman. "Nameless + Harmless = Blameless: When Seemingly Irrelevant Factors Influence Judgment of (Un)ethical Behavior." *Organizational Behavior and Human Decision Processes* 111 (2012): 102–115.

Moore, Don A., Samuel A. Swift, Zachariah S. Sharek, and Francesca Gino. "Correspondence Bias in Performance Evaluation: Why Grade Inflation Works." *Personality and Social Psychology Bulletin* 36 (2010): 843–852.

Related readings:

Chinander, Karen R., and Maurice E. Schweitzer. "The Input Bias: The Misuse of Input Information in Judgments of Outcomes." *Organizational Behavior and Human Decision Processes* 91 (2003), 243–253.

Chapter 8

Based on:

Cable, Dan, Francesca Gino, and Brad Staats. "Breaking Them In or Revealing Their Best? Reframing Socialization Around Newcomers' Self-Expression." Working paper, 2012.

Wiltermuth, Scott S., and Francesca Gino. "'I'll Have One of Each': How Separating Rewards into (Meaningless) Categories Increases Motivation." *Journal of Personality and Social Psychology* 109 (2012): 15197–15200.

Related readings:
Tversky, Amos, and Daniel Kahneman. "The Framing of Decisions and the Psychology of Choice." *Science* 211 (1981): 453–458.

Chapter 9

Based on:
Chance, Zoë, Michael I. Norton, Francesca Gino, and Dan Ariely. "Temporal View of the Costs and Benefits of Self-Deception." *Proceedings of the National Academy of Sciences*, 108 (2011): 15655–15659.

Gino, Francesca, and Lamar Pierce. "The Abundance Effect: Unethical Behavior in the Presence of Wealth." *Organizational Behavior and Human Decision Processes* 109 (2009): 142–155.

Piovesan, Marco, Natalia Montinari, Francesca Gino, and Michael I. Norton. "Usage of the Veil of Fairness Develops Over Childhood." Working paper, 2011.

Shu, Lisa L., Nina Mazar, Francesca Gino, Dan Ariely, and Max H. Bazerman. "Signing at the Beginning Makes Ethics Salient and Decreases Dishonest Self-Reports in Comparison to Signing at the End." *Proceedings of the National Academy of Sciences* (forthcoming).

Zhong, Chen-Bo, Vanessa K. Bohns, and Francesca Gino. "Good Lamps Are the Best Police: Darkness Increases Dishonesty and Self-Interested Behavior." *Psychological Science* 21 (2009): 311–314.

ACKNOWLEDGMENTS

When I was contemplating whether to go to graduate school, I thought of the academic profession as one filled with solitude. I pictured studious professors, scratching their heads in search of good ideas and putting words on paper during long hours of isolation. As it turns out, the images in my mind were quite different from reality. Most of the research discussed in *Sidetracked* is the result of joint projects I embarked on over the last ten years with wonderful colleagues who are also close friends. I feel very fortunate to have spent endless hours talking about research and life more generally with each one of them: Dan Ariely, Shahar Ayal, Max Bazerman, Vanessa Bohns, Alison Wood Brooks, Dan Cable, Lisa Cavanaugh, Zoë Chance, Gavan Fitzsimons, Frank Flynn, Adam Galinsky, Adam Grant, Rick Larrick, Nina Mazar, Natalia Montinari, Don Moore, Mike Norton, Lamar Pierce, Marco Piovesan, Gary Pisano, Maurice Schweitzer, Zach Sharek, Lisa Shu, Brad Staats, Sam Swift, Leigh Tost, Scott Wiltermuth, and Chen-Bo Zhong. You all have contributed to making my academic journey a very inspiring and fun adventure.

I owe a particularly special debt of gratitude to two longtime collaborators, friends, and mentors: Max Bazerman and Don Moore. It is still unclear to me what potential you saw in me when I first landed in the United States and told you I was interested in the world of research. I feel truly grateful for the time and energy you invested in mentoring me, and I feel even more thankful for your creativity and thoughtfulness, which have been a source of constant inspiration since I met you. You always inspire me to be a better scholar as well as a better human being.

I am also especially grateful to my colleague and mentor Gary Pisano, who always challenged me to think about the relevance of my research to the real world. Thank you for your guidance and advice when I was a PhD student; it taught me the value of getting into the field. And thank you also for always keeping an eye on me as I grew as a scholar.

Writing *Sidetracked* was a very gratifying experience, but not always an easy one. I am truly thankful I had help from two genuinely supportive people along the way. Katherine Shonk read every single chapter with great care, and was never afraid to let me know what needed to be rethought or rewritten. With her beautiful touch, Katie helped me make sure my thoughts would come through clearly. I am indebted to you for your helpful and detailed advice on how to improve each chapter. And then there is my editor, Tim Sullivan. From the first time we met to discuss my book proposal, Tim has been an amazingly supportive editor, and his enthusiasm motivated me whenever I found myself staring at a blank page on my computer. Tim patiently read and edited this book multiple times and shared his insightful ideas on how to make it better. Thank you for your support, creativity, and attention to detail; you made this journey truly enjoyable. I am grateful I had the opportunity to work with such a trusting and helpful editor.

As I was writing the book, I often had conversations on how to frame my ideas in more compelling ways. With their creative insights, Deepak Malhotra and Kathleen McGinn helped me get unstuck. Thank you for being generous with your time and for always making yourselves available to think through my arguments. I am so happy to have you both just down the hall!

I am also grateful to Mike Norton. Your innovativeness and ability to generate random yet insightful ideas on the spot continually inspires me. It has been such a pleasure to comanage with you the GiNorton lab, a group of smart and ingenuous students: Lalin Anik, Silvia Bellezza, Ryan Buell, Mika Chance, Zoë Chance, Pinar Fletcher, Julia Lee, Patt Satterstrom, Ovul Sezer, Hee Yeon Shin, Lisa Shu, and Ting Zhang. Our weekly lab meetings, where

I reported my progress on the book, were highly motivating and helped me stay on track. Thanks to you all, getting to work feels as enjoyable as a hobby.

When I finished writing *Sidetracked*, I was eager to get feedback, so I shared the working draft with my colleagues Max Bazerman, Gary Pisano, and Enrico Zaninotto. They all read the book within the span of two weeks and gave me very useful feedback. Thanks to them, you—the readers of this book—did not have to slog through boring anecdotes and lengthy explanations of research details that were not central to the message of each chapter. My assistant, Michael Skocay, and research associates, Austin Crumpton and Taryn Valley, also provided very helpful feedback along the way, when the chapters were still in rough form.

I decided to write this book soon after joining the Negotiation, Organizations & Markets Unit at Harvard Business School in the summer of 2010. I cannot think of a better community to accompany me in the process of writing this book. I feel extremely lucky to have an office close to that of such smart and supportive colleagues, from whom I continue to learn: Nava Ashraf, Max Bazerman, Peter Coles, Amy Cuddy, Ben Edelman, Jerry Green, Brian Hall, Ian Larkin, Michael Luca, Deepak Malhotra, Kathleen McGinn, Al Roth, Jim Sebenius, Bill Simpson, Guhan Subramanian, Andy Wasynczuk, and Mike Wheeler. Thanks to insightful research conversations, exhausting workouts, or delightful lunches on campus, you all make work a fun place to be.

The research I described in this book was carried out while I was on the faculty at three different institutions: Carnegie Mellon University, the University of North Carolina at Chapel Hill, and Harvard Business School. I thank these institutions for their support and for investing in my development as a scholar. Conducting research is not only an investment in time, but also in money. I am deeply grateful for the financial support I received from these institutions. In particular, I owe a special thanks to my research director at HBS, Teresa Amabile, and the director of research at HBS, Paul Healy, for being so supportive of my ongoing research efforts.

I also want to thank the research laboratories at these institutions, where most of the research discussed in this book was conducted: the Center for Behavioral Decision Research at Carnegie Mellon University, the Center for Decision Research at the University of North Carolina in Chapel Hill, and the Computer Lab for Experimental Research at Harvard Business School. I realize how much work goes into running experiments effectively, and how many people there are behind the scenes orchestrating these labs. It has been a privilege to work with the research assistants and staff members who work at these laboratories.

And now, let me turn to those closer to home. I owe a heartfelt *grazie* to my family for understanding the passion that keeps me far away from Italy and for the endless support they give me in all I do.

I am also deeply grateful to my best friend, roommate, and husband, Greg. Listening to an academic who talks like an unstoppable radio about research ideas can certainly be boring, yet you've been amazingly patient in letting me talk over the years we've been together. I am thankful for your understanding of my passion for what I do and for not getting upset when I spend long hours at work.

Finally, I want to thank you, the reader. Reading a book is no small commitment, and I am happy you chose to read *Sidetracked*. I hope you enjoyed it.

—July 31, 2012
Cambridge, Massachusetts

INDEX

ABOUT THE AUTHOR

Francesca Gino is an associate professor of Business Administration in the Negotiation, Organizations & Markets Unit at Harvard Business School. She is also formally affiliated with the Program on Negotiation at Harvard Law School. She has earned major research awards from the National Science Foundation and the Academy of Management. Her research has been featured in leading scholarly journals in psychology and management, and in various popular media outlets, including the *New York Times*, the *New York Times Magazine*, the *Wall Street Journal*, *Business-Week*, the *Boston Globe*, the *Economist*, *Huffington Post*, *Newsweek*, and *Scientific American*. Gino has appeared on CBS Radio and National Public Radio. She lives in Cambridge, Massachusetts.